Praise from the Experts

"This book is an excellent resource for any SAS programmer, packed with gems that most of us don't have time to go hunting for. Whether you read from cover to cover or just dip in now and again, your time will be rewarded with Phil's insights to how SAS can work better for you.

"Phil's style of writing tips encourages readers to try the methods in their own programs, rather than just lift the code wholesale. That's important when the success of some tips in saving time, storage, or other resources will be dependent, as Phil warns us, on your data, your machine, and your operating system.

"Readers at all levels will be rewarded by skimming through and marking their 'favorites' to use in the future. I even found a few that I might try myself, and I've been working with SAS for 25 years!"

Steve Morton
Principal Consultant
Applied System Knowledge Ltd.

"Phil Mason, one of the SAS user community's famous creative tinkerers—the SAS user version of mild-mannered Clark Kent—has updated his 300-page first edition of *SAS Tips and Techniques* with the addition of nearly a third more tips in this second edition. There is an entirely new chapter on ODS with over 30 tips.

"This book is a good read, suitable to curl up with on a quiet evening and think about that problem you had last week or last month—which you kludged rather than solved—and see if Phil has found the solution you need."

Ronald J. Fehd
IT Specialist, Help Desk: SAS
Centers for Disease Control and Prevention

"If you have ever wondered where 'SAS Experts' pick up those little tidbits of knowledge that make all the difference, look no farther. They probably have been reading Phil Mason's *In the Know: SAS Tips and Techniques From Around the Globe*.

"The second edition brings the text up to date with SAS®9, and includes new options and techniques. It also includes some comparisons for SAS 8 vs. SAS®9.

"This book has something for everyone. It is packed with tips, from the obscure to the commonly used. Written in a fairly terse style, Phil's book gets right to the point, and it gets there point after point. It covers topics that you don't know, topics that you don't know of, and most importantly it covers topics that you don't know that you need to know."

Art Carpenter
California Occidental Consultants

"A book of tips is organized differently from one in which each concept is built upon a previous concept. Here each page or two is a gem lying on the surface. Philip Mason is the grand master in the art of the SAS software tip. If you enjoyed his first book of tips, then you will enjoy this new edition."

Ian Whitlock

Publishing

In the know...
SAS® Tips and Techniques
from around the globe

Second Edition

Phil Mason

THE POWER TO KNOW®

The correct bibliographic citation for this manual is as follows: Mason, Phil. 2006. *In the Know ... SAS® Tips and Techniques from Around the Globe, Second Edition*. Cary, NC: SAS Institute Inc.

In the Know ... SAS® Tips and Techniques from Around the Globe, Second Edition

Copyright © 2006, SAS Institute Inc., Cary, NC, USA

ISBN 978-1-59047-702-1 (Hardcopy)
ISBN 978-1-62959-836-9 (PDF)

SAS Institute Inc., SAS Campus Drive, Cary, North Carolina 27513-2414.

April 2015

Contents

Using this book

This book is arranged into chapters that contain collections of related tips. Each chapter also contains a reference to related documentation, which you can refer to for further information.

The tips within each chapter are arranged in order from the most useful to the least useful. Of course this is a very subjective decision and you may disagree with my ordering. My aim in ordering the tips this way is to make the most useful tips available to the reader first. Remember that if you are searching for a tip on a particular subject, then look in the table of contents or the index, since this may take you right to the desired tip.

There is a common organization for each tip. Each tip contains the text of the tip and several other optional sections to help you to grasp the meaning quickly.

Where to find more tips

Apart from tips and discussion that take place on the SAS-L Internet user group, there are many other sources of good SAS tips. Many tips come right from the pages of SAS manuals. Apart from reading obscure parts of the basic manuals (*SAS Language Reference, Base SAS Procedures Guide*), a gold mine of tips can be found in Technical Reports.

There are many collections of SAS tips on the Internet. One great way to find them is doing a search on **SAS tips**. Some of my favorite Web sites are

- www.sas.com, which is the main SAS business portal

- support.sas.com, which is the SAS Customer Support Center portal

- www.sconsig.com, which is the SAS Consultant Special Interest Group (by Charles Patridge), has a large number of SAS tips

- www.sas-l.org, which links to an interface that enables you to search SAS users groups proceedings and subscribe to the SAS-L listserv

Acknowledgments

Though I am the author of this book, there were many others who helped to make it what it is. I would like to thank the following people who were responsible for the technical review of this book:

George Berg	Lynn Mackay	Kevin Russell
Clara A. Bonney	Lynn Matthews	Jane Stroupe
Jennifer Clegg	Kathryn McLawhorn	Ken Thompson
Margaret Crevar	Allison McMahill	Russ Tyndall
Paige Daniels	Chevell Parker	Ed Vlazny
Jeanne Ferneyhough	Nancy Rausch	Cynthia Zender
Bari Lawhorn	Kent Reeve	

I would also like to thank the production team, consisting of the following people:

- Patrice Cherry (cover designer)
- Candy Farrell (technical publishing specialist)
- Shelly Goodin (marketing)
- Mary Beth Steinbach (managing editor)
- Carolyn Sutton (copy editor)
- Liz Villani (marketing)

I would like to extend special thanks to Patsy Poole (acquisitions editor) who was my point of contact at SAS Press for all my dealings with the people above. Thanks, Patsy, for your patience and hard work in making this book a reality.

I'd also like to thank some of the world's leading SAS experts who reviewed this book for me. Thanks to Ian Whitlock, Ron Fehd, Art Carpenter, and Steve Morton.

Last, I'd like to thank my family for supporting me in the writing of this book. Thanks to my wife, Esther, and my children Jake (9), Annie (7), and Reuben (4).

Oh, and thanks to you for buying this book. My hope is that you quickly learn a few things that help you in your work and make the cost worthwhile.

God bless,
Phil Mason
Wallingford, England

Chapter **1**

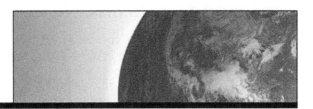

Resource Tips

Some ways to save disk space

Disk space equates to cost. Reducing space means the need for less disk hardware and therefore less cost.

1. Use PROC DATASETS, the DIR window, or the Libraries window to delete temporary and permanent data sets after use.

2. Use the KEEP= or DROP= data set options to limit the data set to only the variables required. You can also use the KEEP or DROP statements to do this.

3. Use the WHERE= data set option or WHERE statement to limit the number of observations processed by procedures or DATA steps. A WHERE statement can be used to replace an IF statement in a DATA step, and can be more efficient.

4. Use _NULL_ as the data set name in the DATA statement when you don't need to create a data set—for example, when creating a report.

5. Use remote library services to enable you to keep only one copy of data on your network.

6. Use data set compression. Data set compression can be done in one of several ways. Using either a data set option, a LIBNAME option, or a system option, you can set the compression to use. COMPRESS=YES is equivalent to COMPRESS=CHAR, and is good for compressing data that has mainly character values. COMPRESS=BINARY is good for compressing data that has mainly numerics. COMPRESS=NO disables compression.

7. Use views, rather than temporary data sets, but remember that this will increase CPU time.

8. Use pipes to compress data (for operating systems that support pipes). These enable compressed data to be read and written in real time. Please see your operating system companion for more information.

9. Use SQL to merge, summarize, sort, and so on, rather than using a combination of procedures and DATA steps with temporary data sets. Using one SQL statement can avoid saving temporary data sets, depending on the data that you are using. Keep in mind that SQL is often not as efficient as DATA step and procedure code.

10. Keep temporary files on tape, cartridge, CD, DVD, or other high-capacity media.

11. Use SQL pass thru for relational database processing to allow SQL to use temporary file space of the server SQL system (which is often a larger complex). This avoids using space on the machine that you are running.

12. Produce a format and store coded values in your data set. These values can be decoded using the format in a DATA step or a procedure.

13. Put your data into something approaching third-normal form, although this can affect system performance. Third-normal form involves splitting data (where appropriate) into more tables where tables with data that have a 1:1 relationship are placed in individual tables. For instance, with address data, you could have a table of zip codes and city names, which would mean the main address data could have zip codes but not city names. Then, when you want to know a city name, you could just take the zip code and look it up in the zip/city file.

14. Store your data in the order in which it is usually required. This avoids the need to re-sort data, thereby saving utility work space. Indexes can be added to avoid re-sorting too. Generating and maintaining indexes can take resources. Also, the index itself will take some space and use CPU time.

15. If you have a large SAS program consisting of many steps, then when reading a file into a data set, you should delete any observation that you don't need as soon as you determine you don't need it. This reduces the size of the data set when it is subsequently used in the rest of the program.

16. Use the LENGTH statement to limit the bytes used to represent a number or character to what is required for the desired precision. You must be careful when doing this for numerics, because the precision can be affected and CPU time will increase slightly. It is safest to do so only for characters and integer numerics, unless you are sure of what you are doing. Consider taking the SAS Programming III course.

17. An ideal technique for reducing the space required to store SAS dates is to reduce the length of the variable to 4. You require only 4 bytes of storage, not 8, to store any date.

18. Minimize the data that you keep in your permanent SAS libraries. Always ask yourself several questions:
    - Do I need this data? (What value is the information that it represents?)
    - Can data within the data set be derived from other information that I have? (For example, don't keep month, year, and day if you have a date.)
    - Is there another copy that I can refer to (for example, data held in DB2)?

- Is the cost of reproducing the data high (i.e., can I re-run my SAS program to reproduce the data)?
- Am I likely to need to refer to this data before it is outdated? (Daily data may be useful only for a day.)
- How much is it costing to keep this data (disk charges, etc.)?
- Can I tell the system to delete my data when it is no longer of use (for example, automatically delete data after 30 days)?
- Can I summarize historical data and delete details if I never again need them?

19. Delete any unused indexes. Make sure that the indexes are not being used by anyone before deleting.

20. Store program code centrally, rather than distributing it to users. Maintaining one copy will save space and make maintenance easier.

21. If the length of numeric ID variables is more than 8 digits (**Note:** default numeric length is 8), save it as a numeric variable, such as account number, Social Security number, employee, ID or student ID (all numbers). This also applies for 8 or fewer digits. For example, a number using 3 bytes of storage (in Windows) can represent a 4-digit number up to 8,192, and a number using 6 bytes of storage can represent a 12-digit number up to 137,438,953,472. For example,
   - Don't use: Length ID $ 16 ;
   - Instead use: Length ID 8 ; which will save half the space!

22. Define an index to avoid sorting. (Sorting often takes very large amounts of space.) Of course, indexes use space, but often the space used can be far less than that required for sorting. Indexes are not as efficient as sorted data, however.

23. Delete records not needed when they are read.

24. Don't use audit trails unless you need them.

25. Keep data in permanent libraries only if it will be needed later.

26. Use character variables to store numbers. For instance, if a number will only ever be 0 or 1, then it can be stored in a character of length 1, but a number (under Windows) must be at least 3 bytes long.

27. Use the FTP filename access method to access data on other machines, rather than making a local copy.

28. Use the LENGTH function to shorten characters and numerics when possible. You can write a program to analyze a data set and set lengths appropriately based on data values.

29. Use the SASFILE statement to load data sets into memory, which saves some space that you would otherwise need for them on disk. This also has the benefit of giving faster access to the data set in memory.

How to save space in SAS catalogs

SAS catalogs are not automatically compressed. As you save catalog entries, unused space accumulates. In some cases, less than half the space used by a catalog is actually needed.

To compress and reuse the unused space in a catalog, use REPAIR in PROC DATASETS.

This will compress sasuser.profile:

```
Proc datasets library=sasuser ;
  repair profile / mt=cat ;
quit ;
```

9 ways to minimize input/output

Input/output (I/O) to disk is the factor that usually slows down SAS programs. Reducing I/O will speed up execution and often reduce costs.

Generally, SAS is I/O intensive, rather than CPU intensive. As the great performance and tuning guru Ken Williams says, "The best I/O is the one you didn't do." Thus, a saving in I/O will improve the performance of your SAS program.

Here are 9 ways to minimize I/O:

1. Use LENGTH statements to minimize variable lengths, where possible.

2. Use CLASS statement(s), where possible, rather than BY statements, which might require a SORT.

3. Use DROP and KEEP statements to minimize observation length.

4. Use SORT only when necessary.

5. Create multiple data sets in one DATA step when possible.

6. Use WHERE statements with procedures to avoid subsetting in a DATA step followed by a procedure.

7. Use the _NULL_ DATA step when you don't need to create a data set. For example, you might want to create an external file, produce a report, or just do some calculations.

8. Compress some large SAS data sets, but beware that compression can use more space in some cases, which might actually increase I/O.

9. Develop and test programs on a small subset of the data.

Note: This list is not comprehensive. It merely attempts to provide a few ideas for investigation. Not all of the points will always reduce I/O time.

Implementing application data security

The aim is to let permitted users access data via your application, but to make it very difficult for anyone to access data without your application. The application should detect who the user is and should provide appropriate data access for them.

Data set passwords

You can put passwords on SAS data sets. This prevents accessing them without specifying the password. This also prevents users from accessing SAS data sets in their own batch jobs (unless they know the password). Passwords can be coded into source code so that your program "knows" the password. Using PROC PWENCODE is useful in this case, because it will generate a string, which cannot be recognized as the password, in place of the password.

Operating system security

On z/OS, you may have RACF or ACF2 to secure your data sets. On Windows and UNIX, you can protect directories from unauthorized users. On standalone PCs, you can often specify a startup password.

SAS®9

In SAS®9, the Business Intelligence Architecture enables much more security. By using the SAS Metadata Server, you can define users and groups of users along with information about the resources that they can access and what they can do with them.

Data encryption

An encryption key (or algorithm) can be used to encode numbers or text and can be kept in a secure data set. It can be read in when compiling the application or can even be built by an algorithm in the code. Different encryption keys can be used for different groupings of information to add another level of security. This means that a hacker would need many encryption keys to access all of the data.

There is also the ENCRYPT data set option, which makes SAS encrypt your data sets.

Other points

- You should exit SAS before the application ends.

- Close secured files after they have been used. Free FILENAME and LIBNAME allocations when you are finished with them.

- For z/OS, specify the NOSTAX system option so that the attention key will end the SAS session.

Useful options for tuning

When tuning your SAS program to make it run more efficiently, it is useful to turn on various information options available in SAS. Remember to turn them off when you finish the tuning and run your program, because many options increase the overhead (CPU time, elapsed time, I/Os) of your program.

```
options oplist stats fullstats echoauto source source2 memrpt mprint
stimer ;
```

Option	Description
oplist	Shows settings of SAS system options in SAS log
echoauto	Shows autoexec file in log
stats	Writes performance statistics to log
fullstats	Writes performance statistics in expanded form
stimer	Maintains and prints timing statistics (Don't use this with views.)
memrpt	Shows memory report
source	Shows source code in log
source2	Shows included source code in log
mprint	Shows statements generated by macro facility

Also consider using ARM macros or the Rtrace facility for other approaches to tuning.

Saving resources when the log is long

When writing a lot of information to the log in interactive SAS, you can be slowed down as SAS scrolls the log to display each line as it is written. This is the default behavior, which works well when you don't write much to the log. This tip tells you how to save time and resources by altering the AUTOSCROLL setting.

Activating the Log window (by selecting Log from the View menu or by clicking the Log window) and setting AUTOSCROLL to 0 tells SAS not to bother scrolling the Log window until the DATA step is finished. AUTOSCROLL can be set by using the pull-down menus to choose EDIT then OPTIONS then AUTOSCROLL.

The following example takes 31.25 seconds to run (on my test machine) with AUTOSCROLL=1. Then, running the same code with AUTOSCROLL=0 takes only 0.29 seconds. I ran these tests several times to ensure there was no effect due to caching of data or anything due to the order of the code being run.

```
dm 'log; clear;autoscroll 1' ;
data _null_ ;
  set sashelp.prdsale ;
  do i=1 to 50 ;
    put year= month= actual= ;
  end ;
run ;
dm 'log; clear;autoscroll 0' ;
data _null_ ;
  set sashelp.prdsale ;
  do i=1 to 50 ;
    put year= month= actual= ;
  end ;
run ;
```

```
568    dm 'log; clear;autoscroll 1' ;
569    data _null_ ;
570      set sashelp.prdsale ;
571      do i=1 to 50 ;
572        put year= month= actual= ;
573      end ;
574    run ;
```

Lines deleted

```
NOTE: There were 1440 observations read from the data set
  SASHELP.PRDSALE.
NOTE: DATA statement used (Total process time):
      real time           7.81 seconds
      cpu time            7.39 seconds
```

```
575    dm 'log; clear;autoscroll 0' ;
576    data _null_ ;
577      set sashelp.prdsale ;
578      do i=1 to 50 ;
579        put year= month= actual= ;
580      end ;
581    run ;
```

Lines deleted

```
NOTE: There were 1440 observations read from the data set
  SASHELP.PRDSALE.
NOTE: DATA statement used (Total process time):
      real time           0.29 seconds
      cpu time            0.29 seconds
```

Several ways to tune a SORT

Here is a brief list of things you can look at if you want to make your PROC SORT go faster, use less space, or use less CPU time. Always test the methods and combinations to see what works best for you.

- SAS®9 can use a product called SyncSort to perform sorts, which can be faster than the SAS sort. It is also multi-threaded to make use of multiple processors. SyncSort was also available in SAS 8 and later for z/OS and UNIX. You need to use the SORTPGM= option to select SyncSort, because the SAS sort is usually the default. You should always check the actual default for your installation of SAS, as this could vary between operating systems and releases of SAS, or be set by your SAS administrator.

- In SAS®9, the standard SAS sort is multi-threaded and performs very well on multi-processor machines.

```
Proc sort data=x threads ;
  By y ;
Run ;
```

- Use TAGSORT where the BY variables combined length is short compared to observation length, and data set is huge. I have had cases where I was sorting very large data sets and a plain PROC SORT took a long time to run, but using TAGSORT cut the time down to less than half.

```
Proc sort data=x tagsort ;
  By y ;
Run ;
```

- You usually don't need the previous order maintained within the new order, so specify NOEQUALS.

```
proc sort data=data-set NOEQUALS ;
  by y ;
run ;
```

- Allocate more sort work data sets to improve sort efficiency (if you are using z/OS).

```
Options sortwkno=6 ;
```

- Reduce observations sorted by using a WHERE clause.

```
proc sort data=xxx(where=(price>1000)) out=yyy ;
  by y ;
run;
```

- Use all available memory for sorting.

```
options sortsize=max ;
```

- If data is grouped, but not sorted, then use NOTSORTED to avoid the need to sort.

```
proc print data=calendar ;
  by month NOTSORTED ;
run;
```

- If external data (perhaps coming from another database via an import) is pre-sorted, then tell SAS it is sorted in a particular order.

```
Data new(SORTEDBY=year month) ;
   Set x.y ;
run ;
```

Chapter 2

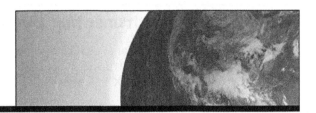

Functions

Incrementing and truncating by time intervals

Some coders devote large chunks of code to the task of figuring out which is the last day of the month, whether it is leap year, etc. That is totally unnecessary if they make use of the INTNX function.

Syntax: INTNX(*interval, from, n*)

This function returns a SAS date, time, or datetime value that is incremented a number of time intervals (days, hours, or whatever you specify).

The function can be used to set the value to the start of the specified interval by incrementing by 0 time intervals.

```
480   data _null_ ;
481     format date date7. datetime datetime16. time time8. ;
482     date=intnx('month','8sep07'd,0) ;
483     datetime=intnx('dtday','8sep07:12:34:56'dt,0) ;
484     time=intnx('hour','12:34't,0) ;
485     put date= / datetime= / time= ;
486   run ;

date=01SEP07
datetime=08SEP07:00:00:00
time=12:00:00
NOTE: DATA statement used (Total process time):
      real time            0.00 seconds
      cpu time             0.00 seconds
```

One other fine use of INTNX is to get the last day of a month or year:

```
/* SASDAY is a SAS variable containing a SAS date */
/* LASTDAY is the last day of the month of SASDAY */
LASTDAY = INTNX("MONTH",SASDAY,1) - 1;
```

Another feature of the INTNX function is an added argument that causes the function to return a value aligned to either the beginning, middle, or end of the interval specified. You can even use SAMEDAY to get the same day of the month.

```
data test ;
  first=intnx('month',date(),-2,'beginning') ;
  same=intnx('year','19nov2006'd,20,'sameday') ;
run ;
```

INTNX is one of those incredibly useful features of SAS that makes it stand out from many other languages and that saves you a lot of time and effort.

Counting words

Rather than using a more convoluted technique for counting the number of occurrences of a word in a character string, in SAS®9 you can now use the COUNT function. It will simply count the number of sub-strings that occur in a string, optionally ignoring the case (as in the following example).

```
15    data _null_ ;
16      sentence='This is ONE way of using one in One sentence' ;
17      num=count(sentence,'one','i') ;
18      put num= ;
19    run ;

num=3
NOTE: DATA statement used (Total process time):
      real time           0.00 seconds
      cpu time            0.00 seconds
```

Using PERL regular expressions for searching text

In SAS®9 there are new functions available for using PERL regular expressions to search text for sub-strings. There are two parts to using these, which I demonstrate in the following code:

1. Parse your PERL regular expression using the PRXPARSE function. This returns a pattern-ID that can be used in other PERL functions.

2. Search using the parsed expression by using the PRXSUBSTR function. This returns the position and length of the text found, or 0 if none is found.

Note: For a useful quick reference on PERL regular expressions, see http://www.erudil.com/preqr.pdf.

```
data _null_;
    retain patternID;
  if _N_=1 then
    do;
      pattern = "/ave|avenue|dr|drive|rd|road/i";
      patternID = prxparse(pattern);
    end;
  input street $80.;
  call prxsubstr(patternID, street, position, length);
  if position ^= 0 then
    do;
      match = substr(street, position, length);
      put match : $QUOTE. "found in " street : $QUOTE.;
    end;
  datalines;
153 First Street
6789 64th Ave
4 Moritz Road
7493 Wilkes Place
;
  run ;
```

```
"Ave" found in "6789 64th Ave"
"Road" found in "4 Moritz Road"
```

Concatenating strings the easy way

In SAS®9 there is a new function called CATX, which makes concatenating strings easy. It will concatenate any number of character strings, remove leading and trailing blanks, and insert a separator. The maximum length returned is limited to 32767 in the DATA step, 200 in WHERE clauses, and 65534 in macro variables. Truncation will occur without warning if these limits are exceeded.

```
1     data test ;
2       a='  Phil         ' ;
3       b='   Mason ' ;
4       c=trim(left(a))!!' '!!left(b) ;
5       d=catx(' ',a,b) ;
6       put c= d= ;
7     run ;

c=Phil Mason d=Phil Mason
NOTE: The data set WORK.TEST has 1 observations and 4 variables.
NOTE: DATA statement used (Total process time):
      real time           0.55 seconds
      cpu time            0.06 seconds
```

Putting numbers in macro variables a better way

In SAS®9 there is a new routine called SYMPUTX, which creates a macro variable from a numeric variable without writing a note to the log, and trims leading and trailing blanks. It will use a field up to 32 characters wide, and you can optionally tell it which symbol table to put the macro variable into.

The following two routines are equivalent:

```
Call symput('name',left(trim(my_name))) ;
Call symputx('name',my_name) ;
```

The following example shows how SAS does an automatic type conversion and uses BEST12.2 to convert a numeric to character in line 44. The following line shows how you can explicitly do the conversion and trim the result. The next line shows how to use SYMPUTX to simplify the process.

```
5      data test ;
6         my_val=12345 ;
7         call symput('value0',my_val) ; * auto conversion done ;
8         call symput('value1',trim(left(put(my_val,8.)))) ; * v8 ;
9         call symputx('value2',my_val) ; * SAS 9 ;
10     run ;

NOTE: Numeric values have been converted to character values at the
   places given by:
        (Line):(Column).
        7:24
NOTE: The data set WORK.TEST has 1 observations and 1 variables.
NOTE: DATA statement used (Total process time):
        real time           0.17 seconds
        cpu time            0.02 seconds


11     %put value0 (using symput with auto conversion) is &value0;
value0 (using symput with auto conversion) is           12345
12     %put value1 (using symput with explicit conversion) is &value1;
value1 (using symput with explicit conversion) is 12345
13     %put value2 (using symputx) is &value2;
value2 (using symputx) is 12345
```

Writing messages to the log, while writing text elsewhere

In SAS®9 there is a new statement called PUTLOG, which explicitly writes to the SAS log. This means that you can direct regular PUT statements to write to another destination, and write to the log using PUTLOG without the need to redirect output to the log with a FILE LOG statement.

Remember that NOTE:, WARNING: and ERROR: write out the words NOTE:, WARNING:, or ERROR:, followed by the text in the appropriate color.

```
55    data test ;
56      put 'This goes to LOG by default' ;
57      file print ;
58      put 'This goes to OUTPUT window, since I selected print' ;
59      putlog 'but this still goes to the LOG' ;
60      put 'This goes to OUTPUT' ;
61      putlog 'NOTE: and I can write proper messages using colours' ;
62      putlog 'WARNING: ...' ;
63      putlog 'ERROR: ...' ;
64    run ;

This goes to LOG by default
but this still goes to the LOG
NOTE: and I can write proper messages using colours
WARNING: ...
ERROR: ...
NOTE: 2 lines were written to file PRINT.
NOTE: The data set WORK.TEST has 1 observations and 0 variables.
NOTE: DATA statement used (Total process time):
      real time           0.00 seconds
      cpu time            0.01 seconds
```

Logic and functions

For a useful page of links with interesting tips about logic and functions in the DATA step, see http://support.sas.com/techsup/faq/data_step/logifunc.html. I have summarized some of the gems of information below.

How to find week of year for a date variable DATEVAR

```
data getweek;
   datevar=today();
   week=intck('week',intnx('year',datevar,0),datevar)+1;
run;
```

How to calculate age

```
data one;
   bday='19jan1973'd;
   current=today();
   age=int(intck('month',bday,current)/12);
   if month(bday)=month(current) then
     age=age-(day(bday)>day(current));
run;
```

How to calculate the value of pi

```
Before version 8 use …
   pi=arcos(-1);
From version 8 use …
   pi=constant('pi');
```

How to calculate factorials

```
Before version 8 use …
   sixfact=gamma(7);
From version 8 use …
   sixfact=fact(6);
```

Inverse trigonometry functions

```
inv(cosh)
   arcosh_x=log(x+sqrt(x**2-1));
inv(sinh)
   arsinh_x=log(x+sqrt(x**2+1));
inv(tanh)
   artanh_x=0.5*log((1+x)/(1-x));
```

Are your random numbers really random?

It is important to understand how random numbers work in SAS. If you set an initial seed value for the CALL RANUNI routine or the RANUNI function, you will get a sequence of random numbers that are repeatable. If you use the same seed again, you will get the same series.

If you change the seed using the CALL RANUNI routine, then you will begin a new sequence of random numbers. If you change the seed using the RANUNI function during execution of a DATA step, then the seed will not actually change.

This applies to the other SAS random functions also (RANTRI, RANPOI, etc.).

```
data case;
  retain Seed_1 Seed_2 Seed_3 1 ;
  do i=1 to 10;
    call ranuni(Seed_1,X1) ; * call with unchanging seed ;
    call ranuni(Seed_2,X2) ; * call with seed changing half way
                                 through ;
    X3=ranuni(Seed_3) ;       * function with seed changing half way
                                 through ;
    output;
    * change seed for last 5 rows ;
    if i=5 then
      do;
        Seed_2=2;
        Seed_3=2;
      end;
  end;
run;

proc print;
  id i;
  var Seed_1-Seed_3 X1-X3;
run;
```

I	SEED_1	SEED_2	SEED_3	X1	X2	X3
1	397204094	397204094	1	0.18496	0.18496	0.18496
2	2083249653	2083249653	1	0.97009	0.97009	0.97009
3	858616159	858616159	1	0.39982	0.39982	0.39982
4	557054349	557054349	1	0.25940	0.25940	0.25940
5	1979126465	1979126465	1	0.92160	0.92160	0.92160
6	2081507258	794408188	2	0.96928	0.36993	0.96928
7	1166038895	2019015659	2	0.54298	0.94018	0.54298
8	1141799280	1717232318	2	0.53169	0.79965	0.53169
9	106931857	1114108698	2	0.04979	0.51880	0.04979
10	142950581	1810769283	2	0.06657	0.84321	0.06657

The following log also demonstrates a random sequence, which will be the same every time the code is run.

```
66   data _null_ ;
67     do i=1 to 3 ;
68       a=ranuni(123) ;
69       put a= ;
70     end ;
71   run ;

a=0.7503960881
a=0.3209120251
a=0.178389649
NOTE: DATA statement used (Total process time):
      real time          0.00 seconds
      cpu time           0.01 seconds
```

Various forms for function argument lists

You can specify arguments to functions in various ways. For instance, you can nest functions within functions as in the following example:

```
sum(mean(x,y,log(z)),a+12,sqrt(total)) ;
```

You can also specify various lists of variables. (**Note:** The SUM function is merely used as an example.)

sum(a,b,c,d)	Uses all the listed elements.
sum(of a b c d)	Uses all the listed elements.
sum(of x1-x99)	Uses the 99 variables from x1 to x99 (ie. x1, x2, x3, ... x99)
sum(of array(*))	Uses all elements of an array.
sum(of _numeric_)	Uses all numeric variables in DATA step.
sum(of x--a)	Uses all variables defined in the Program Data Vector in order from "x" to "a."
Sum(of a:)	Uses all variables that begin with "a."

Using the INDEX function to treat blanks as nulls

The INDEX function will distinguish between spaces and nulls, whereas using the INDEXW function will treat blanks and nulls as being equal. So a single space and null string " " are equivalent. This is shown in the following log extract.

```
1     data _null_;
2        result1 = indexw(' ',' ');
3        put result1 =;
4        result2 = indexw(' ', '');
5        put result2 =;
6        result3 = indexw('',' ');
7        put result3 =;
8        result4 = indexw('Any Chars',' ');
9        put result4 =;
10    run;

result1=1
result2=1
result3=1
result4=0
NOTE: DATA statement used (Total process time):
      real time            0.14 seconds
      cpu time             0.04 seconds
```

Determining if you have SAS products

Determining which SAS products you have can be quite useful in applications development to make the most of whatever facilities are available. You can check to see if SAS/GRAPH is available. If so, you produce a high-resolution graph; otherwise, use the Base SAS PROC CHART.

There is a DATA step function called SYSPROD. This is used to determine if a SAS product is licensed at your site.

The function returns 1 if a product is licensed, 0 if it is not, or –1 if it is not a product name.

```
x=sysprod('graph') ;
```

Sometimes a product may be licensed but not installed. In such cases it is useful to not only check if the product is licensed, but look to see if something exists that is installed only for that product. The following code checks if you have SAS/GRAPH installed and also if a catalog exists that is there only if it has been installed.

```
if sysprod('GRAPH') and cexist('SASHELP.DEVICES') then ...
```

Another way to detect the existence of a product is to check for its directory, since in current releases of SAS each product creates a directory for its files.

Peculiarities of the LENGTH function

You may expect the length of a null character string to be 0, but that is not correct.

The documentation for the LENGTH function states "Returns the length of a non-blank character string, excluding trailing blanks, and returns 1 for a blank character string."

The length of a space (" ") or missing value (" ") is 1, not 0 as you might expect.

```
1    data _null_ ;
2      blank=length(' ') ;
3      missing=length('') ;
4      normal=length('sas') ;
5      put blank= / missing= / normal= ;
6    run ;

blank=1
missing=1
normal=3
NOTE: DATA statement used (Total process time):
      real time           1.77 seconds
      cpu time            0.11 seconds
```

Using the TRIM function makes no difference to the length, since LENGTH reports the position of the right-most non-blank character. In addition, the length of the value returned by the TRIM function is the length of the argument; therefore, it has no effect.

```
7    data _null_ ;
8       blank=length(trim(' ')) ;
9       missing=length(trim('')) ;
10      normal=length(trim('sas')) ;
11      put blank= / missing= / normal= ;
12   run ;

blank=1
missing=1
normal=3
NOTE: DATA statement used (Total process time):
      real time           0.10 seconds
      cpu time            0.03 seconds
```

If you try the LENGTH function on numbers, then you will have 12 returned by default. You even get 12 returned if the numeric variable had a missing value. The reason for this is that the format BEST12. is used when converting the numbers to characters for use with the LENGTH function. The numbers are right justified and, therefore, show as being 12 long.

```
13   data _null_ ;
14      length a 4 ;
15      length b 6 ;
16      length c 8 ;
17      a=-123.3;
18      b=9999999999;
19      len_a=length(a) ;
20      len_b=length(b) ;
21      len_c=length(c) ;
22      put len_a= / len_b= / len_c= ;
23   run ;

NOTE: Numeric values have been converted to character values at the
  places given by:
      (Line):(Column).
      19:16    20:16    21:16
NOTE: Variable c is uninitialized.
len_a=12
len_b=12
len_c=12
NOTE: DATA statement used (Total process time):
      real time           0.15 seconds
      cpu time            0.05 seconds
```

Minimum/maximum arithmetic operators

These operators are executed from right to left, like the leading minus sign and unlike virtually all the other operators. This leads to the amazing result that

```
-3 >< -3
```

is positive three when it obviously should be negative three!

The reason that SAS returns positive 3 is that the expression is treated as being:

```
- (3 >< -3)
```

```
24    data _null_ ;
25        x=-3><-3 ;
26        put x= ;
27    run ;


x=3
NOTE: DATA statement used (Total process time):
      real time           0.01 seconds
      cpu time            0.02 seconds
```

There are operators that can be used for returning minimum and maximum in arithmetic expressions. Minimum uses the operator ><, and maximum uses <>.

If you wanted to assign the maximum of two variables X and Y to a third variable Z, then rather than coding

```
if x>y then
   z=x ;
else
   z=y ;
```

you could code the following. Note that the problem mentioned with negative numbers above does not occur in this code since the problem occurs only when there is a literal as the first argument and both numbers are negative. Having the first argument as a variable avoids the problem.

```
z=x<>y ;
```

Min/max confusion

In SAS arithmetic >< means minimum.

In SAS PROC SQL (and standard SQL) <> means not-equal.

In WHERE clauses <> also means not-equal.

```
28    proc print data=sashelp.class ;
29      where sex<>'Alaska' ;
NOTE: The "<>" operator is interpreted as "not equals".
30    run ;

NOTE: There were 19 observations read from the data set SASHELP.CLASS.
      WHERE 1 /* an obviously TRUE where clause */ ;
NOTE: PROCEDURE PRINT used (Total process time):
      real time           1.76 seconds
      cpu time            0.20 seconds
```

It may be advisable to use the MAX and MIN functions, which would seem to be more self-documenting to the casual reader. These functions work the same in SAS arithmetic and in SQL. You can have two or more arguments to these functions.

For example:

```
z = MIN(x,y,z);
```

Getting the remainder of a division

The MOD function returns negative values when the first argument is negative. This could be thought to be mathematically incorrect.

```
31   data _null_ ;
32      x=mod(-3, 2) ;
33      put 'mod(-3, 2)=' x ;
34      x=mod(-3,-2) ;
35      put 'mod(-3,-2)=' x ;
36      x=mod( 3, 2) ;
37      put 'mod( 3, 2)=' x ;
38      x=mod( 3,-2) ;
39      put 'mod( 3,-2)=' x ;
40   run ;

mod(-3, 2)=-1
mod(-3,-2)=-1
mod( 3, 2)=1
mod( 3,-2)=1
NOTE: DATA statement used (Total process time):
      real time           0.16 seconds
      cpu time            0.05 seconds
```

The "trap" with the MOD function is not that it produces mathematically incorrect results, but that the function name (MOD) implies *modulo* or *clock* arithmetic.

It is (and has always been) simply the "remainder" function.

It represents (arg1 - (int(arg1/arg2) * arg2)).

"The MOD function returns the remainder when the integer quotient of argument-1 divided by argument-2 is calculated." Here is the output produced by the code shown above.

arg-1	arg-2	integer quotient= int(arg1/arg2)	remainder
-3	2	-1	-1
-3	-2	1	-1
3	2	1	1
3	-2	-1	1

As in other cases throughout SAS (for example, LAG), MOD does exactly what it is designed to do, but not what many of us would expect given its name. Read the documentation carefully and you will find that it behaves as described.

Chapter 3

DATA Step

Rearranging variables in a data set

To rearrange the order of variables in your SAS data set, you can use the RETAIN statement before the SET statement. This sets the order of the variables in the Program Data Vector (PDV) since they will be put in the PDV in the order in which they are used.

Alternatively, you can use other statements before the SET statement (e.g. LENGTH, LABEL, FORMAT, INFORMAT). Some statements can't be used to rearrange the order of variables (e.g. KEEP). For example:

```
data new ;
  retain this that theother ;
  set old ;
run ;
```

Using pattern matching in WHERE clauses

Pattern matching provides a lot more flexibility in specifying criteria for selecting data using a WHERE clause.

The LIKE operator in the WHERE clause enables you to use pattern matching in DATA and PROC steps.

- An underscore (_) in a pattern will match any single character in that position.

- A percent sign (%) in a pattern will match any number of characters in that position.

- A colon modifier (for example =:) used at the end of any comparison operator lets you match the first characters of the longer value with those of the shorter value.

- The contains operator searches for the occurrence of a string within the value of another string.

- The sounds-like operator or an asterisk (*) can be used to match slight spelling variations.

All the following examples would match name='Phil Mason':

```
where name=:'Ph' ;
where name like 'P_il M_s_n' ;
where name like '%son' ;
where name contains 'il' ;
where name ? 'hil' ;
where name=*'PFil Mason' ;
where name>:'Phil' ;
where name le: 'Phim' ;
```

Conditionally generating code with CALL EXECUTE

Sometimes, depending on data from some source, you might want to conditionally generate SAS code from a SAS program. The CALL EXECUTE routine is an efficient way to do this.

You can use CALL EXECUTE to set up SAS code that will be executed after a DATA step ends. This is similar to the traditional method of putting statements out to a temporary file, and then including them in the SAS stream using %INCLUDE.

This takes care of about 90% of the reasons that most people would like to use %IF macro statements in open code, which, of course, cannot be done since %IF statements work only inside a macro.

The following SAS log shows an example that uses data from a data set to generate a format that uses CALL EXECUTE.

Log: Example using a DATA step

```
60    data one;
61       x=1;
62       y='A';
63       output;
64       x=2;
65       y='B';
66       output;
67    run;

NOTE: The data set WORK.ONE has 2 observations and 2 variables.
NOTE: DATA statement used (Total process time):
      real time           0.01 seconds
      cpu time            0.02 seconds


68
69    data _null_;
70       set one end=last;
71       if _n_=1 then
72         call execute('proc format; value myfmt');
73       call execute( x);
74       call execute('=');
75       call execute(quote(y));
76       if last then
77         call execute(";run;");
78    run ;
```

(continued)

(continued)

```
NOTE: Numeric values have been converted to character values at the
      places given by:
      (Line):(Column).
      73:18
NOTE: There were 2 observations read from the data set WORK.ONE.
NOTE: DATA statement used (Total process time):
      real time           0.03 seconds
      cpu time            0.04 seconds


NOTE: CALL EXECUTE generated line.
1    + proc format;
1    +                value myfmt
2    +             1
3    + =
4    + "A"
5    +             2
6    + =
7    + "B"
8    + ;
NOTE: Format MYFMT is already on the library.
NOTE: Format MYFMT has been output.
8    +  run;

NOTE: PROCEDURE FORMAT used (Total process time):
      real time           0.02 seconds
      cpu time            0.03 seconds
```

The following log demonstrates how macro programs are executed immediately as a DATA step executes.

Log: Example using macros

```
79    %macro x;
80       %put Line 1 ;
81       %put Line 2 ;
82    %mend x;
83
84    %macro y;
85       %put Line 3 ;
86       %put Line 4 ;
87    %mend y;
88    data _null_ ;
89      call execute('%x %y %x %y');
90    run;

Line 1
Line 2
Line 3
Line 4
Line 1
Line 2
Line 3
Line 4
NOTE: DATA statement used (Total process time):
      real time           0.04 seconds
      cpu time            0.03 seconds


NOTE: CALL EXECUTE routine executed successfully, but no SAS statements
      were generated.
```

DDE: Writing to Microsoft Word

Writing data from SAS to Microsoft Word requires a slightly different Dynamic Data Exchange (DDE) triplet than writing to a spreadsheet. The triplet is made up of the program name, document name, and bookmark name. A bookmark can be inserted into Microsoft Word using the Edit menu. Bookmarks can then be referred to by defining a FILEREF for each one.

This example uses two bookmarks defined in doc1.doc. The first is positioned so that a name can be inserted. The second is positioned in the text of a letter so that some text can be inserted.

```
filename name dde 'WinWord|doc1.doc!name' notab ; *** First bookmark ;
filename problem dde 'WinWord|doc1.doc!problem' notab ; *** Second
   bookmark ;

data _null_ ;
  file name ;
  put 'Rod Krishock' ;
  file problem ;
  put 'stay in a cheap hotel' ;
run ;

NOTE: The file NAME is:
      FILENAME=WinWord|doc1.doc!name,
      RECFM=V,LRECL=256

NOTE: The file PROBLEM is:
      FILENAME=WinWord|doc1.doc!problem,
      RECFM=V,LRECL=256

NOTE: 1 record was written to the file NAME.
      The minimum record length was 12.
      The maximum record length was 12.
NOTE: 1 record was written to the file PROBLEM.
      The minimum record length was 21.
      The maximum record length was 21.
NOTE: The DATA statement used 0.93 seconds.
```

DDE: Operating other programs from SAS

Using DDE, SAS can control other programs by issuing commands that they recognize. The commands used depend on the application being controlled. A simple way to find out which commands to use is to turn on the applications macro recorder, perform an action, and then edit the macro recorded to see what the commands are.

Use these steps to remotely control applications from SAS.

1. Decide which commands to use, either with manual or macro recorder.

2. Allocate the FILEREF. Remember to use the applications program name and the word SYSTEM, separated by a vertical bar.

3. Write commands to the FILEREF. Commands should be contained within square brackets.

Following are two examples, one controlling Lotus 123 and the other controlling Microsoft Word.

Log: Example 1

```
filename lotus dde '123w|system' notab ;   *** Program name is 123w.exe ;
data _null_ ;
  file lotus ;
  put '[run({CHART-NEW A:A1..A:F14})]' ; *** Create a new chart ;
  put '[run({SELECT "CHART 1";;"CHART"})]' ; *** Select it ;
  put '[run({CHART-RANGE "X";A:A1..A:A4;"Line";"NO"})]' ; *** Set the X
  range ;
  put '[run({CHART-RANGE "A";A:B1..A:B4;"Bar";"NO"}dd)]' ; * Set the Y
                                                             range and
                                                             plot a bar
                                                             chart ;
run ;

NOTE: The file LOTUS is:
      FILENAME=123w|system,
      RECFM=V,LRECL=256

NOTE: 4 records were written to the file LOTUS.
      The minimum record length was 30.
      The maximum record length was 48.
NOTE: The DATA statement used 1.37 seconds.
```

Log: Example 2

```
filename word dde 'winword|system' notab ; *** Program name is
  Winword.exe ;
data _null_ ;
  file word ;
  put '[FileOpen .Name = "phil1.DOC"]' ; *** Open a file called
  phil1.doc ;
  put '[macro1]' ; *** Execute a macro called macro1 ;
run ;

NOTE: The file WORD is:
      FILENAME=WinWord|system,
      RECFM=V,LRECL=256

NOTE: 1 record was written to the file WORD.
      The minimum record length was 30.
      The maximum record length was 30.
NOTE: The DATA statement used 3.62 seconds.
```

Adding variables with similar names

Sometimes you may have groups of variables whose names start with the same characters. These can be added (or some other operation done) by putting the variables into an array and then handling each variable as an element of the array using a DO loop.

Example: All variables that describe international phone calls begin with the International Direct Dialing (IDD) prefix and then have a suffix describing the country the call goes to.

```
data _null_ ;
* Sample data ;
  iddusa=10 ;
  iddaus=33 ;
  iddtai=44 ;
  idduk=99 ;
  iddbel=1 ;
  iddcan=11 ;
* Define array to hold all the IDD variables ;
  array idd(*) idd: ;
* Add them up ;
  do i=1 to dim(idd) ;
    total+idd(i) ;
  end ;
* Calculate average ;
  avg=total/dim(idd) ;
  put _all_ ;
run ;
```

```
IDDUSA=10 IDDAUS=33 IDDTAI=44 IDDUK=99 IDDBEL=1 IDDCAN=11 TOTAL=198 I=7
AVG=33 _ERROR_=0 _N_=1
```

Inputting data using text value positioning

There are various ways of positioning the pointer for reading in data using the INPUT statement. One of the ways is to use INPUT @*text*. This statement searches the input line for *text* and positions the pointer directly after it, which allows data following *text* to be read by SAS. This technique could be used to read CPU times from the SAS log, for example.

The following example is a SAS log from one of my SAS jobs. Note that the filename SASLOG is not a special automatic FILEREF, but one that I have assigned to a file in which I have stored a previous SAS log.

```
data logstats ;
   infile saslog ;
   input @'used' duration 6.2 ;
run ;

proc print data=logstats ;
run;
```

```
OBS     DURATION

 1         0.05
 2         2.72
 3         6.74
 4        69.09
 5         2.74
 6         3.03
 7        13.10
 8        12.29
 9       109.70
```

Reading unaligned data that require informats

With list input, SAS scans the data line for the fields specified in the INPUT statement. Fields don't have to be aligned, but must be separated by at least one delimiter (which could be a space, comma, tab, or other delimiter by using the DLM= or DSD option in the INFILE statement). Format modifiers provide more flexibility in reading data in this way.

Syntax: INPUT *<pointer-control> variable* <format-modifier> <informat.>
<@!@@> ;

Format modifiers

  &   The ampersand allows character values to have single embedded blanks. The field is read until either two consecutive blanks or the end-of-line is reached.

  :   The colon allows an informat to be used to read data in. This is useful for truncating values when the field is longer than the informat specifies. You must put an informat after the colon.

  ~   The tilde, when used in conjunction with the DSD INFILE option, keeps quotation marks rather than stripping them off (as is the default).

```
data test ;
  infile datalines dsd ;
  input name     :  $20.
        title    ~  $40.
        address  &  $30. ;
  datalines ;
"Phil Mason","SAS Tips guy",Melbourne - Australia
"Mark Bodt","Expert in SAS, Microsoft & more",Wellington - New Zealand
;
proc print ; run ;
```

```
                          The SAS System                                3

Obs     name      title                                      address

1 Phil Mason "SAS Tips guy"                     Melbourne - Australia
2 Mark Bodt  "Expert in SAS, Microsoft & more"  Wellington - New Zealand
```

Using _NULL_ DATA steps when not creating data sets

Use a _NULL_ DATA step where you need to do DATA step processing, but do not need to create a data set—for example, when creating a report or using CALL SYMPUT to create a macro variable. This avoids the overhead involved in writing to a disk and taking up disk space when you create a data set.

Be aware that using the DATA statement with no argument will create a default data set called DATA1, DATA2, etc. Using DATA _NULL_ does not create a data set. See the following example.

```
    data ;
      x=1 ;
    run ;

NOTE: The data set WORK.DATA1 has 1 observations and 1 variables.
NOTE: The DATA statement used 0.01 CPU seconds and 1426K.

    data _null_ ;
      x=1 ;
    run ;

NOTE: The DATA statement used 0.01 CPU seconds and 1426K.
```

Determining the number of observations in a data set

The NOBS= option in the SET statement assigns the number of observations in the SAS data set to a variable. However, this does not work for either SQL or DATA step views.

Views

The NOBS= option returns 2**53 if the data set being read is a view. If you want to know the number of observations available to a view, you must use a different approach. See the following example.

```
52    DATA a_view / view=a_view ;
53       set sashelp.class ;
54    run ;

NOTE: DATA STEP view saved on file WORK.A_VIEW.
NOTE: A stored DATA STEP view cannot run under a different operating
      system.
NOTE: DATA statement used (Total process time):
      real time              0.04 seconds
      cpu time               0.01 seconds


55
56    DATA _null_ ;
57       if 0 then
58          set a_view nobs=nobs ;
59       put "For a View: " nobs= ;
60       stop ;
61    Run ;

For a View: nobs=9.0071993E15
NOTE: View WORK.A_VIEW.VIEW used (Total process time):
      real time              0.01 seconds
      cpu time               0.00 seconds

NOTE: DATA statement used (Total process time):
      real time              0.01 seconds
      cpu time               0.00 seconds
```

(continued)

(continued)

```
62
63   DATA temp ;
64     if 0 then
65       set sashelp.class nobs=nobs ;
66     put "For a Disk dataset: " nobs= ;
67     stop ;
68   Run ;

For a Disk dataset: nobs=19
NOTE: The data set WORK.TEMP has 0 observations and 5 variables.
NOTE: DATA statement used (Total process time):
      real time            0.04 seconds
      cpu time             0.00 seconds
```

Note: We used `if 0 then` in the code in the preceding example. This is a useful technique when you do not want a statement to execute. Since the NOBS= parameter is set at compile time, its value will be set even though the SET statement is not executed.

OBS and FIRSTOBS

NOBS is unrelated to the OBS= argument and the FIRSTOBS= argument, and is ignored. Also, WHERE clauses and deleted records are not taken into account when assigning NOBS. If you use these parameters to limit the number of observations that your DATA step is processing, the NOBS parameter will still return the total number of observations, including observations that you do not process. Deleted observations, which have been flagged but not removed, are also included in the NOBS count. See the following example.

```
103   data temp ;
104     if 0 then
105       set sashelp.prdsale(firstobs=20 obs=25) nobs=nobs ;
106     put "with firstobs & obs: " nobs= ;
107     stop ;
108   run ;

with firstobs & obs: nobs=1440
NOTE: The data set WORK.TEMP has 0 observations and 10 variables.
NOTE: DATA statement used (Total process time):
      real time            0.01 seconds
      cpu time             0.02 seconds
```

(continued)

(continued)

```
109   data temp ;
110      if 0 then
111         set sashelp.prdsale nobs=nobs ;
112      put "without firstobs & obs: " nobs= ;
113      stop ;
114   run ;

without firstobs & obs: nobs=1440
NOTE: The data set WORK.TEMP has 0 observations and 10 variables.
NOTE: DATA statement used (Total process time):
      real time           0.03 seconds
      cpu time            0.04 seconds
```

Tape data sets

On mainframe tape data sets, the number of observations in the data set is not stored in the descriptor portion of the SAS data set (which is at the beginning of the data set, of course), because SAS cannot possibly know when beginning to write the tape data set how many observations it will write. For disk data sets, SAS just goes back to the descriptor portion and writes the number of observations into the correct slot once the data set is finished. It's easy to see why this isn't a feature with tape data sets.

You can use the TAPE engine to have sequential data sets stored on disk. In this case, the number of observations is also not available. See the following example.

```
LIBNAME v9305 V606SEQ ;

NOTE: Libref V9305 was successfully assigned as follows:
      Engine:         V606SEQ
      Physical Name:  IVXXX.REQ3339.CARTVX2.SAS9305

DATA temp ;
  if 0 then
    set v9305.ServBill nobs=nobs ;
  put nobs= ;
  stop ;
Run ;

NOBS=2147483647
NOTE: The data set WORK.TEMP has 0 observations and 3 variables.
NOTE: The DATA statement used 0.03 CPU seconds.
```

NOBS=*variable* available prior to SET statement execution

The number of observations in a data set can be obtained using the NOBS keyword in the SET statement. The variable that you specify to hold the number of observations is set at compile time, so you can access it at runtime prior to SET statement execution.

You can get the number of observations and store it in a macro variable without reading observations in. This could be useful if you wanted to run code conditionally depending on whether you had data available.

```
* code to test if a data set has any obs. ;
data _null_ ;
  if 0 then set work.ytd nobs=count ;
  call symput('numobs',left(put(count,8.))) ;
  stop ;
run;

%macro reports ;
%if &numobs =0
%then %do ;
data _null_ ;
  file ft20f001 ;
  %title ;
  put ////
     @10 "NO records were selected using the statement " //
     @15 "&where" //
     @10 "for any month from &start to &end" //
     @10 'THIS RUN HAS COMPLETED SUCCESSFULLY.' ;
run ;
%end ;
%else
  %do ;
* generate graph of costs vs cycle;
proc chart data=work.ytd ;
    by finyear ; vbar pcycle / type=sum sumvar=cost discrete; format
       pcycle $2. ; run;
  %end ;
%mend ;

%reports;
```

Creating views from a DATA step

Apart from SQL views, we also have the DATA step view available within SAS. This is a compiled DATA step that is stored away, able to run at a later time. It can be used anywhere a data set can be used, which means that complicated DATA steps can be written and stored once, then be used over and over for reporting, even as the data changes.

For example, if you had a log file that came to you each month in the form of a large flat file (or CSV, etc.), then you could set up a view to read the records in. This view could then be used in various procedures and other DATA steps to analyze and report on the data.

In the following example, we read in a member that has JCL and SAS code in it. We keep only the lines of JCL in our data set, and make a variable for the account number (if it is there). The PRINT procedure then prints only the line with the account number.

```
    filename x 'IVCGI.REQ3300.CNTL(SQL)' ;
    data sasuser.readx / view=sasuser.readx ;
    infile x ;
    input line $80. ;
    if index(line,'//') ; * keep jcl lines ;
    acc=index(line,' JOB ')+5 ;
    if acc>5 then
    account=scan(substr(line,acc),1,"'") ;
    run ;

NOTE: DATA STEP view saved on file SASUSER.READX.
NOTE: The original source statements cannot be retrieved from a stored
      DATA STEP view nor will a stored DATA STEP view run under a
      different release of the SAS system or under a different operating
      system.
      Please be sure to save the source statements for this DATA STEP
      view.
NOTE: The DATA statement used 0.01 CPU seconds and 1985K.
    proc print ;
    where account>'' ;
    run ;

NOTE: The infile X is:
Dsname=XXXGI.REQ3300.CNTL(SQL),
Unit=3380,Volume=D00106,Disp=SHR,Blksize=23440,
Lrecl=80,Recfm=FB
NOTE: 45 records were read from the infile X.
NOTE: The view SASUSER.READX.VIEW used 0.02 CPU seconds and 2066K.
NOTE: The PROCEDURE PRINT used 0.01 CPU seconds and 2066K.
```

```
OBS                                LINE
1 //XXMSPM00 JOB 'XXXGI002','A_3300 (PM9992306)',CLASS=V,

OBS    ACC    ACCOUNT

 1      16    XXXGI002
```

In some cases, you may find that another excellent use of DATA step views is to improve the performance of pre-processing DATA steps. For example:

```
data work.temp;
   set work.large;
   if variable >=0 then flag=1;
   else flag=0;
run;
proc freq data=work.temp;
   table flag;
run;
```

This requires three I/Os per observation (a read/write by the DATA step and a read by PROC FREQ). Changing work.temp to a view reduces the I/Os to one read, as the DATA step passes the modified observation directly to PROC FREQ. (Adding the keep reduces the data vector.) For example:

```
data work.temp / VIEW=WORK.TEMP;
  KEEP FLAG;
  set work.large;
  if variable >=0 then flag=1;
                  else flag=0;
run;

proc freq data=work.temp;
   table flag;
run;
```

Also, with the original code a work file of a greater size than the original data is required. However, this is not the case using a view, as the modified observations are not kept. The work file needs only to be big enough to hold the compiled view.

Of course, if the view is required frequently, the extra processing cost may outweigh the savings. However, for occasional use the savings can be very significant.

Using the DATA step debugger

The DATA step debugger operates in much the same way as the SCL debugger of SAS/AF, which has been available for a long time. It can be used to step through your DATA step, executing a line at a time. At any stage, you can examine the values of variables. You can set break points and run the DATA step until the code gets to your breakpoint.

To invoke the DATA step debugger, simply put / DEBUG in your DATA statement. See the following example.

Screen shot of the DATA step debugger

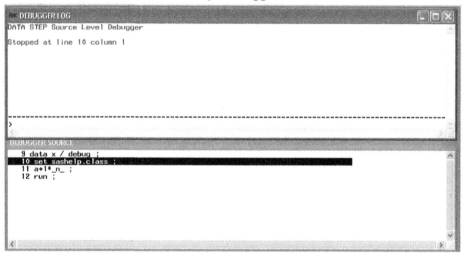

Here are some of the debugger commands. In the following commands, I use the pipe symbol (|) to separate alternate parameters.

Commands

BREAK *line-num*	suspends program execution at an executable statement.
DESCRIBE *arg-list|_all*	displays the attributes of variable(s).
ENTER *command-list*	assigns one or more debugger commands to the ENTER key.
EXAMINE *arg-list|_all*	displays the value of one or more variables.
GO *line-num|label*	starts or resumes execution of the DATA step.
JUMP *line-num*	acts like a GOTO command.
LIST *B|W|_all_*	displays all breakpoints, watch variables, or both.
QUIT	terminates the debugger session.
SET *variable-expression*	assigns new values to a variable.
STEP	executes statements one at a time.
WATCH *variable*	suspends DATA step execution when the value of a specified variable has been modified.

Help

The DATA step debugger is very similar to the SCL debugger. Here are a few interesting notes:

- The Help command describes (in detail) the complete syntax and functionality.

- Pmenus are available with all the options.

- Function keys are defined for some of the common commands (except END).

- You can define macros of debugger commands. I haven't had time to play with this, but it could be useful.

See the SAS Help and Documentation for more information.

Putting variable labels into titles

There are several ways to put a variable label into a title:

1. Use the CALL LABEL routine to put the label into a variable and then SYMPUT to put it into a macro variable. The macro variable can then be used in a TITLE statement.

2. Use SQL to get the label from a data dictionary table and into a macro variable.

3. Get the label from the SASHELP column view, either in SQL or a DATA step.

The following examples show each of the three methods, using SASUSER.FITNESS.

CALL LABEL

```
507   data _null_ ;
508      length agelabel $ 40 ;
509      set sasuser.fitness ;
510      call label(age,agelabel) ;
511      call symput("agemacro",agelabel) ;
512   stop ;
513   run ;

NOTE: There were 1 observations read from the data set SASUSER.FITNESS.
NOTE: DATA statement used (Total process time):
      real time            0.09 seconds
      cpu time             0.00 seconds


514   title "&agemacro" ;
515   proc print data=sasuser.fitness(obs=1) ;
516   run ;

NOTE: There were 1 observations read from the data set SASUSER.FITNESS.
NOTE: PROCEDURE PRINT used (Total process time):
      real time            0.00 seconds
      cpu time             0.00 seconds
```

				Age in years				
Obs	age	weight	runtime	rstpulse	runpulse	maxpulse	oxygen	group
1	57	73.37	12.63	58	174	176	39.407	2

DICTIONARY.COLUMNS

```
517  proc sql ;
518    SELECT label into: wmacro
519      FROM dictionary.columns
520        WHERE libname='SASUSER'
521          & memname='FITNESS'
522          & name='WEIGHT' ;
NOTE: No rows were selected.
522!                               * note: text is case-sensitive ;
523  quit ;
NOTE: PROCEDURE SQL used (Total process time):
      real time           0.14 seconds
      cpu time            0.04 seconds


WARNING: Apparent symbolic reference WMACRO not resolved.
524  title "&wmacro" ;
525  proc print data=sasuser.fitness(obs=1) ;
526  run ;

NOTE: There were 1 observations read from the data set SASUSER.FITNESS.
NOTE: PROCEDURE PRINT used (Total process time):
      real time           0.00 seconds
      cpu time            0.00 seconds
```

```
Weight in kg

Obs  age  weight  runtime  rstpulse  runpulse  maxpulse  oxygen  group

  1   57   73.37   12.63      58       174       176     39.407    2
```

SASHELP.VCOLUMN

```
proc sql ;
   SELECT label INTO :gmacro
      FROM sashelp.vcolumn
      WHERE libname='SASUSER'
      & memname='FITNESS'
      & name='GROUP' ;
title "&gmacro" ;
NOTE: The PROCEDURE SQL used 0.02 CPU seconds and 2722K.
proc print data=sasuser.fitness(obs=1) ;
run ;
NOTE: The PROCEDURE PRINT used 0.01 CPU seconds and 2722K.
```

```
                      Experimental group
OBS  AGE  WEIGHT  RUNTIME  RSTPULSE  RUNPULSE  MAXPULSE  OXYGEN  GROUP
 1   57   73.37   12.63       58       174       176    39.407    2
```

Commenting out code

Adding the CANCEL option to the RUN statement, as illustrated in the following examples, will cause a DATA step or PROC to not run. This option is useful to disable a DATA step or PROC without deleting or commenting the code out. Beware, though, that if the data set does not exist, then the code will still generate an error even though SAS does not attempt to run it.

Code for a PROC example

```
proc contents data=sasuser._all_ ;
run cancel ;

NOTE: The procedure was not executed at the user's request.
NOTE: The PROCEDURE CONTENTS used 0.00 CPU seconds and 1537K.
```

Log for a DATA step example

```
    data ;
      put "This is a test on &sysday" ;
    run ;

This is a test on Friday
NOTE: The data set WORK.DATA1 has 1 observations and 0 variables.
NOTE: The DATA statement used 0.01 CPU seconds and 1435K.

    data ;
      put "This is a test on &sysday" ;
    run cancel ;

NOTE: Data step not executed at user's request.
NOTE: The DATA statement used 0.00 CPU seconds and 1435K.
```

Altering processing within a DO loop, based on a condition

Leaving a loop based on a condition

The LEAVE statement ceases processing the current DO loop or SELECT group. Execution continues with the statement following the DO loop or SELECT group. This is very useful should you want to leave a loop (or group) if some condition is met.

There is a trap with nested DO loops in that the LEAVE statement leaves only the current DO loop, not all of the DO loops in which the statement may be nested.

```
    data temp ;
      set random ;
    *** Put all the variables starting with x into an array ;
      array scores(*) x: ;
    *** Loop through the variables looking for a score over 90% ;
      do i=1 to dim(scores) ;
        if scores(i)>.9 then
          leave ; *** If we find one then leave the loop ;
      end ;
      put scores(i)= ; *** Write out the score that we ended up with ;
    run ;

X2=0.9700887157
NOTE: The data set WORK.TEMP has 1 observations and 21 variables.
NOTE: The DATA statement used 0.02 CPU seconds and 1881K.
```

Going on to the next iteration of a DO loop

The CONTINUE statement stops processing the current iteration of a DO loop and continues with the next iteration. It can be used to terminate processing an iteration based on a condition.

In the following example, if an element of the crimes array is less than 100, then you go on to the next iteration of the loop. Otherwise, you write out information about it.

```
    data over100 ;
       set sasuser.crime(drop=state) ;  * Dont need this variable ;
       array crimes(*) _numeric_ ;       * Put all the crime rates in an
array ;
       do i=1 to dim(crimes) ;          * Loop through each of the crime
variables ;
          if crimes(i)<100 then
             CONTINUE ;                  * If a rate is under 100 then
                                           proceed to next iteration ;

          put 'State: ' staten
              'has ' crimes(i)= ;        * These are >= 100 ;
       end ;
    run ;

State: Alabama has ASSAULT=278.3
State: Alabama has BURGLARY=1135.5
State: Alabama has LARCENY=1881.9
State: Alabama has AUTO=280.7
State: Alaska has ASSAULT=284
 etc. etc. etc.
```

Editing external files in place

You can use PUT statements to make modifications to large external files (flat files, VSAM, etc.) rather than reading data into SAS variables, modifying variables, and writing them out.

There are two ways to accomplish this:

1. Use put _infile_ to write out the data you read in, and then overwrite the parts you want to change.

2. Use the SHAREBUFFERS option in the INFILE statement, which causes the FILE and INFILE statements to use the same buffer. This enables you to write the same data out that you read in, but making any changes as you do it, as in the following example. This might also save CPU time by eliminating the need to copy the input buffer to the output buffer.

Basic example code

```
data _null_ ;
  infile 'c:\very-long-recs.txt'
        sharebuffers ;   /* Define input file */
  input ;                /* Read a record into the input buffer */
  file out ;             /* Point to where you want to write output */
  put @33  'ABC'         /* write changes */
      @400 '12345'       /* write another change */
      @999 'Wow' ;       /* write the last change */
run ;
```

Alternate example code

```
Data _null_ ;
infile 'c:\very-long-recs.txt' ;
input ;
file 'c:\out.txt' ;
put _infile_ ',this,that' ;  * Appends 2 fields to the end of a CSV
                                file ;
run ;


Data _null_ ;
infile 'c:\very-long-recs.txt' ;
input ;
file 'c:\out.txt' ;
put first ',' second ',' _infile_ ; * Puts 2 fields at the start of
                                       a CSV file ;
run ;
```

DDE: Making sure numbers are numeric

Sometimes when writing out data using DDE, you might find that you can't do calculations on the numbers that you have written to your spreadsheet or database. This is because the numbers have been written out as character values, rather than numbers.

When you use DDE to write numbers to a spreadsheet or database, the numbers can sometimes be inadvertently read in as character values. This can happen if you use a variable to hold your tab character, because after a variable is output, a space is written. To get around this, position the column pointer over the space that was written (see the following example).

```
filename lotus dde '123w|test.wk4!a:a1..a:b3' notab ;

* Writing numeric values directly to spreadsheet via DDE ;
data _null_ ;
  retain tab '09'x ; ** Define a tab character ;
  file lotus ; ** Directs output to spreadsheet via DDE link ;
* In Lotus: 1 is numeric, but 2 is character due to implicit space
            after variable TAB ;
*           3 & 4 are numeric, since implicit space is overwritten ;
*           5 & 6 are numeric since there is no implicit space, due to
            constant being used ;
  put '1'     tab
      '2'     /
      '3'     tab +(-1)
      '4'     /
      '5'     '09'x
      '6'     ;
run ;

NOTE: The file LOTUS is:
      FILENAME=123w|test.wk4!a:a1..a:b3,
      RECFM=V,LRECL=256

NOTE: 3 records were written to the file LOTUS.
      The minimum record length was 3.
      The maximum record length was 4.
NOTE: The DATA statement used 0.66 seconds.
```

Data of views can't change

If the structure of data sets on which views are based changes, then the view will no longer work. In the following example, I create a DATA step view and use it successfully. Then I add a variable to the data that the view references, and the view no longer works. You must also keep the libref (sasuser in this example) the same.

```
data v_house / view=v_house ;
  set sasuser.houses ;
run ;

NOTE: DATA STEP view saved on file WORK.V_HOUSE.
NOTE: The original source statements cannot be retrieved from a stored
      DATA STEP view nor will a stored DATA STEP view run under a
      different release of the SAS system or under a different operating
      system.
      Please be sure to save the source statements for this DATA STEP
      view.
NOTE: The DATA statement used 0.44 seconds.


proc print data=v_house(obs=1) ;
run;

NOTE: The view WORK.V_HOUSE.VIEW used 0.39 seconds.

NOTE: The PROCEDURE PRINT used 0.44 seconds.


data sasuser.houses ;
  set sasuser.houses ;
  obs=_n_ ;
run ;

NOTE: The data set SASUSER.HOUSES has 15 observations and 7 variables.
NOTE: The DATA statement used 0.66 seconds.


NOTE: The view WORK.V_HOUSE.VIEW used 0.22 seconds.

proc print data=v_house(obs=1) ;
ERROR: The variable OBS from data set SASUSER.HOUSES is not defined in
       the INPUT view
       WORK.V_HOUSE.
ERROR: Failure loading view WORK.V_HOUSE.VIEW with request 4.
```

Views don't use indexes

If you create a view (DATA step or SQL) of an indexed SAS data set, the index of that data set will not be used when using the view. See the following example.

Log: DATA step view

```
options msglevel=i ; *** Tell me when SAS uses an index ;

proc datasets library=mis ;
  modify item ;
  index create _type_ ;
NOTE: Single index _TYPE_ defined.
run;

NOTE: The PROCEDURE DATASETS used 3.02 seconds.

*** This shows that the index is being used when using the data set
    directly ;
proc print data=mis.item ;
  where _type_=0 ;
INFO: Index _TYPE_ selected for WHERE clause optimization.
run;

NOTE: The PROCEDURE PRINT used 0.22 seconds.

*** Make a DATA step view ;
data v_item / view=v_item ;
  set mis.item ;
  year=substr(servmth,1,2) ;
run ;

NOTE: DATA STEP view saved on file WORK.V_ITEM.
NOTE: The original source statements cannot be retrieved from a stored
      DATA STEP view nor will a stored DATA STEP view run under a
      different release of the SAS system or under a different operating
      system.
      Please be sure to save the source statements for this DATA STEP
      view.
NOTE: The DATA statement used 0.55 seconds.

*** Use the DATA step view, and notice that the index is not used ;
proc print data=v_item ;
  where _type_=0 ;
run;
```

(continued)

(continued)

```
NOTE: The view WORK.V_ITEM.VIEW used 1.41 seconds.
NOTE: The PROCEDURE PRINT used 1.59 seconds.

===> Example 2: SQL view

proc sql ;
  create view v_item as
  select *,
        substr(servmth,1,2) as year
  from mis.item ;
NOTE: SQL view WORK.V_ITEM has been defined.
quit ;
NOTE: The PROCEDURE SQL used 0.39 seconds.


proc print data=v_item ;
  where _type_=0 ;
run;

NOTE: The PROCEDURE PRINT used 3.62 seconds.
```

Bringing environment variables into macro variables

This tip is very useful for determining system information. In SAS, under Windows and UNIX, there's a function called SYSGET that gets DOS or SAS environment variables into macro variables. It can also be used as a way to pass information from DOS to SAS so that the information could then be used in SAS programs.

In this example, I extract one system environment variable and then two variables that I set in my AUTOEXEC.BAT.

```
    %let comspec=%sysget(comspec);
    %let temp=%sysget(temp);
    %let name=%sysget(name);
    %put comspec=&comspec ;
comspec=C:\COMMAND.COM
    %put temp=&temp ;
temp=C:\TEMP
    %put name=&name ;
name=Philip Mason
```

Using stored compiled programs

By compiling a program and storing it away, you save the CPU time that would be used to compile it each time it is run. If the program is quite long and is used often, then this may help to improve performance. However, there won't typically be much of a savings.

You can compile DATA steps and save the compiled code to be executed later. The main advantage of this is that you need to compile the code only once, but can run it many times, saving resources used in doing the compile each time you run. See the following examples.

```
    data test / pgm=sasuser.prog1 ;
      set sasuser.class ;
      if age<10 then
       child='YES' ;
    run ;

NOTE: DATA STEP program saved on file SASUSER.PROG1.
NOTE: The original source statements cannot be retrieved from a stored
      DATA STEP program nor will a stored DATA STEP program run under a
      different release of the SAS system or under a different operating
      system.
      Please be sure to save the source statements for this stored
      program.
NOTE: The DATA statement used 0.01 CPU seconds and 1600K.
```

```
    data pgm=sasuser.prog1 ;
    run ;

NOTE: DATA STEP program loaded from file SASUSER.PROG1.
NOTE: The data set WORK.TEST has 19 observations and 6 variables.
NOTE: The DATA statement used 0.01 CPU seconds and 1694K.

proc print data=test ;
run ;
```

Treatment of macros

Be aware that when you use compiled programs in SAS together with macro variables, those macro variables are resolved at compile time. This goes for compiled DATA steps and SCL programs. If you want to use the value of a macro variable at execution time, then you should use the SYMGET function, as shown in the following example.

```
data test ;
  set sashelp.class ;
  value=SYMGET('macrovar') ; * Specify macro name without a leading &
    or % ;
run ;
```

Logic variations using IF and WHERE statements

Usually the conditions used with an IF statement and a WHERE statement will produce the same results, but not in all cases.

A SAS trap is not a bug, but a feature. Most of the traps are documented, but often they are counterintuitive and dangerous for even the experienced user. Some are avoidable, some have historical rationales, and some are simply bizarre. Here is one such trap.

Usually WHERE *var;* and IF *var;* will produce the same result. However, if the value of the variable is a character value of "0", then the WHERE will return TRUE and the IF will return FALSE. The following example demonstrates this.

```
data x ;
  zero='0' ;
run ;

NOTE: The data set WORK.X has 1 observations and 1 variables.
NOTE: The DATA statement used 0.01 CPU seconds and 1383K.
data If ;
  set x ;
  if zero ;
run ;

NOTE: Character values have been converted to numeric
      values at the places given by: (Line):(Column).
42:6
NOTE: The data set WORK.IF has 0 observations and 1 variables.
NOTE: The DATA statement used 0.01 CPU seconds and 1383K.
data Where ;
  set x ;
    where zero ;
run ;

NOTE: The data set WORK.WHERE has 1 observations and 1 variables.
NOTE: The DATA statement used 0.01 CPU seconds and 1399K.
```

The WHERE statement does not do automatic variable type conversions, whereas the IF statement does. ZERO is a character variable. The log shows a character to numeric conversion with the IF statement. It does not do so with the WHERE statement because if you use the name of a character variable by itself as a WHERE expression, SAS selects observations where the value of the character variable is not blank. And "0" is not blank.

DDE: Using more advanced commands

DDE system commands are issued by setting up a FILEREF to point to an application, as in the example below. The commands can then be sent to the application by writing to the FILEREF. When issuing commands to the application, the SYSITEMS system command can be used to discover what commands the program supports. These commands offer a greater level of interaction between SAS and the other program. Using the SYSITEMS command on Lotus 123, I discovered that it supports six commands (see example below), whereas Microsoft Word 6 supports only three of those.

Lotus 123

SysItems	returns commands available for server (see example below)
Topics	returns topics
Formats	returns file formats handled by server (for example, RTF, text, WK3, etc.)
RangeNames	returns name of range and its specification (for example, Sales A:C4..A:E8)
Selection	returns name of data file and range selected (for example Untitled A:A1..A:C3)
Status	returns status of server (for example, Ready)

```
** Define the sysitems topic to find which commands are supported
   by the application for DDE ;
filename lotus dde '123w|system!sysitems' notab ;

data _null_ ;
  length cmd $ 40 ; * Otherwise first command read in sets maximum
  length ;
  infile lotus pad dsd dlm='09'x ; * One tab delimited record is
  returned ;
  input cmd $ @@ ;
  put cmd ;
run ;

NOTE: The infile LOTUS is:
      FILENAME=123w|system!sysitems,
      RECFM=V,LRECL=256
```

(continued)

(continued)

```
SysItems
Topics
Formats
RangeNames
Selection
Status
NOTE: 1 record was read from the infile LOTUS.
      The minimum record length was 51.
      The maximum record length was 51.
NOTE: SAS went to a new line when INPUT statement reached past the end
      of a line.
NOTE: The DATA statement used 0.82 seconds.
```

Microsoft Word

```
** Define the sysitems topic to find which commands are supported
   by the application for DDE ;
filename word dde 'winword|system!sysitems' notab ;

data _null_ ;
  infile word pad dsd dlm='09'x ; * One tab separated record is returned
  ;
  input cmd $ @@ ;
  put cmd ;
run ;

NOTE: The infile WORD is:
      FILENAME=winword|system!sysitems,
      RECFM=V,LRECL=256

SYSITEMS
TOPICS
FORMATS
NOTE: 1 record was read from the infile WORD.
      The minimum record length was 23.
      The maximum record length was 23.
NOTE: SAS went to a new line when INPUT statement reached past the end
      of a line.
NOTE: The DATA statement used 0.81 seconds.
```

Generation data sets

A generation data set is a historical copy of a data set. The generation data set feature enables you to keep multiple copies of data sets by defining a maximum number to keep. Generation data sets are supported in SAS 8 and later.

To define the number of generations to keep, you can use the GENMAX= data set option.

```
* keep multiple copies of data sets ;
data x(genmax=5) ;
a=1 ;
run ;
* each time we create the data set again it makes another generation ;
data x ;
a=2 ;
run ;
data x ;
a=3 ;
run ;
data x ;
a=4 ;
run ;
* current generation is 0, or just dont specify the one you want ;
data y ;
  set x(gennum=0) ;
  put a= ;
run ;
* generation 2 is the 2nd one created - actually called x#002 ;
data y ;
  set x(gennum=2) ;
  put a= ;
run ;
* generation -1 is the previous one created, not the current one but
the one before ;
data y ;
  set x(gennum=-1) ;
  put a= ;
run ;
```

Automatic checking of the log

Here is a useful technique for times when you have a huge log and want to check to see if it has any error or warning messages. You could use DLGFIND and search for "ERROR", but that would find occurrences of the word "ERROR" that may not be error messages (e.g. the variable _error_).

This technique copies the log to a catalog member and then checks each line from it to see if there are any error or warning messages. These are put into a data set and then displayed in an HTML report. If there are no errors or warnings, then a message appears to say so. This can, of course, be modified to look for other messages or text.

To make this technique really useful, you can define a tool on the toolbar. The command for the tool should be something like the following example:

```
sub '%include "c:\demo\anal.sas";'
```

```
*** need to assign this macro call to a button on toolbar
    so that pressing the button will analyze the log ;
filename cat catalog 'work.test.test.log' ;
dm 'log;file cat' ; * write log to catalog member ;
ods listing close ;
ods html file='analyze.htm' ;
data analyze ;
  length line $200 ;
  label line='Line from LOG'
        _n_='Line number' ;
  infile cat end=end truncover ;
  file print ods=(vars=(_n_ line)) ;
  input line & ;
  if substr(line,1,5)='ERROR' then
    put _ods_ ;
  else
    if substr(line,1,7)='WARNING' then
      put _ods_ ;
    else
      n+1 ;
  if end & n=_n_ then
    do ;
      window status rows=15 columns=40 color=gray
                #5 'No errors or warnings were found.' color=yellow
                #9 'Press enter to continue' ;
      display status ;
    end ;
run ;
```

```
ods html close ;
filename cat ; * free catalog member ;
dm 'del work.test.test.log' ; * delete it ;
ods listing ;
```

Using data sets without librefs

In SAS 8 and later you can directly reference SAS data sets, without needing to define a libref. This is done by enclosing the physical file name in quotation marks. See the following example.

```
15    * Create a version 6 data set ;
16    data 'c:\test.sd2' ;
      run ;

NOTE: c:\test.sd2 is a Version 6 data set.  In future releases of SAS
      you may not be able to create or update Version 6 data sets. Use
      PROC COPY to convert the data set to Version 9.
NOTE: The data set c:\test.sd2 has 1 observations and 0 variables.
NOTE: DATA statement used (Total process time):
      real time           0.00 seconds
      cpu time            0.00 seconds


17    * Create a version 8 data set ;
18    data 'c:\test.sas7bdat' ;
      run ;

NOTE: The data set c:\test.sd7 has 1 observations and 0 variables.
NOTE: DATA statement used (Total process time):
      real time           0.01 seconds
      cpu time            0.01 seconds


19    * Create a version 9 data set ;
20    data 'c:\v9\test.sas7bdat' ;
      run ;

NOTE: The data set c:\v9\test.sas7bdat has 1 observations and 0
      variables.
NOTE: DATA statement used (Total process time):
      real time           0.01 seconds
      cpu time            0.01 seconds


21
22    * access a data set directly ;
23    proc print data='c:\test.sas7bdat' ;
      run ;

NOTE: No variables in data set c:\test.sas7bdat.
NOTE: PROCEDURE PRINT used (Total process time):
      real time           0.01 seconds
      cpu time            0.00 seconds
```

Using wildcards to read external files

To read many identically structured and consecutively named files (i.e. Tab1.dat, tab2.dat, etc.) in a single DATA step of Windows or UNIX, you can use the filename statement with a wildcard (asterisk or question mark).

```
filename in 'c:\tab*.dat' ;

data report ;
  infile in ;
  input a b c ;
run ;
```

Data encryption for the beginner

The data stored in some SAS data sets is sensitive and needs protection. This tip provides sufficient protection for many security requirements.

The BXOR function presents budding encrypters with a basic tool for encrypting numbers. The function works by returning the result of a binary exclusive OR between the two arguments. The following example shows how a key can be used to change original numbers into coded numbers. Using the BXOR function against those coded numbers with the same key returns the numbers to the original value.

This technique truncates values to the nearest 1 (see the value 34.4 in the following example program). If using decimal places (for example, as with money), then you should convert numbers to integers (for example, express the value in cents).

If you want to see where the bits are set in keys and data, then use the following format. This will enable you to easily check the function by hand.

Format	Description	Width Range	Default Width	Alignment
BINARY w.	converts numeric values to binary	1-64	8	left

```
data coded ;
  * set the value of the key ;
  retain key 1234567 ;
  input original ;
  * encode the original value using the key ;
  coded=bxor(original,key);
  put key= original= coded= ;
  datalines ;
1
1234567
999999
34.4
0
run ;
```

```
data decode ;
 * the value of the key must be the same,
   or else the number will not decode correctly ;
 retain key 1234567 ;
 set coded ;
 * decode the coded value using the key ;
 decoded=bxor(coded,key);
 put coded= decoded= ;
run ;
```

The following log shows the results of the first DATA step, which encodes the numbers.

```
KEY=1234567 ORIGINAL=1          CODED=1234566
KEY=1234567 ORIGINAL=1234567 CODED=0
KEY=1234567 ORIGINAL=999999   CODED=1938616
KEY=1234567 ORIGINAL=34.4     CODED=1234597
KEY=1234567 ORIGINAL=0          CODED=1234567
NOTE: The data set WORK.CODED has 5 observations and 3 variables.
NOTE: The DATA statement used 0.01 CPU seconds and 1451K.
```

The following log shows the results of the second DATA step, which decodes the numbers.

```
CODED=1234566 DECODED=1
CODED=0        DECODED=1234567
CODED=1938616 DECODED=999999
CODED=1234597 DECODED=34
CODED=1234567 DECODED=0
NOTE: The data set WORK.DECODE has 5 observations and 4 variables.
NOTE: The DATA statement used 0.01 CPU seconds and 1471K.
```

Note: Other ways to do encryption include:

■ using the data set option encrypt=yes

■ using encryption within the operating system, such as going into the file properties in Windows XP and selecting **Encrypt**.

Dealing with missing values

Here are several things to be aware of when dealing with missing values:

- Most operators propagate missing values, but comparison operators treat them as negative infinity, so X < 0 is true when X is missing.

- Adding and/or subtracting several numbers using the plus (+) and minus (–) operators will return a missing value if any of the numbers are missing. To get around this, you should use the SUM function. The SUM function will return a missing value only if all of the values or variables being added are missing. If you always want a 0 returned, rather than a missing value, use SUM(0,var1,var2,...).

- Many procedures (for example, SUMMARY, TABULATE, FREQ, CALENDAR, etc.) ignore missing values, or at least treat them in a different way. Usually, missing values are ignored by default, and you should override the default if you want them included.

- Some procedures have different statistics for missing and non-missing variables. For instance, SUMMARY has N for the number of non-missing observations and NMISS for the number of observations with missing values. If you use PROC MEANS with a class statement, you can get the NOBS statistic, which is the sum of missing and non-missing observations.

See the following example.

```
data _null_ ;
 * Initialize values ;
  a=. ;
  b=0 ;
  c=-7 ;
  d=99 ;
 * Try various forms of addition involving missing values ;
  add=a+b+c+d ;
  put 'Addition of missing & non-missing values :   ' add= ;
  sum=sum(a,b,c,d) ;
  put 'Sum of missing & non-missing values :   ' sum= ;
  summiss=sum(.,a) ;
  put 'Sum of missing values only :   ' summiss= ;
  sumzero=sum(0,.,a) ;
  put 'Sum of 0 and missing values :   ' sumzero= ;
 * See how the missing value compares to zero ;
  if a<0 then
    put 'Missing is less than 0' ;
  else if a>0 then
    put 'Missing is greater than 0' ;
run ;
```

In the following log, you can see the results of performing various operations on missing values. You can also notice the note about missing values being generated. This note warns you that some calculations in your code contain missing values and have therefore resulted in missing values. Usually you don't want this to happen, so be aware of this message and use the line and column reference from the log to locate the places that it occurs to verify that it is OK or to fix it.

```
Addition of missing & non-missing values :  ADD=.
Sum of missing & non-missing values :  SUM=92
Sum of missing values only :  SUMMISS=.
Sum of 0 and missing values :  SUMZERO=0
Missing is less than 0

NOTE: Missing values were generated as a result of performing an
operation on missing values.
Each place is given by: (Number of times) at (Line):(Column).
1 at 77:8    1 at 77:10    1 at 77:12    1 at 81:11
NOTE: The DATA statement used 0.02 CPU seconds and 1420K.
```

■ Special missing values are handled in a way you might not necessarily expect. They are not handled incorrectly, but when I assumed that if I did something with a special missing value, it would be propagated as a special missing value, I was surprised! See the following example.

```
data temp;
  missing Z;
  input a;
  b = a + 0;
datalines;
7
4
.Z
5
;
run;
proc print ;
run ;
```

In the output, I would have expected that the special missing value when added to 0 would result in the same special missing value (i.e. .Z). However, it results in a normal missing value (i.e. .). Note that the "Z" shown in the output is actually the missing value ".Z". SAS does not yet print it as ".Z".

```
OBS     A     B

 1      7     7
 2      4     4
 3      Z     .
 4      5     5
```

Note: .Z is a special missing value, which is different from a normal missing value.

You could use a custom format to display the special missing value in another form. See the following example.

```
proc format ;
  value miss
     .z='Missing data' ;
run ;
```

Writing to an external log, rather than to the SAS log

Sometimes you may want to record specific information to a log so that you can keep track of activity. The following macro shows how to use a simple general purpose technique to write that information to a file in a standardized way.

```
%macro log(action,who,what,where) ;
* Description - This method will record a record to a Log file ;
* action ... 1=write to GUI log
             2=write to data log
* return ... we return the return code from the (un)lock operation ;
  %if &action=1 %then
    %let file=system.gui_log ;
  %else
    %if &action=2 %then
      %let file=system.data_log ;
    %else
      %do ;
        %put WARNING: invalid action specified for LOG macro. ;
        %goto out ;
      %end ;
  data line ;
    who="&who" ;
    what="&what" ;
    where="&where" ;
    when=datetime() ;
  run ;
  proc append base=&file data=line force ;
  run ;
%out:
%mend log ;
/*%log(1,phil,test log macro,on ashe) ;*/
```

Adding a progress bar to a DATA step

If you have a long-running DATA step, then you may find yourself wondering if SAS is actually doing anything or not. One way to indicate what is happening is to display a progress indicator to the user. The following macro will show the number of the record currently being read in. If you were to show this for every record, it would slow down the DATA step while the display was updated, so you need to specify how often to update the display. Typically, updating about every 1000 records will give a good indication without slowing things down.

Of course, if you don't have a large file, you may not even see the progress bar pop up on the screen before it is gone again.

The PROGRESS macro

```
%macro progress(every) ;
  window progress irow=4 rows=7 columns=40
    #1 @6 'Processing record: ' _n_ persist=yes ;
  if mod(_n_,&every)=0 then
    display progress noinput ;
%mend progress ;
```

How to use it

All you need to do is to add the macro call to your DATA step. The following DATA step updates the record count every 1000 records read in.

```
data x ;
  infile 'm:\datasets\x.txt' ;
  input name $30. phone $18. ;
  %progress(1000) ;
run ;
```

Progress bars in DATA steps

This macro relies on a variable called NOBS, which exists in the DATA step and holds the number of observations. The macro then updates the progress bar at the interval specified in the parameter EVERY.

```
%macro progress2(every) ;
 * this macro relies on NOBS=NOBS & END=END being on input data set ;
 * progress will change every%, e.g. progress2(10) changes every 10% ;
  pct=round(_n_/nobs*100) ;
  window progress irow=4 rows=7 columns=40
    #1 @6 'Percent Complete: ' pct '%' persist=yes ;
  if mod(pct,&every)=0 then
    display progress noinput ;
%mend progress2 ;
*** use it ;
data test ;
  set xxx nobs=nobs ;
  %progress2(10) ; * update progress every 10% ;
run ;
```

Using bit flags

Sometimes you may want to use a single number in a variable and set bits within it to represent different things. You can use the binary format to display a number in binary form, so you can see what each bit is set to. You can also use the BXOR function to set individual bits. The following example demonstrates some techniques for doing this.

```
* maximum binary format can handle is 64 ;
data _null_ ;
  max=2**64;
  put max= comma27. ;
  flag=max-1;
  put flag binary64. ' - ' flag comma27. ;
run ;
* test setting bits ;
data _null_ ;
  flag=0 ;
  bit=3 ;
  link setflag ;
  bit=6 ;
  link setflag ;
  bit=20 ;
  link setflag ;
  return ;
setflag:
  flag=bor(flag,2**(bit-1)) ;
  put flag binary32. flag 12. ;
return ;
run ;
```

Taking a sample of data

Sometimes you may want to take a small sample of a large file so you can test your code against it. The following code shows how you can take the second 100 records from a file and save to another file.

```
data _null_ ;
   infile 'M:\My big file.txt' firstobs=101 obs=200 ;
   file 'm:\system\small.txt' ;
   input ;
run ;
```

Using unusual variable names

In SAS 8 and later,

- Variable names can be upper and lower case.

- Variable names can be up to 32 characters long.

- Referencing variables is case insensitive.

- Spaces and some special symbols are allowed (depending on options).

To use embedded spaces and special symbols, you need to specify the following option:

```
options validvarname=any;
```

The following example shows how to create a variable name and use it.

```
data test ;
  '#1 @ the "Top"'n='John' ;
  "Applied Statistician's"N=1 ;
run ;
proc print ;
  id '#1 @ the "Top"'n ;
  var "Applied Statistician's"N ;
run ;
```

Partial output from a PROC CONTENTS on the data set TEST follows.

```
Alphabetic List of Variables and Attributes

#    Variable                  Type    Len

1    #1 @ the "Top"            Char     4
2    Applied Statistician's    Num      8
```

Renaming variables

You can rename individual variables using a RENAME statement, using the
RENAME= data set option, or you can rename a range of variables as shown in the
following example.

```
data x ;
  array a(10) $ 2 ;
run ;
* Renaming one at a time ;
proc print data=x(rename=(a1=b1 a2=b2 a3=b3 a4=b4 a5=b5
                          a6=b6 a7=b7 a8=b8 a9=b9 a10=b10)) ;
* Renaming a range of variables ;
proc print data=x(rename=(a1-a10=b1-b10)) ;
run ;

data y ;
  array x(50) $ 2 ;
  rename x1-x50=something_else1-something_else50 ;
run ;
```

IN operator now accepts integer ranges

In SAS®9 and later, the IN operator has been enhanced to accept integer ranges. This works well with IF statements, but doesn't work with WHERE statements. See the following example.

```
73   data sample ;
74     set sashelp.class ;
75       if age in (11, 13:15, 18:25) ;
76   run ;

NOTE: There were 19 observations read from the data set SASHELP.CLASS.
NOTE: The data set WORK.SAMPLE has 13 observations and 5 variables.
NOTE: DATA statement used (Total process time):
      real time             0.03 seconds
      cpu time              0.02 seconds
```

Using compiled DATA steps

For those who haven't seen compiled DATA steps before, here is the basic code. The example shows how %SYSFUNC is executed at compile time so that the COMPILE_TIME value does not change once the code is compiled. Then each time you run the code, the TIME() function is run and gives the current time.

```
data test / pgm=test ;
  format compile_time exec_time time8. ;
  compile_time=%sysfunc(time()) ; * gets the current time, when
compiled ;
  exec_time=time() ; * gets the current time when run ;
  put compile_time= exec_time= ;
run ;
data pgm=test ;
run ; * run a compiled data step ;
```

```
33   data pgm=test ;
34   run ;

NOTE: DATA STEP program loaded from file WORK.TEST.
compile_time=13:21:34 exec_time=13:22:38
NOTE: The data set WORK.TEST has 1 observations and 2 variables.
NOTE: DATA statement used:
      real time             0.01 seconds
      cpu time              0.01 seconds
```

EXECUTE and DESCRIBE

Prior to SAS 8.2, source code was not kept with compiled code, which meant that if you lost the source code, then it might be difficult to rewrite the code. However, in SAS 8.2 and later, you can use the DESCRIBE statement to display the original source code. You can also use the EXECUTE statement to rerun the original source code to produce a newly compiled DATA step. See the following example.

```
34    data pgm=test ;
35       describe ;
36    run ;

NOTE: DATA step stored program WORK.TEST is defined as:

data test / pgm=test ;
   format compile_time exec_time time8. ;
   compile_time=48093.5910000801 ;
   exec_time=time() ;
   put compile_time= exec_time= ;
run ;


NOTE: DATA statement used:
      real time              0.00 seconds
      cpu time               0.00 seconds


37    data pgm=test ;
38       execute ;
39    run ;

NOTE: DATA STEP program loaded from file WORK.TEST.
compile_time=13:21:34 exec_time=13:28:12
NOTE: The data set WORK.TEST has 1 observations and 2 variables.
NOTE: DATA statement used:
      real time              0.01 seconds
      cpu time               0.01 seconds
```

Running macro code from a DATA step

The CALL EXECUTE macro can be used to submit code enclosed in quotation marks as a parameter to CALL EXECUTE. The code will be run as soon as possible. This means that if it is macro code, it will often be run immediately as the DATA step is running. If the code is DATA step or PROC code, then it will be queued up and run right after the current DATA step ends. The following example shows how a macro assignment statement is executed during a DATA step, and then the RESOLVE function gets the value that was just assigned.

```
353  %let x=0 ;
354  data _null_ ;
355    call execute ('%let x=1 ;') ;
356    x=resolve ('&x') ;
357    put x= ;
358  run ;

NOTE: DATA statement used (Total process time):
      real time           0.01 seconds
      cpu time            0.01 seconds

x=1

NOTE: CALL EXECUTE routine executed successfully, but no SAS statements
      were generated.
```

Using the PUT statement

The PUT statement is a very flexible tool in the DATA step programmer's toolkit. Here are some different ways of using it. Hopefully, there will be one or two you have not seen before.

Statement	Explanation
`put x y z ;`	writes values of 3 variables out separated by a space.
`put 'hello' '09'x ;`	writes text followed by hexadecimal 09—which is a tab character (in ASCII).
`put 132*'_' ;`	writes 132 underscores.
`put #3 @44 cost ;`	writes the value of cost out, beginning at line 3 column 44.
`put var 1-5 ;`	writes the value of var out into the columns from column 1 to column 5.
`put cost dollar12.2 ;`	writes the value of cost out using the dollar12.2 format.
`put (a b) (1. ','` `$3.) ;`	writes the value of a out using a 1. format, then a comma, then the value of b using a $3. format.
`put _infile_ ;`	writes the current input buffer, as read by the last input statement.
`put _all_ ;`	writes the values of all variables, including _error_ and _n_.
`put _ods_ ;`	writes the default or previously defined variables to the ODS destination.
`put a b c @ ;`	writes the values of variables a, b, and c, separated by spaces and keep line open so that the next PUT statement will continue on. If we reach the end of the DATA step iteration, then the line is closed.
`put d e @@ ;`	writes the values of variables d and e, separated by spaces and keep line open, even if we reach the end of the DATA step iteration.
`put @10 name ;`	writes the value of name at column 10.
`put @pos name ;`	writes the value of name at the column specified in variable pos.

(continued)

(continued)

Statement	Explanation
`put @(3*pos) name ;`	writes the value of name at the column calculated by value of pos multiplied by 3.
`put a +3 b ;`	writes the value of a, followed by 3 spaces and then the value of b.
`put a +gap b ;`	writes the value of a, followed by a number of spaces specified in the variable gap, and then the value of b.
`put a +(2*gap) b ;`	writes the value of a, followed by a number of spaces calculated by the value of gap multiplied by 2, and then the value of b.
`put #2 text ;`	writes the value of text at line 2.
`put #line text ;`	writes the value of text at the line specified in the variable line.
`put #(line*3) text ;`	writes value of text at the line calculated by the value of line multiplied by 3.
`put line1 / line2 ;`	writes the value of line 1, then goes to a new line, and writes the value of line 2.

`put @1 title`
`overprint @1`
`'_____' ;`
	writes the value of title and then overprints underscores on that value. This works only on some print destinations and usually looks wrong on the screen.

`put _blankpage_ ;`	ensures that a totally blank page is produced. This means that if we had written even 1 character on a page, then that page will be written as well as another totally blank page.
`put _page_ ;`	finishes the current page, causing the next thing we write to be on a new page.
`put name= phone= ;`	writes the text "name=" followed by the value of name, and then "phone=" followed by the value of phone.
`put my_big_array(*) ;`	writes each element of my_big_array in the form variable=value.

Interesting options on the FILE statement

The FILE statement has a multitude of options available. Here are some of the more interesting ones that you may find useful.

Statement	Explanation
Column=var	sets var to current column number.
Delimiter=',' | var	sets delimiter to a character (e.g. comma) or variable value.
Dropover	drops data too long for line.
Dsd	writes data items with delimiters (default delimiter is the comma).
Filename=var	sets var to physical filename in use.
Filevar=var	determines the physical file to be written to.
Flowover	writes to the next line anything that doesn't fit on the current line.
[no]footnotes	prints footnotes.
Header=label	runs statements at label for each new page.
Line=var	contains current logical line number.
Linesize=	indicates columns per line.
Linesleft=var	contains lines left on page.
Mod	writes after whatever is in file.
Ods=	defines ODS sub-options.
Old	wipes file before writing.
Pagesize=	indicates lines per page.
Stopover	stops DATA step if trying to write beyond end of line.
[no]titles	prints titles.
file=var	contains current output buffer and is read/write.

Reading the next value of a variable

When reading a data set in the DATA step, you can use the LAG() function to read previous values of a variable. The LAG function returns the value of the argument from the last time lag was executed, not necessarily from the previous observation.

For example:

```
data x;
  set sasuser.class;
  if sex ne lag(sex)  then y='ABC';
  if sex ne lag(sex) then z=lag(name);
run;
```

That's handy, but what if you would also like to look ahead and read the next value(s)? Well, you can do this by reading the same data set again, only starting at a later record.

For example, if you wanted to read the next value of name from a data set, then you would use the SET statement to read the data set as usual, but then you would use another SET statement to read the data set starting at the second record. So as to not overwrite other variables, just keep the variable you are interested in, and rename it to something that makes its meaning clear (next_name). The following SAS Log shows some code that does this and you can see that it has worked by looking at the values it wrote out.

Of course, if you want to also read the next observation at the same time, then you could just add another SET statement starting at record 3 and rename the variable to something like next_name2.

```
1    data name ;
2      set sashelp.class ; * read this record ;
3      set sashelp.class(firstobs=2
4                        keep=name
5                        rename=(name=next_name)) ; * just read one
  variable from the next record ;
6      put _n_ name= next_name= ;
7    run ;

1 Name=Alfred next_name=Alice
2 Name=Alice next_name=Barbara
3 Name=Barbara next_name=Carol
4 Name=Carol next_name=Henry
5 Name=Henry next_name=James
6 Name=James next_name=Jane
7 Name=Jane next_name=Janet
8 Name=Janet next_name=Jeffrey
9 Name=Jeffrey next_name=John
10 Name=John next_name=Joyce
11 Name=Joyce next_name=Judy
12 Name=Judy next_name=Louise
13 Name=Louise next_name=Mary
14 Name=Mary next_name=Philip
15 Name=Philip next_name=Robert
16 Name=Robert next_name=Ronald
17 Name=Ronald next_name=Thomas
18 Name=Thomas next_name=William
NOTE: There were 19 observations read from the data set SASHELP.CLASS.
NOTE: There were 18 observations read from the data set SASHELP.CLASS.
NOTE: The data set WORK.NAME has 18 observations and 6 variables.
NOTE: DATA statement used:
      real time              0.35 seconds
      cpu time               0.05 seconds
```

Flexible new date format

In SAS®9, there is a new date informat that interprets dates being read based on the value of a system option. The system option is called DATESTYLE, and it is used to identify sequence of month, day, and year when the ANYDATE informat data is ambiguous. When dates being read are not ambiguous, then the option is ignored and date is read correctly.

Specifying DATESTYLE=LOCALE will set the order of day, month, and year according to the value of the LOCALE system option.

```
33   options datestyle=mdy;
34   data _null_;
35     date=input('01/02/03',anydtdte8.); * ambiguous date ;
36     put date=date9.;
37   run;

date=02JAN2003
NOTE: DATA statement used (Total process time):
      real time            0.51 seconds
      cpu time             0.00 seconds


38   options datestyle=ydm;
39   data _null_;
40     date=input('01/02/03',anydtdte8.); * ambiguous date ;
41     put date=date9.;
42   run;

date=02MAR2001
NOTE: DATA statement used (Total process time):
      real time            0.00 seconds
      cpu time             0.00 seconds


43   options datestyle=myd;
44   data _null_;
45     date=input('01/31/2003',anydtdte10.); * unambiguous date, so
  option ignored ;

46     put date=date9.;
47   run;

date=31JAN2003
NOTE: DATA statement used (Total process time):
      real time            0.00 seconds
      cpu time             0.00 seconds
```

Sorting array elements

In SAS®9, there is a new routine that can be used to sort the values of a list of variables passed to it. SORTN should be used for sorting numerics, and SORTC for character values. If the variables belong to an array, then these sort routines effectively sort the values of the array. The sorts are always done in ascending sequence, but by specifying the variables in reverse order you can effectively sort in descending sequence. See the following example.

Note: Character variables must be the same length.

```
data test ;
  array v(50) 8 ;
  do i=1 to dim(v) ;
    v(i)=i+1 ;
  end ;
  call sortn(of v1-v50);
  put 'Up: ' v(1)= v(2)= v(3)= v(48)= v(49)= v(50)= ;
  call sortn(of v50-v1);
  put 'Down: ' v(1)= v(2)= v(3)= v(48)= v(49)= v(50)= ;
* sort values between 3 character variables ;
* note: character variables must be same length to avoid errors ;
  x='3 dogs ' ;
  y='1 cat  ' ;
  z='2 frogs' ;
  call sortc(x,y,z) ;
  put x= y= z= ;
run ;
```

```
86    data test ;
87      array v(50) 8 ;
88      do i=1 to dim(v) ;
89        v(i)=i+1 ;
90      end ;
91      call sortn(of v1-v50);
92      put 'Up: ' v(1)= v(2)= v(3)= v(48)= v(49)= v(50)= ;
93      call sortn(of v50-v1);
94      put 'Down: ' v(1)= v(2)= v(3)= v(48)= v(49)= v(50)= ;
95      * sort values between 3 character variables ;
96      * note: character variables must be same length to avoid errors ;
97      x='3 dogs ' ;
98      y='1 cat  ' ;
99      z='2 frogs' ;
100     call sortc(x,y,z) ;
101     put x= y= z= ;
102   run ;

NOTE: The SORTN function or routine is experimental in release 9.1.
Up: v1=2 v2=3 v3=4 v48=49 v49=50 v50=51
Down: v1=51 v2=50 v3=49 v48=4 v49=3 v50=2
NOTE: The SORTC function or routine is experimental in release 9.1.
x=1 cat y=2 frogs z=3 dogs
NOTE: The data set WORK.TEST has 1 observations and 54 variables.
NOTE: DATA statement used (Total process time):
      real time           0.05 seconds
      cpu time            0.06 seconds
```

Accessing the clipboard from SAS

Here is a technique that you can use if you want to use a SAS program to access the clipboard when running SAS under Windows in display manager mode. By using this technique, you can cut or copy something from one application and then run your program in SAS to make use of what you cut or copied.

You can use a very similar technique to copy data to the clipboard so that it can then be used by another Windows application.

Getting data from the clipboard

1. Use the DM command to open a SAS notepad window, clear it, paste the contents of the clipboard into it, and end (saving contents).

```
dm 'notepad work.temp.temp.source;clear;paste;end';
```

2. Read that file in.

```
filename c catalog 'work.temp.temp.source';
data _null_;
  infile c;
  input;
  put _infile_;
run;
```

Putting data on the clipboard

You can use a similar technique to write data to the clipboard.

```
filename c catalog 'work.temp.temp.source';
data _null_;
  file c;
  put 'hello';
run;
dm 'notepad work.temp.temp.source;curpos 1 1;mark;curpos max
max;store;end';
```

Flexible date formats

There are a number of date formats that are useful when you want to vary the separators used. These are MMDDYY*xw*, DDYYMM*xw*, and YYMMDD*xw*. The x specifies a separator or no separator, where:

- *B* separates with a blank

- *C* separates with a colon

- *D* separates with a dash

- *N* indicates no separator

- *P* separates with a period

- *S* separates with a slash

The *w* specifies the width of the output field (default: 8; range: 2–10).

Note that when *w* is from 2 to 5, SAS prints as much of the month and day as possible. When *w* is 7, the date appears as a two-digit year without separators, and the value is right-aligned in the output field.

```
205   data _null_ ;
206     now=today() ;
207     put 'Blanks ... ' now yymmddb10. ;
208     put 'Colon ... ' now yymmddc10. ;
209     put 'Dash ... ' now yymmddd10. ;
210     put 'No Separator ... ' now yymmddn8. ;
211     put 'Period ... ' now yymmddp10. ;
212     put 'Slash ... ' now yymmdds10. ;
213   run ;

Blanks ... 2005 03 22
Colon ... 2005:03:22
Dash ... 2005-03-22
No Separator ... 20050322
Period ... 2005.03.22
Slash ... 2005/03/22
NOTE: DATA statement used (Total process time):
      real time           0.00 seconds
      cpu time            0.00 seconds
```

Sending e-mail from SAS

You can send e-mail directly from a SAS DATA step. SAS will use your default e-mail settings so you don't have to specify anything other than a FILENAME statement using the e-mail access device, and a TO address. E-mail can also be sent using SCL or macro language.

E-mail can be very handy for doing things like:

■ notifying users about errors

■ interfacing through an SMS gateway to send messages to mobile phones

■ sending reports to customers

See the following examples.

Simple example

```
35     filename mail email to="phil@woodstreet.org.uk" ;
36     data ;
37       file mail ;
38       put 'hello' ;
39     run ;

NOTE: The file MAIL is:
      E-Mail Access Device

Message sent
      To:             phil@woodstreet.org.uk
      Cc:
      Subject:
      Attachments:
NOTE: 1 record was written to the file MAIL.
      The minimum record length was 5.
      The maximum record length was 5.
NOTE: The data set WORK.DATA2 has 1 observations and 0 variables.
NOTE: DATA statement used:
      real time          6.82 seconds
      cpu time           0.06 seconds
```

Another example

```
40    filename mail email ' '
41                    to=('phil@woodstreet.org.uk')
42                    cc=('john@woodstreet.org.uk'
  'peter@woodstreet.org.uk')
43                    subject="Here are your graphs for &sysdate"
44                    attach =('c:\gchart1.gif' 'c:\gchart2.gif') ;
45    data _null_;
46      file mail;
47      put "I could put some text in here to describe the graphs.";
48      put " ";
49    run;

NOTE: The file MAIL is:
      E-Mail Access Device

Message sent
      To:            ('phil@woodstreet.org.uk' )
      Cc:            ('john@woodstreet.org.uk' 'peter@woodstreet.org.uk' )
      Subject:    Here are your graphs for 18JUL03
      Attachments: ('c:\gchart1.gif' 'c:\gchart2.gif' )
NOTE: 2 records were written to the file MAIL.
      The minimum record length was 1.
      The maximum record length was 53.
NOTE: DATA statement used:
      real time          13.89 seconds
      cpu time           0.08 seconds
```

Specifying character and numeric variable ranges

Many people know about the _character_ , _numeric_, and _all_ variables, which can be used to specify all character, numeric, or any variables currently defined in a DATA step. There are other common ways of specifying variable ranges using single or double-dashed ranges. A less common method is to specify to use all variables of a particular type between two variables. This selects variables in the order they are defined to the data set, not alphabetical order.

a-numeric-b   uses all numeric variables between a and b

a-character-b   uses all character variables between a and b

```
data _null_ ;
  set sashelp.prdsale ;
  put actual-numeric-month ; * numeric range ;
  put country-character-product ; * character range ;
run ;
```

Using a wildcard in variables lists

Using a wildcard in variable lists can save you a lot of typing and make your code much more generic (in some instances).

The colon can be used as a wildcard in variable lists; for example, ABC: means all variable names beginning with ABC.

```
data x(keep=a:) ;
  a1=1 ;
  a2=10 ;
  a3=100 ;
  b1=1000 ;
  b2=10000 ;
run;

NOTE: The data set WORK.X has 1 observations and 3 variables.
NOTE: The DATA statement used 0.01 CPU seconds and 1435K.
```

Notice that the three variables starting with the letter "a" have been kept. We can also use "a:" in procedures.

```
proc print ;
  var a:;
run ;

NOTE: The PROCEDURE PRINT used 0.01 CPU seconds and 1489K.
```

The colon must be at the end of the name, not embedded. For example, AB:C is invalid. Colons can be used in most places where other abbreviated variable lists such ABC1–ABC99 are allowed. It cannot be used in a SUM function in place of a list of variables.

Creating CSV files from a DATA step, easily

You can write all values from a DATA step in CSV format using one statement:

```
Put (_all_) (:) ;
```

This writes all variables in the DATA step program data vector, except for _N_ and _ERROR_. It separates each of them by a comma.

```
32     filename out 'c:\out.csv' ;
33     data _null_;
34       file out dsd;
35       set sashelp.class;
36       put (_all_) (:);
37     run;
bb
NOTE: The file OUT is:
      File Name=c:\out.csv,
      RECFM=V,LRECL=256

NOTE: 19 records were written to the file OUT.
      The minimum record length was 17.
      The maximum record length was 21.
NOTE: There were 19 observations read from the data set SASHELP.CLASS.
NOTE: DATA statement used (Total process time):
      real time           0.13 seconds
      cpu time            0.04 seconds


38     filename out ;
NOTE: Fileref OUT has been deassigned.
```

Chapter 4

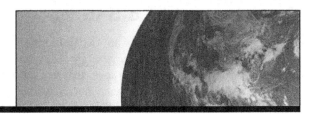

Options

Capturing part of a SAS log

Sometimes you may want to capture the SAS log for further examination, analysis, or storage. However, you might really be interested only in a part of the SAS log, or perhaps you want to save different parts of the log to different places. The following technique uses a macro, which will copy a selected part of the log to a text file. This file could then be viewed, stored, or even analyzed for problems. The technique mimics the commands that you might use to navigate the log, highlight what you want to copy, and paste the highlighted text into a file to save.

There are other ways to capture the log, but one key advantage of the technique shown here is that you can capture what you want, but still have the entire SAS log available in the log window.

The CLIPLOG macro

```
%macro cliplog(marker1,marker2,pos=last,file=c:\test.txt) ;
  * note: split search text in half so we dont go and find it in our
          macro call ;
  * note: save mprint option since we want mprint turned off for the
          macro run, otherwise we get our search text written to the
          log and we will find it ;
  %let o=%sysfunc(getoption(mprint)) ;
  options nomprint ;
/* log;
   find '&marker1&marker2' &pos;
   rfind;
   mark;
   bottom;
   mark;
   store;
   unmark;
   notepad;
   clear;
   paste;
   file '&file';
   end
*/
  dm "log;find '&marker1&marker2'
&pos;mark;bottom;mark;store;unmark;notepad;clear;paste;file
'&file';end" ;
  * view the file in windows notepad ;
  x "notepad &file" ;
  options &o ;
%mend cliplog ;
```

Capturing part of a log

The following skeleton code shows how you might mark the start of a section you want to copy. You then run the SAS code for the section that you want the log to capture. Once that is done, you call the macro to capture that section of the log.

```
***BEGIN***; /* this marks where to start the copying from the log */

/* now run all the SAS code you would like to capture */

%cliplog(***BEGIN,***) ; /* finally we call the macro which captures the
log from the point we previously marked */
```

Useful secret options

To discover some secret SAS options, you can run PROC OPTIONS with the INTERNAL parameter, which lists the internal, undocumented, unsupported options. This code produces a listing consisting of four sections:

```
proc options internal;
run;
```

- internal portable options
- portable options
- internal host options
- host options

Running this code in SAS 9.1.2 reveals some interesting options such as:

NOUNBUFLOG   The log is buffered. Switching to UNBUFLOG can be useful for viewing the log in a file while SAS is running.

IWEIGHT=100   Weighting factor for index costing, which can be adjusted to alter the way indexes are used.

IBUFNO=0   Number of index file buffers, which can be altered to assist performance.

TKG   Threaded kernel code generator.

There are many other options, and it is worth looking through the list to see if anything might be of interest to you.

Limiting options by group

If you want to limit the number of options you see when you use PROC OPTIONS, then you can select a specific group to get only those options relating to that group.

```
proc options group = inputcontrol;
run ;
```

Acceptable group names in SAS®9 are:

COMMUNICATIONS	GRAPHICS	MACRO
DATAQUALITY	HELP	MEMORY
EMAIL	INPUTCONTROL	META
ENVDISPLAY	INSTALL	ODSPRINT
ENVFILES	LANGUAGECONTROL	PERFORMANCE
ERRORHANDLING	LISTCONTROL	SASFILES
EXECMODES	LOG_LISTCONTROL	SORT
EXTFILES	LOGCONTROL	

Registering the location of the SAS System

If your SAS System is not registered properly during an installation, or if you have installed SAS 8 and SAS®9 on the same machine, you could use the undocumented system option –REGSERVER to register the default location of the sas.exe program. This configuration option can be used in a command prompt:

```
!SASROOT\sas.exe -regserver
```

Preventing the appearance of pop-up windows

The undocumented option –NOSLEEPWINDOW prevents the appearance of the pop-up windows that normally appear when you use the SLEEP and WAKEUP functions. This invocation option can be used in the startup command of your SAS session shortcut, with your RUN command, or in your sasv9.cfg file.

Resetting the date on output

Usually the date on SAS output is set to the date when the SAS session began. You can now use the option DTRESET to reset this date to the current date. This might be useful in very long-running SAS sessions so that the date on the output represents the date the output was actually produced.

The following example shows how to do this.

```
options date dtreset ;
ods rtf file='c:\test.rtf' ;
proc print data=sashelp.prdsale ;
run ;
ods rtf close ;
```

Getting a list of paper sizes

You can use PROC REGISTRY to get a list of available paper sizes and their dimensions. This is useful to see what paper sizes are supported and can be selected from the Output Delivery System (ODS).

```
proc registry list startat="CORE\PRINTING\PAPER SIZES";
run;

* We can set the paper size to a pre-defined size, or enter
  measurements ;
options papersize=a3;

* Now we produce output and can verify in MS Word
  that the page size is A3 as selected ;
ods rtf file='c:\test.rtf' ;
proc print data=sashelp.prdsale;
run ;
ods rtf close ;
```

```
[    Letter]
    Height=double:11
    Units="IN"
    Width=double:8.5
...
[    ISO A4]
    Height=double:29.7
    Units="CM"
    Width=double:21
```

Creating permanent data sets

This technique enables you to use single-level names to create permanent data sets. If you have a single-level data set name, then by default it will go to the Work library. However, another feature within SAS indicates that if you allocate a library called User, then all single-level data sets will be stored there, rather than in Work.

This means that you can write some code using single-level data set names, and while testing they will be put in Work and deleted at the end of the SAS session. You could then decide to keep those data sets by simply allocating the User library and pointing it to a directory to keep those data sets.

The following SAS log demonstrates this.

```
1     * Test code, and all single level datasets go to work library,
  which is cleared when SAS
1   ! ends ;
2     data test ; x= 1 ; run ;

NOTE: The data set WORK.TEST has 1 observations and 1 variables.
NOTE: DATA statement used:
      real time           0.27 seconds
      cpu time            0.03 seconds


3
4     * Once tested, define the USER libref, sending all single level
      datasets to a permanent
4   ! location ;
5     libname user 'c:\' ;
NOTE: Libref USER was successfully assigned as follows:
      Engine:         V8
      Physical Name: c:\
6     data test ; x= 1 ; run ;

NOTE: The data set USER.TEST has 1 observations and 1 variables.
NOTE: DATA statement used:
      real time           0.01 seconds
      cpu time            0.01 seconds


7     * when finished free the USER fileref to redirect datasets to WORK ;
8     libname user ;
NOTE: Libref USER has been deassigned.
```

Turning comments on and off

You can set up comments that can be activated and deactivated by setting a couple of macro variables at the top of your program. This is achieved by defining macro variables, which contain parts of a begin comment symbol. We need to define a and b (see below) separately, since if we put them together they are treated as a comment.

This is quite useful for debugging since debugging code can be effectively switched on and off.

Enabling comments
Set macro variables a and b to nulls, so that &a&b resolves to a null and has no effect. */; also has no effect since it behaves as a normal comment starting with a * and ending with a semi-colon.

Disabling comments
Set macro variable a to / and b to *. When they are put together as &a&b they produce /* which starts a comment. */ then ends the comment.

```
%let a=/;   * debug code inactive ;
%let b=*;   * debug code inactive ;
*** to activate set A & B to blanks ***;
&a&b
proc print data=x ;
run ;
*/;
data _null_ ;
run ;
```

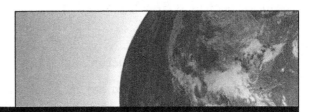

Chapter 5

Macros

Automatic macro variables

The SAS System keeps a set of automatic macro variables, which can be used by the programmer.

The macro variables provide information such as the date, current device, completion codes of procedures, etc.

They can be used in DATA steps with the SYMGET function or elsewhere with macro facility statements. In DATA steps you can substitute macro variables when the DATA step is compiled by using the macro variable (e.g. `&sysdate`), but the SYMGET function will get the macro value when the DATA step is executed. See the following example.

Log: Very simple example

```
%put Session for &sysjobid started on &sysday &sysdate at &systime ;
Session for XV02341 started on Thursday 29SEP06 at 06:51
```

Here is a list (from SAS Help and Documentation) of the automatic macro variables available. Note that different SAS products provide extra automatic macro variables. Also, different operating systems have some different automatic macro variables. Your list may vary from the one listed here.

Automatic Macro Variables	Contains
SYSBUFFR	text entered in response to a %INPUT statement that the macro processor cannot match with any variable in the statement.
SYSCC	the current condition code that SAS returns to your operating environment (the operating environment condition code).
SYSCHARWIDTH	the character width value.
SYSCMD	the last command from the command line of a macro window that was not recognized by display manager.
SYSDATE	the character value representing the date the job started execution in DATE6. or DATE9. format.*
SYSDATE9	the character value representing the date that a SAS job or session began executing in DATE9. format.*

(continued)

Automatic Macro Variables	Contains
SYSDAY	the character value representing the day of the week the job or session started execution.*
SYSDEVIC	the name of the current graphics device.
SYSDMG	the return code that reflects an action taken on damaged SAS data set.
SYSDSN	the name of the most recently created SAS data set.
SYSENV	FORE if the SAS program was entered from the keyboard. If input does not come from the keyboard, or if the macro executes in noninteractive mode, the value is BACK.*
SYSERR	the return code set by SAS procedures.* Values are: 0 Execution completed successfully. 1 Execution canceled by user with a RUN CANCEL statement. 2 Execution canceled by user with an ATTN or BREAK command. 4 Execution completed successfully but with warning messages. >4 An error occurred.
SYSFILRC	the return code set by the FILENAME statement. 0 if last filename statement executed O.K.; otherwise is set to the return code of the filename operation.
SYSINDEX	the number of macros that have started execution in the current SAS job or session.*
SYSINFO	the return code information provided by some SAS procedures.
SYSJOBID	the name of the currently executing batch job. The value and behavior are system dependent. Please refer to the SAS documentation for your operating system.
SYSLAST	the name of the most recently created SAS data set.

(continued)

Automatic Macro Variables	Contains
SYSLCKRC	the return code set by the LOCK statement. 0 if last LOCK statement executed O.K.; otherwise, is set to the return code of the lock operation.
SYSLIBRC	the return code set by the LIBNAME statement.
SYSMACRONAME	the name of the currently executing macro.*
SYSMENV	the current macro execution environment.*
	Values:
	S macro was part of the SAS program.
	D macro was invoked from display manager or full-screen procedure command line.
SYSMSG	the message for display in the message area of a macro window.
SYSNCPU	the current number of processors available to SAS.
SYSPARM	the value specified by the DATA step function SYSPARM().
SYSPBUFF	the text supplied as macro parameter values in the macro call.
SYSPROCESSID	the process ID for the current SAS process.
SYSPROCESSNAME	the process name for the current SAS process.
SYSPROCNAME	the name of the SAS procedure currently being processed.
SYSRC	the return code from X statement, X command, or any other operating system command.
SYSSCP	the abbreviation for the operating system being used.*
SYSSCPL	the long name for the operating system being used.*
SYSSITE	the site number for this SAS installation.
SYSSTARTID	the ID generated from last start SAS command.
SYSSTARTNAME	the name generated from last start SAS command.
SYSTIME	the time the job started execution (hh:mm).*

(*continued*)

Automatic Macro Variables	Contains
SYSUSERID	the user ID or logon ID of current SAS process
SYSVER	the version of SAS software you are using.
SYSVLONG	the release number and maintenance level of SAS software that is running.

* indicates that the variable is read-only.

Listing macro variables and their values

SAS provides the ability to display macro variables.

You can use keywords like _USER_, _GLOBAL_, _LOCAL_, _AUTOMATIC_, and _ALL_ with %PUT to write macro variables and their values to the log. Only one keyword can be used at a time, and there can be no other text in the %PUT statement.

- _LOCAL_ shows macro variables defined in the current macro definition

- _GLOBAL_ shows all macro variables in the SAS session

- _USER_ shows all user-defined macro variables

- _ALL_ shows all macro variables

- _AUTOMATIC_ shows all pre-defined automatic SAS macros

```
372   %let mg = i am global ;
373   %macro t ;
374       %local l1 l2 ;
375       %let l2 = i am local ;
376       %q
377   %mend t ;
378   %macro q ;
379       %local l3 ;
380       %let l3 = inner local ;
381       %put ***** local ***** ;
382       %put _local_ ;
ERROR: Macro keyword PUT appears as text.  A semicolon or other
       delimiter may be missing.
383       %put ----- user ----- ;
384       %put _user_ ;
385       %put ===== all ===== ;
386       %put _all_ ;
387       %mend q ;
388   %t
***** local *****
----- user -----
Q L3 inner local
T L1
T L2 i am local
GLOBAL MG i am global
===== all =====
Q L3 inner local
T L1
T L2 i am local
GLOBAL MG i am global
```

(continued)

(continued)

```
AUTOMATIC AFDSID 0
AUTOMATIC AFDSNAME
AUTOMATIC AFLIB
AUTOMATIC AFSTR1
AUTOMATIC AFSTR2
AUTOMATIC FSPBDV
AUTOMATIC SYSBUFFR
AUTOMATIC SYSCC 3000
AUTOMATIC SYSCHARWIDTH 1
AUTOMATIC SYSCMD
AUTOMATIC SYSDATE 22MAR05
AUTOMATIC SYSDATE9 22MAR2005
AUTOMATIC SYSDAY Tuesday
AUTOMATIC SYSDEVIC ACTIVEX
AUTOMATIC SYSDMG 0
AUTOMATIC SYSDSN WORK     DATA1
AUTOMATIC SYSENDIAN LITTLE
AUTOMATIC SYSENV FORE
AUTOMATIC SYSERR 0
AUTOMATIC SYSFILRC 0
AUTOMATIC SYSINDEX 2
AUTOMATIC SYSINFO 0
AUTOMATIC SYSJOBID 3300
AUTOMATIC SYSLAST WORK.DATA1
AUTOMATIC SYSLCKRC 0
AUTOMATIC SYSLIBRC 0
AUTOMATIC SYSMACRONAME Q
AUTOMATIC SYSMAXLONG 2147483647
AUTOMATIC SYSMENV S
AUTOMATIC SYSMSG
AUTOMATIC SYSNCPU 2
AUTOMATIC SYSPARM
AUTOMATIC SYSPBUFF
AUTOMATIC SYSPROCESSID 41D54421E93800004020000000000000
AUTOMATIC SYSPROCESSNAME DMS Process
AUTOMATIC SYSPROCNAME
AUTOMATIC SYSRC 0
AUTOMATIC SYSSCP WIN
AUTOMATIC SYSSCPL XP_PRO
AUTOMATIC SYSSITE 0031371006
AUTOMATIC SYSSIZEOFLONG 4
AUTOMATIC SYSSIZEOFUNICODE 2
AUTOMATIC SYSSTARTID
AUTOMATIC SYSSTARTNAME
AUTOMATIC SYSTIME 21:37
AUTOMATIC SYSUSERID Philip Mason
AUTOMATIC SYSVER 9.1
AUTOMATIC SYSVLONG 9.01.01M2P033104
AUTOMATIC SYSVLONG4 9.01.01M2P03312004
```

Accessing all macro variable values

There is a predefined view (sashelp.vmacro) that shows the contents of the macro symbol table. This is extremely useful in keeping track of macro variables and their definitions. Also, you can use the %PUT _ALL_ macro statement, which will list all macro values. The advantage of using the macro table view is that its contents can be used programmatically.

Another source of this information is DICTIONARY.MACROS, which is available when using SQL. Remember that macro variable values are split into 200-byte chunks, and OFFSET is used when a macro variable has gone beyond 200 characters. See the following examples.

```
%let name=Phil ;
%macro test ;
  %let count=1 ;
  proc print data=sashelp.vmacro ;
  run ;
%mend test ;
%test ;
```

Obs	scope	name	offset	value
1	TEST	COUNT	0	1
2	GLOBAL	NAME	0	Phil
3	AUTOMATIC	AFDSID	0	0
4	AUTOMATIC	AFDSNAME	0	
5	AUTOMATIC	AFLIB	0	
6	AUTOMATIC	AFSTR1	0	
7	AUTOMATIC	AFSTR2	0	
8	AUTOMATIC	FSPBDV	0	
9	AUTOMATIC	SYSBUFFR	0	
10	AUTOMATIC	SYSCC	0	0
11	AUTOMATIC	SYSCHARWIDTH	0	1
12	AUTOMATIC	SYSCMD	0	
13	AUTOMATIC	SYSDATE	0	08JUL05
14	AUTOMATIC	SYSDATE9	0	08JUL2005
15	AUTOMATIC	SYSDAY	0	Friday
16	AUTOMATIC	SYSDEVIC	0	
17	AUTOMATIC	SYSDMG	0	0
18	AUTOMATIC	SYSDSN	0	WORK X
19	AUTOMATIC	SYSENDIAN	0	LITTLE
20	AUTOMATIC	SYSENV	0	FORE
21	AUTOMATIC	SYSERR	0	0
22	AUTOMATIC	SYSFILRC	0	0

(continued)

(continued)

23	AUTOMATIC	SYSINDEX	0	1
24	AUTOMATIC	SYSINFO	0	0
25	AUTOMATIC	SYSJOBID	0	3736
26	AUTOMATIC	SYSLAST	0	WORK.X
27	AUTOMATIC	SYSLCKRC	0	0
28	AUTOMATIC	SYSLIBRC	0	0
29	AUTOMATIC	SYSMACRONAME	0	TEST
30	AUTOMATIC	SYSMAXLONG	0	2147483647
31	AUTOMATIC	SYSMENV	0	
32	AUTOMATIC	SYSMSG	0	
33	AUTOMATIC	SYSNCPU	0	2
34	AUTOMATIC	SYSPARM	0	
35	AUTOMATIC	SYSPBUFF	0	
36	AUTOMATIC	SYSPROCESSID	0	41D567BC0584FDF44020000000000000
37	AUTOMATIC	SYSPROCESSNAME	0	DMS Process
38	AUTOMATIC	SYSPROCNAME	0	PRINT
39	AUTOMATIC	SYSRC	0	0
40	AUTOMATIC	SYSSCP	0	WIN
41	AUTOMATIC	SYSSCPL	0	XP_PRO
42	AUTOMATIC	SYSSITE	0	0084110018
43	AUTOMATIC	SYSSIZEOFLONG	0	4
44	AUTOMATIC	SYSSIZEOFUNICODE	0	2
45	AUTOMATIC	SYSSTARTID	0	
46	AUTOMATIC	SYSSTARTNAME	0	
47	AUTOMATIC	SYSTIME	0	22:05
48	AUTOMATIC	SYSUSERID	0	Philip Mason
49	AUTOMATIC	SYSVER	0	9.1
50	AUTOMATIC	SYSVLONG	0	9.01.01M3P021605
51	AUTOMATIC	SYSVLONG4	0	9.01.01M3P02162005

Alternatively, you could use the following code:

```
proc sql ;
  select * from
    dictionary.macros ;
quit ;
```

Using arithmetic calculations in macros

The macro language compares numbers with dot characters (decimal points) as character strings. The EVAL macro function is usually used for doing simple integer calculations in macro language such as:

```
let x=%eval(1+2) ;
```

You must be careful since the EVAL macro function works properly on integers, but if you include decimal points it doesn't work as expected. The following log shows this.

```
68      %put result=%eval(1+2) ;
result=3
69      %put result=%eval(1.0+2.0) ;
ERROR: A character operand was found in the %EVAL function or %IF
       condition where a numeric operand is required. The condition
       was: 1.0+2.0
result=
```

The %EVAL macro function always evaluates digit-strings as integers, even if they are quoted with a macro quoting function. Hence, long digit strings will cause overflow. This example raises 9 to the power 99, which causes an overflow error.

```
%put =======> %eval(9**99) ;
ERROR: Overflow has occurred; evaluation is terminated.
```

Note: Using the %SYSEVALF macro function will get around this problem.

Matching quotation marks in macro comments

Quotation marks must be matched if used in macro comments, but this doesn't apply to other comments. If the quotation marks are not matched, then SAS searches for the next quotation mark before it deals with any other code. This can lead to unexpected and confusing errors.

Note also that /* */ comments are slightly more efficient than macro comments, so when you have a choice, use them. Another reason to use /* */ comments rather than macro comments is because of the inconsistent way in which macro comments treat quotation marks.

SAS gives you a clue to the reason for this error. If you have more than 200 characters between your quotation marks, you will get the following warning:

```
WARNING: The current word or quoted string has become more than 200
         characters long.  You may have unbalanced quotation marks.
```

Make sure your quotation marks are matched. This example demonstrates unmatched quotation marks.

```
%* This is Phil's unmatched quote which will cause problems ;

data x ;
  put "This single quote ' will not match with the previous one'" ;
 * since it was in quotes ;
  put 'But the first one used here will' ;
 * Note there is one single quote left unmatched ;
run ;

 * These quotes "' are O.K., since this kind of comment doesn't mind ;
/* These quotes '" are also O.K., since these comments don't mind
either */
```

If you do have an unmatched quotation mark, then you can submit another quotation mark from the editor, to close the previous one. For example, ';

Quotation marks in non-macro comments outside of macros do not need to be matched.

```
* This comment has 1 quote ' and is O.K. ;
proc print data=sasuser.crime(obs=1) ;
run ;
```

Quotation marks in macros or macro statements, including macro comments, need to be matched unless you use something like %STR(%').

```
%* This is not OK ` ;
proc print data=sasuser.crime(obs=1) ;
run ;
WARNING: The current word or quoted string has become more than 200
characters long.  You may have unbalanced quotation marks.
%* because the proc print ends up between quotes ` and never runs ;
```

Forcing SAS to store macro symbol tables on disk

Macro symbol tables are usually stored in memory; however, specifying OPTIONS MSYMTABMAX=0 will cause the tables to be stored to disk. Global macro variables will be stored in WORK.SAS0ST0. Local macro variables will be stored in a series of catalogs starting with WORK.SAS0ST1.

Some macro variable values are not available in this way. For instance, in variables in a %DO expression (i.e. %do i=1 %to 10), the macro variable &I would not be available in the disk file, since it is kept only in memory.

If you browse the catalog using the Explorer window from SAS, you will not actually be able to see anything in the catalogs, since the entries are hidden.

```
* Store macro symbol table to work library ;
options msymtabmax=0 ;

*** Define some macro variables ;
%let a=1 ;
%let b=2 ;

%macro fred ;
  %let c=3 ;
%mend fred ;

%fred

*** Now look in your Work library and you can see the SAS0STn catalogs ;
***    each one has a member for each macro variable ;
```

Producing files for import into other applications

In earlier versions of SAS, you typically wrote code to create comma-separated or tab-separated files that could be produced from a DATA step and then imported into other applications. In current releases of SAS, you can use the ODS statement to simplify this immensely.

```
ods csv file='c:\test.csv' ;
proc print data=sashelp.prdsale ;
run ;
ods csv close ;
```

First few lines of CSV file produced

```
"Obs","ACTUAL","PREDICT","COUNTRY","REGION","DIVISION","PRODTYPE","PRODU
  CT","QUARTER","YEAR","MONTH"
"1",925.00,850.00,"CANADA","EAST","EDUCATION","FURNITURE","SOFA",1,1993,
  "Jan"
"2",999.00,297.00,"CANADA","EAST","EDUCATION","FURNITURE","SOFA",1,1993,
  "Feb"
"3",608.00,846.00,"CANADA","EAST","EDUCATION","FURNITURE","SOFA",1,1993,
  "Mar"
```

Using merge macros

Here is a useful macro for general purpose merging. You can use it to modify the default behavior of the MERGE statement when used without a BY statement.

This macro is particularly useful with data representing a series of measurements over time. If measurements are missing, then the previous non-missing value will be used in the merge.

The quoting functions used in the code are used to enable macro variables to be passed into the invocation of the macro—e.g. %MERGEBY *(&sales1, &sales2, year month)* ;

Macro code

```
%**************************** mergeby ****************************;
%* mergeby acts like a MERGE statement with a BY statement even if
there are no BY variables;

%macro mergeby(data1, data2, byvars);
  %if %bquote(&byvars) NE %then
    %do;
      merge %unquote(&data1) %unquote(&data2);
        by %unquote(&byvars);
    %end;
  %else
    %do;
      if _end1 & _end2 then
        stop;
      if ^_end1 then
        set %unquote(&data1) end=_end1;
      if ^_end2 then
        set %unquote(&data2) end=_end2;
    %end;
%mend mergeby;
```

Example code

```
* Create some sample data - firstly data set x ;
data x;
  do x=1 to 5;
    output;
  end;
run;
```

```
* Create some sample data - secondly data set y ;
data y;
  do y=1 to 3;
    output;
  end;
run;

*** Now we merge the two data sets with a standard merge statement ;
*** - notice that there is no BY statement ;
data xy;
  merge x y;
run;

proc print data=xy;
run;

*** Now we merge the two data sets with the MERGEBY macro ;
data xy;
  %mergeby(x,y);
run;
proc print data=xy;
run;
```

Example output

```
                          The SAS System

                                   Obs     x     y

                                    1      1     1
                                    2      2     2
                                    3      3     3
                                    4      4     .
                                    5      5     .

                          The SAS System

                                   Obs     x     y

                                    1      1     1
                                    2      2     2
                                    3      3     3
                                    4      4     3
                                    5      5     3
```

Another way to accomplish general purpose merging is by using the following non-macro code. This non-macro code has the disadvantage that it must be recoded each time.

Example code

```
data xy(drop=last_y) ;
  retain last_y ;
  merge x y ;
  if y NE . then
    last_y=y ;
  else
    y=last_y ;
run ;
```

Automatically documenting your programs

By using some simple coding standards, we can use the following program to automatically document the programs. The macro will take all the text from the first comment block, delimited by a /* and */. If you code all your programs with an initial header in that form, then you will be able to use this macro to scan through a directory and automatically extract all those comments. The macro then creates a rich text format (RTF) document. See the following example.

Documentation macro

```
/***
Program Name : Doc
Date         : 5Feb2007
Written By    : Phil Mason
Overview      : Scans a directory and looks at all SAS code,
                extracts the comments to creating a
                MS Word file for documentation
Parms         : target ... directory where modules are
                            located that we wish to document
***/
%macro doc(target) ;

filename dir pipe "dir ""&target""" ;

data files(keep=file line) ;
  length file line $ 200
         next $ 8 ;
  label file='Filename'
        line='Header' ;
  if _n_=1 then
    put '*** Processing files ***' / ;
  infile dir missover ;
 * You may need to adjust this depending on the version of the operating
   system you are running on - for my system I am able to read the file
   name from a directory listing at column 37 ;
   input @37 file & ;
 * Only continue if the file is a SAS file ;
   if index(upcase(file),'.SAS')>0 ;
   put '--> ' file ;
   next='' ;
 * Point to that SAS file ;
   rc1=filename(next,"&target\"||file) ;
 * Open it up ;
   fid=fopen(next) ;
   write=0 ;
```

(*continued*)

(continued)

```
* Read through each line of the SAS file ;
  do while(fread(fid)=0) ;
    line=' ' ;
    rc3=fget(fid,line,200) ;
      * if it is the start of a comment block then I will write line ;
  if index(line,'/*')>0 then
    write=1 ;
  if write then
      output ;
      * if its end of comment block I will stop writing lines ;
  if index(line,'*/')>0 then
    write=0 ;
   * we only process comment blocks that start on the first line
     - i.e. headers ;
      * only continue reading lines if I am currently in a comment block
  ;
  if ^write then
    leave ;
  end ;
 * close file ;
  fid=fclose(fid) ;
  rc=filename(next) ;
run ;

* free the file ;
filename dir ;

* point to an rtf file to create ;
ods rtf file='c:\Documentation.rtf' ;

title "Documentation for &target" ;
data _null_ ;
  set files ;
    by file notsorted ;
  file print ods ;
  if first.file then
    put @1 file @ ;
  put @2 line ;
run ;

* close the rtf file ;
ods rtf close ;

%mend doc ;
```

Sample invocation

```
%doc(C:\temp\programs)
```

Programs in c:\temp\programs

I have one program in this directory called **sample.sas**. Here is the code in it.

```
/*
Author: Phil Mason
Date: 28June2006
Purpose: This is just to demonstrate how the documentation macro works
*/
data test ;
  put 'this shouldnt appear in documentation' ;
run ;
```

Documentation produced

Filename	Header
sample.sas	/*
	Author: Phil Mason
	Date: 28June2006
	Purpose: This is just to demonstrate how the documentation macro works
	*/

Capturing part of a SAS log to a file

The following two macros can be used to capture part of a SAS log to a file. This can be very useful if you want to capture a part of the log that applies to a section of code so it can be analyzed or stored. To use these, simply call the START macro when you want to start capturing the log and then call FINISH at the end.

START

This macro uses the mfile option to write all generated macro code to the mprint fileref.

```
%macro start(file=c:\test.sas) ;
  filename mprint "&file" ;
  options mprint mfile ;
%mend start ;
```

FINISH

This macro turns off the writing of macro code to MPRINT, and then frees the file so we can look at it. (Otherwise it will still be in use by SAS and cannot be viewed.)

```
%macro finish ;
  options nomfile ;
  filename mprint ;
%mend finish ;
```

START and FINISH macros

```
%start ;
* put your code here ... ;
%finish ;
```

Modifying the label of a data set

Sometimes you might want to use a data set label for storing information about the data, such as what processing has been done to it. When doing this you can then build up information bit by bit using the following macro. This macro will return the contents of the current data set label.

```
%macro label(ds) ;
   %let dsid=%sysfunc(open(&ds)) ;
%sysfunc(attrc(&dsid,label))
   %let dsid=%sysfunc(close(&dsid)) ;
%mend label ;
*** How to use it ;
data x(label='part 1') ;
run ;
data x(label="%label(x) - part 2") ;
set x ;
run ;
```

Keeping variables on a data set

I once had a situation where I wanted to specify a long list of variables to keep on a range of data sets, but sometimes I did not have all of the variables on the data set due to missing raw data from which our data set was created. Specifying to keep variables that don't exist causes an error. See the following example.

Log showing error produced

```
4020   data x ;
4021   set sashelp.prdsale(keep=x actual) ;
ERROR: The variable x in the DROP, KEEP, or RENAME list has never been
       referenced.
4022   run ;
```

To get around this you can use the following macro, which will return only those variables that exist on a data set from the list of variables that you specify.

Macro code

```
%macro vars_on_dset(dset,vars) ;
  %let dsid=%sysfunc(open(&dset)) ;
  %let vars=%sysfunc(compbl(&vars)) ;
  %let n=%eval(1+%length(&vars)-%length(%sysfunc(compress(&vars)))) ;
  %put n=&n;
  %do i=1 %to &n ;
    %let bit=%scan(&vars,&i) ;
    %if %sysfunc(varnum(&dsid,&bit))>0 %then
      &bit ;
  %end ;
  %let dsid=%sysfunc(close(&dsid)) ;
%mend vars_on_dset ;
```

Log showing how to avoid errors by using macro code

The following log shows how the macro determines which of the variables we want to keep are available, and returns only those variables—in this case, just the variable actual.

```
4042   Data out(keep=%vars_on_dset(sashelp.prdsale,x actual)) ;
n=2
MPRINT(VARS_ON_DSET):   actual
4043    Set sashelp.prdsale ;
4044   Run ;


NOTE: There were 1440 observations read from the data set
      SASHELP.PRDSALE.
NOTE: The data set WORK.OUT has 1440 observations and 1 variables.
NOTE: DATA statement used (Total process time):
      real time              0.01 seconds
      cpu time               0.01 seconds



4045   proc contents data=out ;
4046   run ;


NOTE: PROCEDURE CONTENTS used (Total process time):
      real time              0.07 seconds
      cpu time               0.01 seconds
```

Output of PROC CONTENTS

```
Documentation for C:\temp\Programs

                       The CONTENTS Procedure

Data Set Name     WORK.OUT                        Observations
   1440
Member Type       DATA                            Variables            1
Engine            V9                              Indexes              0
Created           Thursday, May 04, 2006 10:52:53 PM  Observation Length   8
Last Modified     Thursday, May 04, 2006 10:52:53 PM  Deleted Observations 0
Protection                                        Compressed          NO
Data Set Type                                     Sorted              NO
Label
Data Representation  WINDOWS_32
Encoding              wlatin1  Western (Windows)

                    Engine/Host Dependent Information

  Data Set Page Size            4096
  Number of Data Set Pages      4
  First Data Page               1
  Max Obs per Page              501
  Obs in First Data Page        368
  Number of Data Set Repairs    0
  File Name                     C:\DOCUME~1\phil\LOCALS~1\Temp\SAS Temporary
                                  Files\_TD3564\out.sas7bdat
  Release Created               9.0101M3
  Host Created                  XP_PRO
```

(continued)

(continued)

#	Variable	Type	Len	Format	Label
		Alphabetic List of Variables and Attributes			
1	ACTUAL	Num	8	DOLLAR12.2	Actual Sales

Combining small values

Sometimes you might want to combine many small, insignificant values or outliers before you display the data to a user. This practice can highlight the larger, more significant figures and unclutter reports and graphic legends. In applications where many kinds of data are involved, it is advantageous to use generalized techniques to do this.

The following macro can be used to combine small values in a subgrouped bar chart. It can also be easily adapted to work with other data. Additionally, by adding a WHERE clause to PROC GCHART, you can exclude all small values and chart only the large ones.

```
%macro limit(limit=0.01,
             class1=a,
             class2=b,
             anal=x,
             more=.,
             in=in,
             out=out) ;
* Limit ... values less that this percentage are combined ;
* class1 ... 1st classification variable ;
* class2 ... 2nd classification variable ;
* anal ... analysis variable ;
* more ... value to use for values that are combined ;

proc sql ;
  create table &out as
    select &class1,
           &class2,
           sum(&anal) as &anal
       from (select &class1,
             case when(&anal/sum(&anal)<&limit) then &more
                                                 else &class2
             end as &class2,
             &anal
       from &in
         group by &class1)
           group by &class1,
                    &class2 ;
  quit ;
%mend limit ;
```

```
*** Create test data ;
  data in ;
    do a=1 to 10 ;
      do b=1 to 100 ;
        x=ranuni(1)*100 ;
        output ;
      end ;
    end ;
run ;

filename graph 'c:\g1.png' ;
goptions device=png gsfname=graph ;
proc gchart data=in ;
  vbar a / subgroup=b sumvar=x discrete ;
run ;
quit ;

*** Use limit macro to avoid large confusing legends and
imperceptibly tiny  bar segments ;
%limit(limit=0.02) ;

filename graph 'c:\g2.png' ;
proc gchart data=out ;
  vbar a / subgroup=b sumvar=x discrete ;
run ;
quit ;
```

Default graph produced

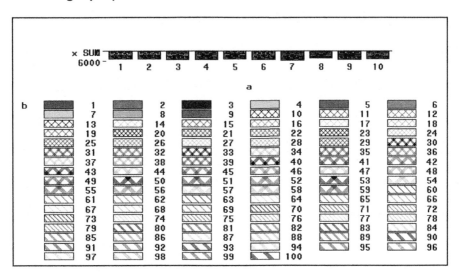

Graph with small values combined

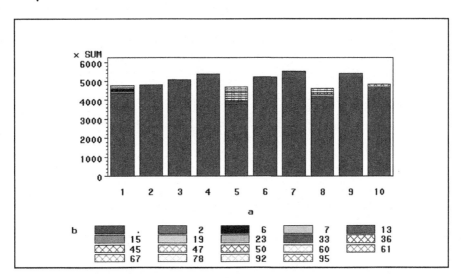

Chapter 6

Assorted Tips

Outputting multiple procedures to a page

Sometimes the output from a procedure will use only a few lines, which can result in a lot of wasted paper. This tip tells you how to avoid that.

You can stop SAS from going to a new page each time a procedure finishes by changing the character that it uses for jumping to a new page (on z/OS this is a 1). Set the FORMDLIM option to a blank to replace the new page character with a blank. See the following example.

Note: This applies to the Output Delivery System (ODS) listing destination.

```
* Setting it to a space causes SAS to fill each page before going to
the next one ;
Options formdlim=' ' ;


* Setting it to a null string resets the value of formdlim to the
default,
   so that each new Proc will start on a new page ;
Options formdlim='' ;
```

Printing graphs in landscape or portrait

If your printer is set to print as portrait by default, then graphs will also print that way. This tip tells you how to make the graphs print in landscape so that they fit the page better.

If your graphs come out portrait rather than landscape when printing them from Windows, then try the following:

```
GOPTIONS ROTATE ;
```

This will rotate the graph, whereas page orientation (landscape or portrait) applies only to text. Use NOROTATE to get back to unrotated.

Putting BY variables into titles

You can insert labels and or values of BY variables into titles. For example, suppose you have a data set sorted by the variable ST, with label "STATE" and formatted values "Victoria," "Tasmania," etc.

You need to specify NOBYLINE, which will get the #BYVAR feature to work. The option NOBYLINE will force a page eject after each BY group.

One BY variable

```
OPTIONS NOBYLINE;

PROC PRINT;
TITLE "List for #BYVAR1 - #BYVAL1";
  BY ST;
  VAR Var1-Var10;
run;
```

For each BY group, you'll get titles such as the following:

```
List for STATE - Tasmania
List for STATE - Victoria
```

The NOBYLINE option suppresses the printing of the BY lines as part of the output, so you don't also see following output:

```
BY STATE=Tasmania
BY STATE=Victoria
```

You can turn BY lines back on with OPTIONS BYLINE;

Two BY variables

The following example shows DIV and DEPT, where DEPT is nested within DIV. DIV has one formatted value "Academic Affairs," with DEPTs "Art" and "History," and another formatted value "Administration," with DEPTs "Admissions" and "Registrar."

```
BY DIV DEPT;
TITLE "Budget - #BYVAL1/#BYVAL2";
```

Partial output

```
Budget - Academic Affairs/Art
Budget - Academic Affairs/History
Budget - Administration/Admissions
Budget - Administration/Registrar
```

Putting multiple graphs on a page

Warren Sarle has kindly provided some macros that are helpful for putting multiple graphs on a page and adding titles to graphs in a catalog. You can look for these on the SAS online samples available over the Internet.

```
/******************************************************************

        name: grid
       title: Replay graphs in a regular grid
     product: graph
      system: all
       procs: greplay gslide
     support: saswss                          update:  10jul95

DISCLAIMER:

       THIS INFORMATION IS PROVIDED BY SAS INSTITUTE INC. AS A SERVICE
TO ITS USERS.  IT IS PROVIDED "AS IS".  THERE ARE NO WARRANTIES,
EXPRESSED OR IMPLIED, AS TO MERCHANTABILITY OR FITNESS FOR A
PARTICULAR PURPOSE REGARDING THE ACCURACY OF THE MATERIALS OR CODE
CONTAINED HEREIN.

The %GRID macro lets you easily replay graphs in a regular grid with
one or more rows and one or more columns. The %GRID macro also
supports titles and footnotes for the entire replayed graph. For
example, if you have run GPLOT four times and want to replay these
graphs in a 2-by-2 grid with the title 'Four Marvellous Graphs', you
could submit the following statements:

   title 'Four Marvellous Graphs';
   %grid( gplot*4, rows=2, cols=2);

The %GRID macro allows 10% of the vertical size of the graph for
titles by default. You can adjust this percentage via the TOP=
argument in %GRID. Determining the best value for TOP= requires
trial and error in most cases. To allow space for footnotes, use
the BOTTOM= argument.

The graphs to replay must be stored in a graphics catalog with
library and member names specified by the macro variables &glibrary
and &gout. By default, SAS/GRAPH stores graphs in WORK.GSEG, which
is the catalog that the %GRID macro uses by default.  If your
graphs are in another catalog, you must specify &glibrary and/or
&gout using %LET statements as shown below.
```

(continued)

(continued)

Each graph that is stored in a catalog has a name. Each procedure
assigns default names such as GPLOT, GPLOT1, GPLOT2, etc. Most
SAS/GRAPH procedures let you specify the name via a NAME= option
which takes a quoted string that must be a valid SAS name. However,
if a graph by that name already exists in the catalog, SAS/GRAPH
appends a number to the name; it does not replace the previous graph
by the same name unless you specify GOPTIONS GOUTMODE=REPLACE, but
this option causes _all_ entries in the catalog to be deleted
every time you save a new graph, so it is not very useful. If you want
to replace a single graph in a catalog, sometimes you can use the
%GDELETE macro to delete the old one and later recreate a graph with
the same name, but this does not work reliably due to a bug in
SAS/GRAPH. By default, %GDELETE deletes _everything_ in the catalog;
this does seem to work reliably.

When you use BY processing, SAS/GRAPH appends numbers to the graph
name to designate graphs for each BY group. For example, if you run
GPLOT with three BY groups and NAME='HENRY', the graphs are named
HENRY, HENRY1, and HENRY2. The %GRID macro lets you abbreviate this
list of names as HENRY*3, where the repetition factor following the
asterisk is the total number of graphs, not the number of the last
graph.

***/

```
%let glibrary=WORK;
%let gout=GSEG;

%macro grid(   /* replay graphs in a rectangular grid */
   list,       /* list of names of graphs, separated by blanks;
                  a name may be followed by an asterisk and a
                  repetition factor with no intervening blanks;
                  for example, ABC*3 is expanded to: ABC ABC1 ABC2 */
   rows=1,     /* number of rows in the grid */
   cols=1,     /* number of columns in the grid */
   top=10,     /* percentage at top to reserve for titles */
   bottom=0);  /* percentage at bottom to reserve for footnotes */

   %gtitle;
   %greplay;
   %tdef(rows=&rows,cols=&cols,top=&top,bottom=&bottom)
   %trep(&list,rows=&rows,cols=&cols)
   run; quit;
%mend grid;
```

(continued)

(continued)

```
%macro gdelete(list); /* delete list of graphs from the catalog;
                         default is _ALL_ */

   %if %bquote(&list)= %then %let list=_ALL_;
   proc greplay igout=&glibrary..&gout nofs;
      delete &list;
   run; quit;
%mend gdelete;


%macro gtitle; /* create graph with titles and footnotes only */

   %global titlecnt;
   %if %bquote(&titlecnt)= %then %let titlecnt=1;
                          %else %let titlecnt=%eval(&titlecnt+1);
   goptions nodisplay;
   proc gslide gout=&glibrary..&gout name="title&titlecnt";
   run;
   goptions display;
%mend gtitle;


%macro greplay( /* invoke PROC GREPLAY */
   tc);         /* template catalog; default is JUNK */

   %if %bquote(&tc)= %then %let tc=junk;
   proc greplay nofs tc=&tc;
      igout &glibrary..&gout;
%mend greplay;


%macro tdef(  /* define a template for a rectangular grid */
   rows=1,    /* number of rows in the grid */
   cols=1,    /* number of columns in the grid */
   top=10,    /* percentage at top to reserve for titles */
   bottom=0); /* percentage at bottom to reserve for footnotes */
   %global tdefname; /* returned: name of template */

   %local height width n row col lower upper left right;
   %let height=%eval((100-&top-&bottom)/&rows);
   %let width =%eval(100/&cols);
   %let tdefname=t&rows._&cols;
   tdef &tdefname
      0/ulx=0 uly=100 llx=0 lly=0 urx=100 ury=100 lrx=100 lry=0
   %let n=1;
   %do row=1 %to &rows;
      %let lower=%eval(100-&top-&row*&height);
```

(continued)

(*continued*)

```
        %let upper=%eval(&lower+&height);
        %do col=1 %to &cols;
            %let right=%eval(&col*&width);
            %let left =%eval(&right-&width);
            &n/ulx=&left uly=&upper llx=&left lly=&lower
                urx=&right ury=&upper lrx=&right lry=&lower
            %let n=%eval(&n+1);
        %end;
    %end;
    ;
    template &tdefname;
%mend tdef;


%macro trep( /* replay graphs using template defined by %TDEF */
    list,      /* list of names of graphs, separated by blanks;
                  a name may be followed by an asterisk and a
                  repetition factor with no intervening blanks;
                  for example, ABC*3 is expanded to: ABC ABC1 ABC2 */
    rows=,     /* (optional) number of rows in template */
    cols=);    /* (optional) number of columns in template */
               /* rows= and cols= default to values set with %TDEF */

    %global titlecnt;
    %local i l n row col name root suffix nrep;
    %if %bquote(&rows)= %then %let rows=%scan(&tdefname,1,t_);
    %if %bquote(&cols)= %then %let cols=%scan(&tdefname,2,t_);
    treplay 0:title&titlecnt
    %let nrep=0;
    %let l=0;
    %let n=0;
    %do row=1 %to &rows;
        %do col=1 %to &cols;
            %let n=%eval(&n+1);
            %if &nrep %then %do;
                %let suffix=%eval(&suffix+1);
                %if &suffix>=&nrep %then %do;
                    %let nrep=0;
                    %goto tryagain;
                %end;
                %let name=&root&suffix;
                %goto doit;
            %end;
%tryagain:
```

(*continued*)

(continued)

```
            %let l=%eval(&l+1);
            %let name=%qscan(&list,&l,%str( ));
            %if &name= %then %goto break;
            %let i=%index(&name,*);
            %if &i %then %do;
                %let nrep=%substr(&name,&i+1);
                %if &nrep<=0 %then %goto tryagain;
                %let root=%substr(&name,1,&i-1);
                %let name=&root;
                %let suffix=0;
            %end;
%doit:
            &n:&name
        %end;
    %end;
%break:
    ;
%mend trep;

 /****************** Examples for the %GRID macro ******************/

%inc greplay;

data trig;
    do n=1 to 100;
        x1=sin(n/16);
        x2=sin(n/8);
        y1=cos(n/16);
        y2=cos(n/8);
        output;
    end;
run;

goptions nodisplay;
proc gplot data=trig;
    title 'Y1 by X1';
    plot y1*x1;
run;
    title 'Y1 by X2';
    plot y1*x2;
run;
    title 'Y2 by X1';
    plot y2*x1;
run;
    title 'Y2 by X2';
    plot y2*x2;
run;
```

(continued)

(continued)

```
title 'Four Marvellous Graphs';
%grid( gplot*4, rows=2, cols=2);


title 'Adding a Title to a Single Graph';
footnote 'And a Footnote';
%grid( gplot, top=12, bottom=5);
```

Putting multiple graphs and tables on an HTML page

The HTML panel tagset lets you do pretty much anything that you can do with the normal ODS HTML destination, except you can break your page into rows and columns. So you could have two graphs at the top, followed by a table, then perhaps three columns with graphs in each, etc. Just use your imagination.

The following code gives you an idea about what can be done with this tagset. It starts with four columns of bar charts over three rows, a report, and then it has five columns of pie charts over two rows.

Note: If you are using an early version of SAS[®]9 then you will need to download the tagset from the SAS Web site and run the PROC TEMPLATE code in SAS to define it.

```
%let panelcolumns = 4;
%let panelborder = 4;
ods tagsets.htmlpanel file="C:\bypanel2.html" gpath='c:\'
options(doc='help');
goptions device=activex xpixels=320 ypixels=240;
title1 'Product Reports' ;
footnote1 ;
proc summary data=sashelp.shoes nway ;
  class region product ;
  var stores sales inventory returns ;
  output out=sum sum= mean= /autolabel autoname ;
run ;
proc gchart data=sum ;
  by region ;
  vbar product / sumvar=sales_sum pattid=midpoint discrete ;
run;
quit;
proc summary data=sashelp.shoes nway ;
  class region subsidiary ;
  var stores sales inventory returns ;
  output out=sum sum= mean= /autolabel autoname ;
run ;
%let panelcolumns = 5;
%let panelborder = 1;
ods tagsets.htmlpanel ;
title 'Summary data' ;
proc print data=sum ;
run ;
title 'Subsidiary Reports' ;
%let panelcolumns = 5;
%let panelborder = 1;
```

```
ods tagsets.htmlpanel ;
goptions dev=activex xpixels=160 ypixels=120;
proc gchart data=sum ;
  by region ;
  pie subsidiary / sumvar=sales_sum discrete ;
run;
quit;
ods _all_ close;
```

Screenshot of output

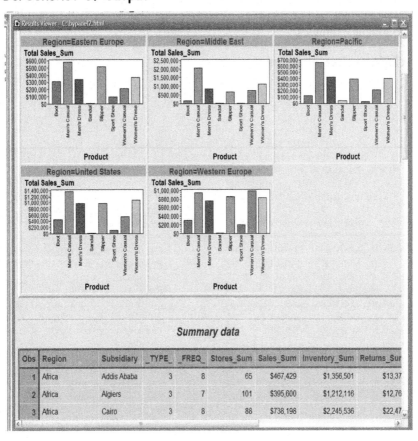

Using nicknames

Nicknames are used in SAS to give shorter or easier to remember names to engines used with the LIBNAME and FILENAME statements.

You can list all the nicknames defined in SAS by using PROC NICKNAME. Nicknames can be used in various places, such as in LIBNAME statements where you would specify an engine.

I have found that using PROC NICKNAME is a good way to find new, experimental, and undocumented engines that may be interesting to try out. See the following examples.

Code to list nicknames

```
proc nickname ; run;
```

```
1     proc nickname ; run ;
NOTE: ENGINE is the default object type.

Current Catalog: SASHELP.CORE

        Nickname  Module    Type  Fileformat Description

P   M   ACCESS    SASIOMDB  ENG   7          SAS/ACCESS Interface to PC Files
    M   ACCESS99  SASECRSP  ENG              Read engine for CRSP ACCESS97
                                             database
    M   BASE      SASE7     ENG   7          Base SAS I/O Engine
P   M   BLOOMBRG  SASIOBLB  ENG   9          SAS/Access Interface To Bloomberg
P   M   BMDP      SASBMDPE  ENG   607        BMDP Save file engine
P   M   CRSPACC   SASECRSP  ENG              Read engine for CRSP ACCESS97
                                             database
P   M   CVP       SASECVP   ENG   9          Character Variable Padding Engine
P   M   DB2       SASIODBU  ENG   7          SAS/ACCESS Interface to DB2
P   M   EXCEL     SASIOXLS  ENG   7          SAS/ACCESS Interface to PC Files
P   M   FAMECHLI  SASEFAME  ENG              Seamless libname interface to FAME
                                             db
P   M   HAVERDLX  SASEHAVR  ENG   9          Read engine for Haver Analytics DLX
                                             db
P       IMDB      SASEIMDB  ENG   9          In Memory Database Engine
P   M   META      SASIOMET  ENG   7          Metadata engine
P   M   MYSQL     SASIOMYL  ENG   7          SAS/ACCESS Interface to MySQL
P   M   ODBC      SASIOODB  ENG   7          SAS/ACCESS Interface to ODBC
P       OLAP      SASEOLAP  ENG   9          SQL Passthru Engine for OLAP
P   M   OLEDB     SASIOOLE  ENG   7          SAS/ACCESS Interface to OLE DB
```

(continued)

(continued)

P	M	ORACLE	SASIOORA	ENG	7	SAS/ACCESS Interface to Oracle
P	M	OSIRIS	SASOSIRI	ENG	607	OSIRIS Data File engine
P		R3	SASIOSR3	ENG	9	SAS Engine for SAP R/3
P	M	REMOTE	SASIORMT	ENG	7	SAS/SHARE Remote access engine
P	M	REMOTE8	SASI8RMT	ENG	7	SAS/SHARE V8 Remote access engine
P	M	REUTERS	SASEREUT	ENG	612	Reuters financial market data interface
	M	SASIOOS2	SASIODBU	ENG	7	SAS/ACCESS Interface to DB2
P	M	SPDE	SASSPDE	ENG	7	Scalable Performance Data Engine
P	M	SPSS	SASSPSS	ENG	607	SPSS Save File engine
P		SQLVIEW	SASESQL	ENG	607	SQL view engine
	M	SXLE	SASEXML	ENG	8	W3C XML input/output engine
P	M	SYBASE	SASIOSYB	ENG	7	SAS/ACCESS Interface to Sybase
P	M	TERADATA	SASIOTRA	ENG	8	SAS/ACCESS Interface to Teradata
P		TRACE	SASETRC	ENG	7	Version 7 trace engine
P	M	V6	SASEB	ENG	607	Base SAS I/O Engine
P	M	V604	SASIO602	ENG	606	Base SAS I/O Engine - 6.06 defaults
	M	V607	SASEB	ENG	607	Base SAS I/O Engine
	M	V608	SASEB	ENG	607	Base SAS I/O Engine
	M	V609	SASEB	ENG	607	Base SAS I/O Engine
	M	V610	SASEB	ENG	607	Base SAS I/O Engine
	M	V611	SASEB	ENG	607	Base SAS I/O Engine
	M	V612	SASEB	ENG	607	Base SAS I/O Engine
	M	V7	SASE7	ENG	7	Base SAS I/O Engine
	M	V701	SASE7	ENG	7	Base SAS I/O Engine
	M	V8	SASE7	ENG	7	Base SAS I/O Engine
P	M	V9	SASE7	ENG	7	Base SAS I/O Engine
P	M	XML	SASEXML	ENG	8	W3C XML input/output engine
P	M	XPORT	SASV5XPT	ENG	607	Version 5 transport datasets
P		BASE	SASXBAM	AM		Base A. M. for external files
P		CACHE	SASXBAMO	AM	9.1	IOM Cache Service
P	M	CATALOG	SASXBAML	AM		Base A. M. for Catalog's
P		CLIPBRD	SASXBAMB	AM	9.1	Clipboard Access Method
P	M	COMMPORT	SASVCOMM	AM		Communication Ports
P	M	DDE	SASVADDE	AM		Dynamic Data Exchange
P	M	DISK	SASXBAM	AM		Base A. M. for Disk files
P	M	DRIVEMAP	SASVDMAP	AM		Drive Map access method
P	M	DUMMY	SASXBAM	AM		Base A. M. for Dummy files
P	M	EMAIL	SASVMAIL	AM		Base A. M. for EMAIL
P	M	FTP	SASXBAMF	AM		FTP A. M.
P		G3270	SASXBAM	AM		Base A.M. for 3270 Graphics terminals
P		GTERM	SASXBAM	AM		Base A. M. for Graphic terminals
P		HTTP	SASXBAMH	AM		Base A.M. for URL
P		LIBRARY	SASXBAML	AM		Base A. M. for Catalog's
P		MESSAGE	SASXBAM	AM		Base A. M. for Message files

(continued)

(continued)

P	M	NAMEPIPE	SASVNPIP	AM		Named Pipes
P	M	NOTESDB	SASVNOTE	AM		Base A. M. for Lotus(tm) Notes
P	M	PIPE	SASVUPIP	AM		Anonymous Pipes
P	M	PLOTTER	SASXBAM	AM		Base A. M. for Plotters
P	M	PRINTER	SASVPRNT	AM		Base A. M. for Printers
P		REAL	SASXBAMR	AM		Real Time A.M
P	M	SOCKET	SASXBAMT	AM		TCP/IP Socket A. M.
P		STREAM	SASXBAMO	AM	9.1	IOM Cache Service
P		TCPIP	SASXBAMT	AM		Base A.M. for TCP/IP Sockets
P	M	TEMP	SASXBAM	AM		Base A. M. for temp files
P		TERMINAL	SASXBAM	AM		Base A. M. for Terminals
P	M	UPRINTER	SASXBAMP	AM		Base A.M. for Universal Printing
P	M	URL	SASXBAMH	AM		Base A.M. for URL

Discovering unknown procedure options

One good way to discover information about undocumented options is to try running a procedure with a parameter specified. If the parameter is wrong, you will get a helpful message back from SAS explaining the valid values of the parameters. See the following example.

```
14    proc nickname ??? ;
                     -
                    22
                     -
                   200
ERROR 22-322: Syntax error, expecting one of the following: ;, ACCESS,
    AM, AMETHOD, C, CALL,
              CAT, CATALOG, ENG, ENGINE, FMT, FNC, FORMAT, FUNC,
    FUNCTION, INF, INFORMAT, SUBR,
              SUBROUTINE.

ERROR 200-322: The symbol is not recognized and will be ignored.
```

Inconsistent treatment of misspelled procedure names

If you misspell procedure names, SAS tries to determine what you meant. Read the warning statements in the SAS log to see whether SAS interpreted your misspelling correctly.

In the following example, SETINIT is derived from SETINITXXXXXXXXX.

```
      proc setinitxxxxxxxxx ;run;
      -----------------
            1
Original site validation data
Site name:    'SAS INSTITUTE AUSTRALIA PTY LTD'.
Site number:  2582050.
Expiration:   15JAN06.
Grace Period:  0 days (ending 15JAN06).
Warning Period: 30 days (ending 14FEB06).
System birthday:   23NOV92.
Operating System:   WIN     .
Product expiration dates:
---BASE Product              15JAN06 (CPU A)
---SAS/GRAPH                  15JAN06 (CPU A)
---SAS/ETS                    15JAN06 (CPU A)
---SAS/FSP                    15JAN06 (CPU A)
---SAS/AF                     15JAN06 (CPU A)
---SAS/CALC                   15JAN06 (CPU A)
---SAS/ASSIST                 15JAN06 (CPU A)
---SAS/CONNECT                15JAN06 (CPU A)
---SAS/INSIGHT                15JAN06 (CPU A)
---SAS/EIS                    15JAN06 (CPU A)
---SAS/ACC-ODBC               15JAN06 (CPU A)

WARNING 1-322: Assuming the symbol SETINIT was misspelled as
               SETINITXXXXXXXXX.

NOTE: The PROCEDURE SETINITXXXXXXXXX used 1.27 seconds.
```

In the next example, OPTIONS is derived from OPTIONSOPTIONSOPTIONS.

```
399   proc optionsoptionsoptions ;run;
      ---------------------
          1

WARNING 1-322: Assuming the symbol OPTIONS was misspelled as
  optionsoptionsoptions.

    SAS (r) Proprietary Software Release 9.1   TS1M2

Portable Options:

<lines removed>

NOTE: The PROCEDURE OPTIONSOPTIONSOP used 8.01 seconds.
```

In the next example, however, SAS can't determine that we really meant to type
PROC PRINT.

```
20    pro cprint data=sasuser.crime ;
      ---
      14
ERROR: Procedure CPRINT not found.
21    run ;

WARNING 14-169: Assuming the symbol PROC was misspelled as PRO.

NOTE: The SAS System stopped processing this step because of errors.
NOTE: The PROCEDURE CPRINT used 0.28 seconds.
```

Tell me what I have...

The following table demonstrates how to get SAS to tell you what you have currently available or defined in your session. For information about undocumented or unsupported options, you can use the INTERNAL parameter in PROC OPTIONS.

For Information about	Use This Option
Products licensed, expiry dates, site info	PROC SETINIT
Librefs defined	LIBNAME _all_ list
Filerefs defined	FILENAME _all_ list
Macro variables defined	%PUT _all_ ;
	%PUT _user_ ;
	%PUT _global_ ;
	%PUT _local_ ;
	%PUT _automatic_ ;
Options, values, and meaning	PROC OPTIONS
ODS styles	PROC TEMPLATE ; list styles ; run;
SAS/GRAPH devices	PROC GDEVICE nofs ; list _all_ ;
SAS/GRAPH fonts	PROC CATALOG cat=sashelp.fonts ; contents ;

The following code is useful because it gives an overview of a SAS system. I often print the overview when I start working with a new client. I save the output for later reference.

```
* what products are licensed here? What is my site number? When will
SAS expire? ;
proc setinit ;
run ;

* what librefs are defined? ;
libname _all_ list ;

* what filerefs are defined? ;
filename _all_ list ;

* what macro variables are defined? ;
```

```
%put _all_ ;

* what options are set? - including undocumented internal ones ;
proc options internal ;
run ;

* what ODS styles are available? ;
proc template ;
  list styles ;
run ;

* what SAS/Graph devices are available? ;
proc gdevice nofs ;
  list _all_ ;
run ;

* what SAS/Graph software fonts do I have? ;
proc catalog catalog=sashelp.fonts ;
  contents ;
run ; quit ;
```

Saving graphs without ODS

You can produce graphs and save them to an external file such as a JPEG or GIF. To do so you must do the following:

- Define a fileref to point to the file.

    □ For a file on the network, use a filename.

    □ For a file on a Web site, use a URL or FTP engine.

- Use GOPTIONS GSFNAME=*fileref.*

- Use GOPTIONS DEVICE=*dev-type ;*

- Produce the graph.

See the following example.

```
filename g 'c:\test.png' ;
goptions device=png gsfname=g ;
proc gchart data=sashelp.class ;
  vbar sex ;
run ;
```

Using pictures as patterns in bar charts

The pattern statement enables you to use a graphic image as the pattern for an area of a graph. This can be any image—for example, a photo or even another graph. The following code demonstrates how to generate a series of pie charts and then to use each corresponding chart as a pattern in a bar of another graph. The following examples show a bar for each age in our data, and a pie chart within that bar showing the male and female proportions for that age.

```
goptions reset=all gsfname=g device=png xmax=6in ymax=4in xpixels=1800
        ypixels=1200 ftext='Arial' htext=5pct;
filename g 'c:\sex11.png' ;
proc gchart data=sashelp.class ;
   where age=11 ;
   pie sex ;
run ;
filename g 'c:\sex12.png' ;
proc gchart data=sashelp.class ;
  where age=12 ;
  pie sex ;
run ;
filename g 'c:\sex13.png' ;
proc gchart data=sashelp.class ;
  where age=13 ;
  pie sex ;
run ;
filename g 'c:\sex14.png' ;
proc gchart data=sashelp.class ;
  where age=14 ;
  pie sex ;
run ;
filename g 'c:\sex15.png' ;
proc gchart data=sashelp.class ;
  where age=15 ;
  pie sex ;
run ;
filename g 'c:\sex16.png' ;
proc gchart data=sashelp.class ;
  where age=16 ;
  pie sex ;
run ;
filename g 'c:\vbar.png' ;
pattern1  image='c:\sex11.png' ;
pattern2  image='c:\sex12.png' ;
```

```
pattern3  image='c:\sex13.png' ;
pattern4  image='c:\sex14.png' ;
pattern5  image='c:\sex15.png' ;
pattern6  image='c:\sex16.png' ;
title c=red 'Male ... ' c=green 'Female' ;
proc gchart data=sashelp.class  ;
   vbar age / subgroup=age discrete width=20 nolegend ;
run; quit;
```

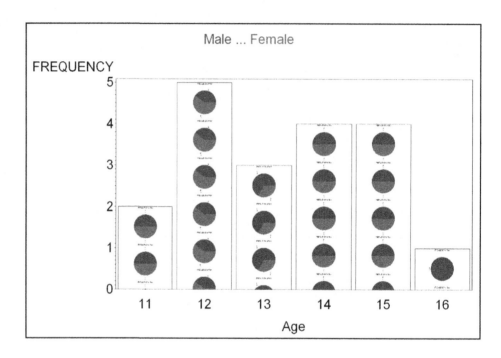

Getting external graphics into a graph

1. Open the graphics editor.

2. Import an image.

   The image can be JPEG or one of many other formats.

3. Save the image as a GRSEG.

   Now you have an external picture in SAS format. The graphic can then easily be Greplayed and combined with other graphs.

12 essential Web sites you should visit

I have looked through my list of SAS Web sites to compile a list that I would recommend visiting particularly if you have not seen them before.

Site	Notes
http://www.lexjansen.com/	Categorizes and indexes a huge amount of information from recent SUGI conferences. Best places to search through: • SUGI, NESUG, PHUSE and PHARMASUG papers • SAS-L archives (via link)
support.sas.com/rnd/base/index-ods-resources.html	Base SAS Community ODS resources. This sight has a huge amount of information about ODS not covered in documentation, particularly in the FAQ section.
www.statsoft.com/textbook/stathome.html	Online statistical text book. This site is great for looking up statistics concepts and methods you're not familiar with.
www.sconsig.com/sastip.htm	SAS Consultant Special Interest Group—SAS coding tips and techniques.
www.prochelp.com	Nice collection of categorized links to useful SAS resources on the Web.
www.ats.ucla.edu/stat/sas/	Resources to learn about and use SAS from UCLA.
support.sas.com/techsup/tnote/tnote_cindex.html	SAS Technical Support documents.
www.views-uk.demon.co.uk/Newsletter/backcopy.htm	VIEWS (Independent UK SAS User Group) newsletters.
www.sas.com/news/newsletter/tech/index.html	SAS Technology Report archive.
www.ratcliffe.co.uk/note_colon/	e-newsletter NOTE:
www.bisug.org	Business Intelligence User Group.
www.woodstreet.org.uk	SAS tips and techniques from Phil Mason.

Getting a list of drivers and information

You can use PROC GDEVICE either to get a list of all graphic drivers or to get details on a specific graphic driver. See the following example. You can then make use of the driver by specifying it in the GOPTIONS statement with DEVICE=.

```
proc gdevice nofs ;
  list _all_ ;
run ;
proc gdevice nofs ;
  list png ;
run ;
```

Chapter **7**

Utility Procedure Tips

More information about space used by catalog members

In PROC CATALOG, you can use the undocumented STAT option on the CONTENTS statement to give you space used by catalog members. See the following examples.

Example code

```
options ls=132 ; * Set linesize wide or output looks a bit weird ;
PROC CATALOG C=sashelp.datafmt ;
  CONTENTS STAT ;
run ;
```

Left side of output

```
# Name      Type    Level      Create Date         Modified Date Description

1 BEANIPA   FILEFMT  12  22FEB2002:14:09:29  04SEP2001:00:00:00 BEA National Income
                                                                and Product Accounts
                                                                Tapes
2 BEANIPAD  FILEFMT  12  22FEB2002:14:09:29  04SEP2001:00:00:00 BEA National Income
                                                                and Product Accounts
                                                                Diskettes
3 BEASPAGE  FILEFMT  12  22FEB2002:14:09:29  04SEP2001:00:00:00 BEA S-Page Current
                                                                Business Statistics
4 BLSCPI    FILEFMT  12  22FEB2002:14:09:29  04SEP2001:00:00:00 BLS Consumer Price
                                                                Index
                                                                Surveys (CU,CW)
5 BLSEENA   FILEFMT  12  22FEB2002:14:09:30  04SEP2001:00:00:00 BLS Employment, Hours,
                                                                and Earnings National
                                                                Survey (EE)
6 BLSEESA   FILEFMT  12  22FEB2002:14:09:30  04SEP2001:00:00:00 BLS State and Area
                                                                Employment, Hours, and
                                                                Earnings Survey (SA)
```

Right side of output

```
                   Last   Last
Page Block Num of Block Block
Size  Size Blocks Bytes  Size Page

4096  4096      1  1438  1530    1
4096  4096      1  1439  1530    1
4096  4096      1  1510  1530    1
4096  4096      1  3533  3570    1
4096  4096      2  1254  1275    1
4096  4096      1  3286  3315    1
4096  4096      1  2047  2295
```

Displaying all characters of a SAS font

You can use PROC GFONT to display the characters from one of the fonts supplied by SAS when you license SAS/GRAPH. This can be useful for fonts that have special characters, because you can see what characters you must specify in order to get the special characters.

The following is a macro that generates a chart that contains a list of all characters within a font. The chart is saved to a graphics file. You can then look at the chart to look up characters you want to use.

```
%macro showfont(font) ;
   filename font "c:\&font..png" ;
   goptions reset=all device=png gsfname=font ;
   title "Font: &font" ;
   proc gfont name=&font
                  nobuild
                  height=.4 cm
                  romcol=red
                  romfont=swissl
                  romht=.3 cm
                  showroman ;
   run;
   quit;
%mend showfont ;

%showfont(math)
%showfont(greek)
```

Charts produced

Font: math

‖	⊥	∠	∴	<	>	±	∓	÷	≠	≡	≤	≥	∝	∼	√	⊂	∪
A	B	C	D	E	F	G	H	I	J	K	L	M	N	O	a	b	c

⊃	∩	∈	→	↑	←	∂	∇	∫	∮	∞	∃	∏	Σ
d	e	f	g	h	i	j	k	l	m	n	o	p	q	r

Font: greek

!	"	#	$	ϑ	&	'	(	)	*	+	,	−	.	/	0	1	2
!	"	#	$	%	&	'	(	)	*	+	,	−	.	/	0	1	2

3	4	5	6	7	8	9	:	;	ϕ	=	ς	?	@	A	B	Ξ	Δ	E
3	4	5	6	7	8	9	:	;	<	=	>	?	@	A	B	C	D	E

Φ	Γ	H	I	E	K	Λ	M	N	O	Π	Θ	P	Σ	T	Υ	∇	Ω	X
F	G	H	I	J	K	L	M	N	O	P	Q	R	S	T	U	V	W	X

Ψ	Z	_	α	β	ξ	δ	ε	φ	γ	η	ι	ε	κ	λ	μ	ν	o	π
Y	Z	_	a	b	c	d	e	f	g	h	i	j	k	l	m	n	o	p

θ	ρ	σ	τ	υ	∂	ω	χ	ψ	ζ	ι	|	ϊ
q	r	s	t	u	v	w	x	y	z	{	|	}

Tuning sorts in SAS

PROC SORT is one of the most resource-intensive procedures in SAS due to the nature of what it does. It is quite important to make it run as efficiently as possible, since large savings can be made here.

There are various ways to make your sort go better. Here a just a few.

1. If you're using PROC SORT and you don't require the data within BY groups to be kept in the same order as they were before the sort, then use the NOEQUALS option. This will save you CPU and elapsed time, particularly on very large data sets.

    ```
    PROC SORT data=fred NOEQUALS ;
      BY this that ;
    run;
    ```

2. Specify more work sort data sets. Often the default is three, but you can have up to six data sets. This is for z/OS only. Specify the following:

    ```
    options sortwkno=6 ;
    ```

3. Use cartridges, tapes, or some other form of mass storage for your sort work data sets. Specify option SORTDEV=<*device-unit-name*>. You will rarely run out of space doing this. The z/OS users should note that SMS has a dataclass that stores a tape data set on disk while being used, but quickly archives it to tape.

4. You can use option SORTSIZE=max to enable sort to use all available main storage.

5. On z/OS, you can use the HIPERSPACE engine option or virtual I/O (VIO) if you have sufficient virtual storage for the amount of data you are sorting. This will speed it up immensely. On Windows, this would be similar to using a RAM disk for your sort work data sets.

6. SAS data sets have a sort indicator that indicates that a data set is already sorted. Then if the data is sorted with PROC SORT in the same order, SAS does not do the sort. Look up the SORTEDBY= data set option. This allows you to tell the SAS System the sort order of data that is read from external sources, without running it through PROC SORT.

7. If your data is grouped, but not sorted in ascending or descending order, then often you don't need to sort. Just use the NOTSORTED option in the BY statement.

Using integrity constraints

Integrity constraints were new in SAS 8. They allow you to define rules that determine which values variables may take on a data set.

There are four types of general integrity constraints, which can be defined for each variable in a data set:

Check   uses a WHERE clause to check for particular values.

Not null   will not allow a null value.

Unique   value must be unique on the data set

Primary key   must be unique and not null; only one of these per data set.

A referential integrity constraint connects a variable in one data set with a primary key in another. Actions are then defined to determine if a value can be changed or what happens when a value is changed. There are three types of referential actions that can occur:

Restrict   If there is a matching foreign key value, then the primary key can't be changed.

Set null   If the primary key is changed or deleted, then the foreign key is set to null.

Cascade   If the primary key is changed or deleted, then the foreign key is also changed.

Note: Some procedures preserve integrity constraints and some destroy them. Sorting data that creates a new data set will not preserve any integrity constraints or indexes.

The SAS Explorer window and the following procedures preserve integrity constraints:

- PROC APPEND
- PROC COPY
- PROC CPORT
- PROC CIMPORT
- PROC SORT[1]
- PROC UPLOAD
- PROC DOWNLOAD

Creating some ICs using PROC DATASETS

```
data people ;
  length sex   $  1
         name $ 32
         serial  8 ;
  delete ;
run ;
data classes ;
  length serial   8
         class $ 32 ;
  delete ;
run ;
proc datasets ;
  modify people ;
    ic create null_name=not null(name) ;
   ic create check_sex=check(where=(sex in ('M','F'))) ;
    ic create one_ser=unique(serial) ;
   ic create prim=primary key(serial) ;
  modify classes ;
    ic create null_class=not null(class) ;
   ic create for_key=foreign key(serial)
      references people
      on delete set null
      on update cascade ;
run ; quit ;
```

---

[1] With PROC SORT, integrity constraints work only when sorting the input data and replacing it with the sorted data.

Creating ICs using PROC SQL

```
proc sql;
    create table people
     (
     name       char(14),
     gender     char(1),
     hired      num,
     jobtype    char(1) not null,
     status     char(10),

     constraint prim_key primary key(name),
     constraint gender check(gender in ('male' 'female')),
     constraint status check(status in ('permanent'
                                'temporary' 'terminated'))
     );

     create table salary
     (
     name       char(14),
     salary     num not null,
     bonus      num,

     constraint for_key foreign key(name) references people
        on delete restrict on update set null
     );
    quit;
```

See the following topics in SAS OnlineDoc for more information:

■ Understanding Integrity Constraints

■ Using PROC DATASETS to Create Integrity Constraints

■ Using SQL to Create Integrity Constraints

Chapter 8

Procedure Tips for Displaying Data

Creating tab-separated output using PROC TABULATE

You may want to get data from SAS to a database or spreadsheet as quickly as possible. This tip is a "quick-and-dirty" method for doing that.

PROC TABULATE can be used to quickly put data in a form suitable for import into EXCEL.

The FORMCHAR option is equal to a comma followed by 10 blanks, and will format the table with a comma separating each column. Alternatively, you can specify a hex value for FORMCHAR if you want to use tabs, rather than commas for separating text. In EBCDIC, that then would be '0540404040404040404040'X. In ASCII it would be '0920202020202020202020'X.

Specify the following:

NOSEPS	to remove horizontal divider lines
NODATE option	to remove date from output
NONUMBER option	to remove page numbers
LINESIZE=254	to allow for a wide page
PAGESIZE=32767	to avoid carriage control for new pages; specifying this makes each page 32767 lines, which is the maximum value allowed.

You can use PROC PRINTTO FILE=ddname; to send the procedure output to a file, or you can assign a file to SASLIST.

Here is an example that uses the LINESIZE= and PAGESIZE= options.

```
options nodate
        nonumber
        ls=254
        ps=32767 ;
proc tabulate data=sashelp.prdsale
              formchar=',                '
              noseps ;
  class country region ;
  var actual ;
  table sum*actual, country all, region all ;
run ;
```

Note: This technique doesn't work as well if you have multiple variables in the column dimension. For instance, if we had a table statement as follows, then the column alignment would not be correct.

```
table sum*actual, country all, region*division all ;
```

Creating data sets from PROC TABULATE

Beginning with SAS 8, we can create an output data set using PROC TABULATE, as well as produce a tabular report. This is done by using OUT=*dataset-name* in the PROC TABULATE statement. This can be useful because we can often write a complex table statement to produce only the statistics we need summarized in the way we want. One tabulation could do what might otherwise require several PROC MEANS or PROC SUMMARY runs. Also in SAS 8 and later, we have extra statistics available to PROC TABULATE, such as median.

The output table contains some extra variables:

■ _TYPE_ contains a bitmap indicating which class variables contributed to each observation. For instance, a value of 10 would indicate the first class variable, but not the second one contributed.

■ _PAGE_ indicates the logical page that contains the observation.

■ _TABLE_ indicates the table that contains the observation.

Note: You can also use the Output Delivery System (ODS) output destination to create data sets from most procedures.

The following example uses PROC TABULATE to create an output data set, TEST. Then you can see the output that is produced.

```
proc tabulate data=sashelp.prdsale out=test ;
  class country region ;
  var actual predict ;
  table country all,
        region*(actual*(sum mean) predict*(min median max)) ;
run ;
proc print data=test ;
run ;
```

The SAS System

	Region				
	EAST				
	Actual Sales		Predicted Sales		
	Sum	Mean	Min	Median	Max
Country					
CANADA	127485.00	531.19	0.00	508.00	986.00
GERMANY	124547.00	518.95	4.00	499.00	993.00
U.S.A.	118229.00	492.62	1.00	494.50	1000.00
All	370261.00	514.25	0.00	503.00	1000.00

(Continued)

	Region				
	WEST				
	Actual Sales		Predicted Sales		
	Sum	Mean	Min	Median	Max
Country					
CANADA	119505.00	497.94	6.00	447.50	1000.00
GERMANY	121451.00	506.05	0.00	448.00	981.00
U.S.A.	119120.00	496.33	22.00	490.00	999.00
All	360076.00	500.11	0.00	457.00	1000.00

(continued)

(continued)

Obs	COUNTRY	REGION	_TYPE_	_PAGE_	_TABLE_	ACTUAL_ Sum	ACTUAL_ Mean	PREDICT_ Min	PREDICT_ Median	PREDICT_ Max
1	CANADA	EAST	11	1	1	127485	531.188	0	508.0	986
2	CANADA	WEST	11	1	1	119505	497.938	6	447.5	1000
3	GERMANY	EAST	11	1	1	124547	518.946	4	499.0	993
4	GERMANY	WEST	11	1	1	121451	506.046	0	448.0	981
5	U.S.A.	EAST	11	1	1	118229	492.621	1	494.5	1000
6	U.S.A.	WEST	11	1	1	119120	496.333	22	490.0	999
7		EAST	01	1	1	370261	514.251	0	503.0	1000
8		WEST	01	1	1	360076	500.106	0	457.0	1000

Traffic lighting with PROC TABULATE

Traffic lighting is to cause colors to change appropriately depending on values. For instance, values below a limit might appear in green, while values over a limit appear in red. This can be easily accomplished in SAS 8 using PROC TABULATE and ODS.

There are a few key things that make this work:

1. Make sure you open and close your ODS destination(s), because this works only with ODS (other than the LISTING and OUTPUT destinations).

2. Create a format that takes ranges and returns the name of a color for each.

3. Use a style override to change the color based on the value. In the example you can see that I set the background color based on my format *traf*, using the total of *actual*.

```
ods html file='test.html' ;
proc format ;
  value traf
    low-120000='red'
    other='green' ;
proc tabulate data=sashelp.prdsale ;
  class country region ;
  var actual ;
  table actual*sum*{style={background=traf.}},country,region ;
run ;
ods html close ;
```

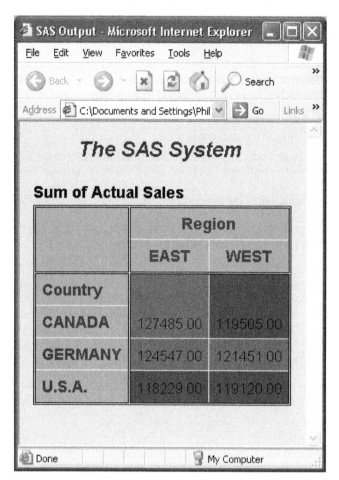

Producing multi-panel reports with PROC REPORT

PROC REPORT has the ability to show multiple logical pages on one physical page. This feature can be used to save paper.

The PANELS=*x* option (default is 1) breaks the page into *x* horizontal panels.

The PSPACE=*y* option (default is 4) puts *y* spaces between panels.

Setting the value of PANELS to a large number will cause SAS to fit as many panels on the page as it can. For example, PANELS=99 might result in two or three panels.

```
234   options ls=132 ps=20 ;
235   proc report data=sashelp.shoes
236              panels=2  /* 2 horizontal panels */
237              nowd ;    /* nowd for running in batch */
238      col (subsidiary product sales) ;  /* Define columns we want */
239   run ;


NOTE: There were 395 observations read from the data set SASHELP.SHOES.
NOTE: PROCEDURE REPORT used (Total process time):
      real time            0.01 seconds
      cpu time             0.02 seconds
```

1st page of output

```
                               The SAS System

Subsidiary    Product        Total Sales   Subsidiary    Product        Total Sales
Addis Ababa   Boot             $29,761     Cairo         Men's Dress        $4,051
Addis Ababa   Men's Casual     $67,242     Cairo         Sandal            $10,532
Addis Ababa   Men's Dress      $76,793     Cairo         Slipper           $13,732
Addis Ababa   Sandal           $62,819     Cairo         Sport Shoe         $2,259
Addis Ababa   Slipper          $68,641     Cairo         Women's Casual   $328,474
Addis Ababa   Sport Shoe        $1,690     Cairo         Women's Dress     $14,095
Addis Ababa   Women's Casual   $51,541     Johannesburg  Boot               $8,365
Addis Ababa   Women's Dress   $108,942     Johannesburg  Sandal            $17,337
Algiers       Boot             $21,297     Johannesburg  Slipper           $39,452
Algiers       Men's Casual     $63,206     Johannesburg  Sport Shoe         $5,172
Algiers       Men's Dress     $123,743     Johannesburg  Women's Dress     $42,682
Algiers       Sandal           $29,198     Khartoum      Boot              $19,282
Algiers       Slipper          $64,891     Khartoum      Men's Casual       $9,244
Algiers       Sport Shoe        $2,617     Khartoum      Men's Dress       $18,053
Algiers       Women's Dress    $90,648     Khartoum      Sandal            $26,427
Cairo         Boot              $4,846     Khartoum      Slipper           $43,452
Cairo         Men's Casual    $360,209     Khartoum      Sport Shoe         $2,521
```

Indenting output using PROC TABULATE

PROC TABULATE supports the INDENT option. This enables nested row titles to be indented, rather than displayed in separate columns, in order to save space and improve appearance.

```
options nocenter ;

data sample ;
  length x y $ 1 ;
  input x y z ;

datalines ;
a b 1
b c 2
a c 3
a b 4
b c 5
a c 6
;

proc tabulate data=sample ;
  class x y ;
  var z ;
  table x*y, z*(min mean max) / INDENT=3 ;
run ;
```

	Z		
	MIN	MEAN	MAX
a			
b	1.00	2.50	4.00
c	3.00	4.50	6.00
b			
c	2.00	3.50	5.00

Wrapping lines with PROC REPORT

PROC REPORT can group variables together by observation. If the variables don't fit on one line, then they will continue on the next line. PROC REPORT can also prefix the value of each variable with its variable name to improve clarity.

Options

The following options are used to wrap data in PROC REPORT.

WRAP   keeps values for an observation together, rather than continuing them on the next page.

NAMED puts each variable label/name and an equal sign before each value.

```
proc report data=sasuser.crime
            WRAP     /* wrap lines */
            nowd ;   * nowd for running in batch ;
     run ;
```

Output using WRAP

State name	FIPS code		MURDER	RAPE	ROBBERY	ASSAULT
BURGLARY	LARCENY	AUTO				
Alabama		1	14.2	25.2	96.8	278.3
1135.5	1881.9	280.7				
Alaska		2	10.8	51.6	96.8	284
1331.7	3369.8	753.3				
Arizona		4	9.5	34.2	138.2	312.3
2346.1	4467.4	439.5				

Program using WRAP and NAMED

```
proc report data=sasuser.crime
            wrap     /* wrap lines */
            NAMED    /* prefix values with var=, instead of col.
                        titles */
            nowd ;   * nowd for running in batch ;
     run ;
```

Output using WRAP and NAMED

```
State name=Virginia          FIPS code=        51  MURDER=           9
RAPE=       23.3  ROBBERY=      92.1  ASSAULT=     165.7  BURGLARY=      986.2
LARCENY=   2521.2  AUTO=      226.7
State name=Washington        FIPS code=        53  MURDER=         4.3
RAPE=       39.6  ROBBERY=     106.2  ASSAULT=     224.8  BURGLARY=     1605.6
LARCENY=   3386.9  AUTO=      360.3
```

Saving space on a page with PROC TABULATE

To remove the divider lines in PROC TABULATE, you can use the NOSEPS option. To remove a line of statistics or labels, you can specify null labels by using either the KEYLABEL statement or ='' against statistics or variables. The RTS (Row Title Space) option can be used to control the size of the row title column(s). The RTS value is the width of the columns plus the vertical divider characters. The FORMAT option can set the default format for columns. (Individual column formats may be overridden too.) The width of the format being used will specify the width of the column in the table. The following is a default tabulate followed by a modified tabulate.

```
proc tabulate data=sashelp.prdsale ;
   class country region ;
   var actual ;
   table country,
         sum*actual*region ;
run ;
```

Subsidiary Reports

	Sum	
	Actual Sales	
	Region	
	EAST	WEST
Country		
CANADA	127485.00	119505.00
GERMANY	124547.00	121451.00
U.S.A.	118229.00	119120.00

Program with labels set to null and no separator lines

```
proc tabulate data=sashelp.prdsale
              format=dollar8.
              noseps ;
  class country region ;
  var actual ;
  table country='',
        sum=''*actual=''*region='' /
        rts=10 ;
run ;
```

Subsidiary Reports		
	EAST	WEST
CANADA	$127,485	$119,505
GERMANY	$124,547	$121,451
U.S.A.	$118,229	$119,120

Defining denominator definitions in PROC TABULATE

Using denominator definitions in PROC TABULATE can be confusing.

- Remember that you cannot use groupings, For example:

      <a*(b c)>

  You must show groupings in their ungrouped form. Therefore, the correct form of the previous example would be:

      <a*b a*c>

Generally, people want either row or column percentages to add up to 100%, which can be achieved as follows:

- To get column percentages, specify the ROW definition as the denominator definition. For example:

      table ROW, column*value*pctn<ROW> ;

```
proc tabulate data=sasuser.houses noseps ;
   class style bedrooms ;
   var price ;
   table style, bedrooms*price*pctn<style> ;
run ;
```

	Number of bedrooms			
	1	2	3	4
	Asking price	Asking price	Asking price	Asking price
	PctN	PctN	PctN	PctN
Style of homes				
CONDO	.	40.00	25.00	25.00
RANCH	50.00	20.00	50.00	.
SPLIT	50.00	.	25.00	25.00
TWOSTORY	.	40.00	.	50.00

To get row percentages, specify the first element of the COLUMN definition as the denominator definition. For example:

```
table row, COLUMN*value*pctn<COLUMN> ;
```

```
proc tabulate data=sasuser.houses noseps ;
  class style bedrooms ;
  var price ;
  table style, bedrooms*price*pctn<bedrooms> ;
run ;
```

	Number of bedrooms			
	1	2	3	4
	Asking price	Asking price	Asking price	Asking price
	PctN	PctN	PctN	PctN
Style of homes				
CONDO	.	50.00	25.00	25.00
RANCH	25.00	25.00	50.00	.
SPLIT	33.33	.	33.33	33.33
TWOSTORY	.	50.00	.	50.00

Other ways to calculate percentages relative to groups

You can use the following statistics to calculate percentages using the value of a cell in relation to the total of values in a group of cells. This is often an easier way to calculate percentages since no denominator definitions are required.

REPPCTN and REPPCTSUM	percentage of value of cell relative to whole report
COLPCT and COLPCTN	percentage of value of cell relative to whole column
ROWPCTN and ROWPCTSUM	percentage of value of cell relative to whole row
PAGEPCTN and PAGEPCTSUM	percentage of value of cell relative to whole page

```
proc tabulate data=sashelp.prdsale ;
  class country region ;
  var actual ;
  table (country all),
        region*
        actual=' '*(sum colpctsum*f=5.1
                        rowpctsum*f=5.1
                        reppctsum*f=5.1)
        all*actual*sum=' ' ;
run;
```

| | | Region | | | | | | | | All |
| | | EAST | | | | WEST | | | | |
		Sum	ColP-ctSum	RowP-ctSum	RepP-ctSum	Sum	ColP-ctSum	RowP-ctSum	RepP-ctSum	Actual Sales
Country										
CANADA		127485.00	34.4	51.6	17.5	119505.00	33.2	48.4	16.4	246990.00
GERMANY		124547.00	33.6	50.6	17.1	121451.00	33.7	49.4	16.6	245998.00
U.S.A.		118229.00	31.9	49.8	16.2	119120.00	33.1	50.2	16.3	237349.00
All		370261.00	100.0	50.7	50.7	360076.00	100.0	49.3	49.3	730337.00

Example using overall percentages

```
proc tabulate data=sasuser.houses noseps ;
  class style bedrooms ;
  var price ;
  table price,
        (style all)*pctsum,
        bedrooms all ;
run ;
```

Asking price

		Number of bedrooms				
		1	2	3	4	All
Style of homes						
CONDO	PctSum	.	15.37	6.40	10.25	32.02
RANCH	PctSum	2.78	5.16	14.16	.	22.11
SPLIT	PctSum	5.31	.	5.94	7.61	18.85
TWOSTORY	PctSum	.	10.08	.	16.94	27.02
All	PctSum	8.09	30.61	26.50	34.80	100.00

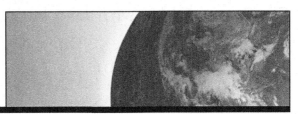

Chapter **9**

Basic Statistical Procedure Tips

Frequency tables with long labels treated differently in SAS 8 and SAS®9

In SAS 8, PROC FREQ truncates variable values to 16 characters and then combines identical truncated values. This can give misleading results as in the following examples. SAS®9 fixes this.

```
data x ;
  length a $ 30 ;
  input a ;
datalines ;
this-is-26-characters-long
this-is-26-characters-long-not
this-is-26-characters-long
run ;

proc freq ;
  table a ;
run ;
```

Output when run in SAS 8.2

A	Frequency	Percent	Cumulative Frequency	Cumulative Percent
this-is-26-chara	3	100.0	3	100.0

Output when run in SAS 9.1.3

a	Frequency	Percent	Cumulative Frequency	Cumulative Percent
this-is-26-characters-long	2	66.67	2	66.67
this-is-26-characters-long-not	1	33.33	3	100.00

To display full variable values with their frequencies in SAS 8, you can use a PROC SUMMARY with the NWAY option, followed by a PROC PRINT. This does not truncate values.

```
proc summary nway ;
  class a ;
  output out=freq ;
run ;

proc print ;
  var a _freq_ ;
run ;
```

OBS	A	_FREQ_
1	this-is-26-characters-long	2
2	this-is-26-characters-long-not	1

Automatic naming in PROC SUMMARY

The following applies to PROC SUMMARY and PROC MEANS, which are essentially the same procedure with different default parameter settings.

We can use multiple class statements, which can be useful if we want to use a number of variables but specify different options for each, such as the order we want class variable values to appear in the output.

Another useful feature is the ability to automatically name statistics generated by an output statement. In SAS 6 we had to explicitly name statistics, unless only generating one statistic for a variable. In the following example, we generate four statistics for each variable, and SAS automatically creates meaningful variable names and labels. For instance, the mean of actual has a variable name of ACTUAL_Mean and a label of Actual Sales_Mean.

```
proc summary data=sashelp.prdsale nway ;
   class country / order=freq ; * countries with most observations come
first ;
   class year month / descending ; * latest data comes first ;
   var actual predict ;
   output sum= mean= min= max= out=stats / autoname autolabel ;
run ;
proc print label ; run ;
```

Obs	Country	Year	Month	_TYPE_	Actual _FREQ_	Predicted Sales_Sum	Actual Sales_Sum	Sales_Mean
1	CANADA	1994	Dec	7	20	$11,722.00	$9,389.00	$586.10
2	CANADA	1994	Nov	7	20	$10,113.00	$9,324.00	$505.65
3	CANADA	1994	Oct	7	20	$8,408.00	$8,085.00	$420.40
4	CANADA	1994	Sep	7	20	$9,954.00	$8,768.00	$497.70
5	CANADA	1994	Aug	7	20	$10,294.00	$9,029.00	$514.70
6	CANADA	1994	Jul	7	20	$9,605.00	$8,866.00	$480.25
7	CANADA	1994	Jun	7	20	$10,493.00	$9,822.00	$524.65
8	CANADA	1994	May	7	20	$11,427.00	$9,355.00	$571.35
9	CANADA	1994	Apr	7	20	$12,654.00	$11,050.00	$632.70
10	CANADA	1994	Mar	7	20	$8,894.00	$10,704.00	$444.70
11	CANADA	1994	Feb	7	20	$10,371.00	$7,967.00	$518.55
12	CANADA	1994	Jan	7	20	$12,035.00	$11,331.00	$601.75
13	CANADA	1993	Dec	7	20	$11,277.00	$8,710.00	$563.85
14	CANADA	1993	Nov	7	20	$8,139.00	$11,163.00	$406.95
15	CANADA	1993	Oct	7	20	$10,739.00	$8,169.00	$536.95
16	CANADA	1993	Sep	7	20	$10,686.00	$9,880.00	$534.30
17	CANADA	1993	Aug	7	20	$8,047.00	$10,009.00	$402.35

(continued)

(continued)

18	CANADA	1993	Jul	7	20	$12,313.00	$11,233.00	$615.65
19	CANADA	1993	Jun	7	20	$11,204.00	$10,671.00	$560.20
20	CANADA	1993	May	7	20	$9,916.00	$10,210.00	$495.80
21	CANADA	1993	Apr	7	20	$9,695.00	$8,594.00	$484.75
22	CANADA	1993	Mar	7	20	$10,458.00	$11,485.00	$522.90

Obs	Predicted Sales_Mean	Actual Sales_Min	Predicted Sales_Min	Actual Sales_Max	Predicted Sales_Max
1	$469.45	$15.00	$71.00	$928.00	$979.00
2	$466.20	$107.00	$0.00	$1,000.00	$923.00
3	$404.25	$35.00	$23.00	$929.00	$947.00
4	$438.40	$112.00	$49.00	$990.00	$839.00
5	$451.45	$51.00	$17.00	$977.00	$955.00
6	$443.30	$20.00	$49.00	$975.00	$969.00
7	$491.10	$14.00	$10.00	$978.00	$992.00
8	$467.75	$3.00	$26.00	$987.00	$839.00
9	$552.50	$43.00	$30.00	$972.00	$987.00
10	$535.20	$24.00	$69.00	$991.00	$966.00
11	$398.35	$92.00	$21.00	$992.00	$871.00
12	$566.55	$88.00	$12.00	$944.00	$1,000.00
13	$435.50	$87.00	$6.00	$954.00	$964.00
14	$558.15	$9.00	$31.00	$993.00	$982.00
15	$408.45	$46.00	$23.00	$981.00	$815.00
16	$494.00	$80.00	$11.00	$981.00	$962.00
17	$500.45	$6.00	$126.00	$923.00	$967.00
18	$561.65	$8.00	$15.00	$968.00	$988.00
19	$533.55	$168.00	$63.00	$983.00	$974.00
20	$510.50	$46.00	$199.00	$854.00	$799.00
21	$429.70	$49.00	$7.00	$895.00	$933.00
22	$574.25	$21.00	$68.00	$995.00	$998.00

PROC MEANS: Specifying confidence limits to calculate

PROC MEANS (which is very similar to PROC SUMMARY) can calculate upper and lower confidence limits.

Options in the PROC statement, which apply to all variables

ALPHA=*value* specifies the confidence level as a percentage, which is (1–*value*)*100. By setting ALPHA=0.1 you will get a 90% confidence interval. The default is 0.5.

CLM calculates upper and lower confidence limits.

LCLM calculates lower confidence limit.

UCLM calculates upper confidence limit.

Keywords for use in the OUTPUT statement, which apply to selected variables

Remember to specify the ALPHA= option, even if using only these keywords:

LCLM calculated lower confidence limit

UCLM calculated upper confidence limit

```
options ls=110 ;
proc means data=sashelp.tourism alpha=.05 clm ;
run ;
```

```
                                  The MEANS Procedure

                                                           Lower 95%      Upper 95%
Variable Label                                             CL for Mean    CL for Mean

year     Year                                              6122.40        8488.36
vsp      the number of holidays in Spain taken by US residents  3.1962536   4.5685257
pdi      UK real personal disposable income                264875.38      312637.51
puk      the implicit deflator of UK consumer expenditure  0.4353734      0.7088667
exuk     an exchange rate index of the UK pound            0.7836988      0.961084
         against the US dollar
pop      the UK population                                 56.1448900     56.8435928
cpisp    the consumer price index in Spain                 0.3784453      0.6684071
exsp     an exchange rate index of Spanish pesetas against 0.7119274      0.9561957
         the US dollar
```

```
proc summary data=sashelp.tourism alpha=.12345 ;
  var pop pdi ;
  output out=stats lclm=low_pop low_pdi uclm=big_pop big_pdi ;
run ;
proc report data=stats nowd ;
  format low_pdi big_pdi comma12. ;
run ;
```

		the UK population	UK real personal disposable income	the UK population	UK real personal disposable income
__TYPE__	__FREQ__				
0	29	56.223362	270,240	5 6.765121	307,273

PROC UNIVARIATE: Mode is the minimum when there are multiples

In PROC UNIVARIATE, the mode of a continuous variable (i.e. one with all values unique) is the minimum value in the data set. If two or more values are the same, then the mode functions correctly. If there are several modes (for example, three of two different numbers), then SAS seems to report the smallest mode.

```
data sample ;
  input x ;
datalines ;
1
1
2
3.1
3.5
3.9
4
;
run ;
proc univariate data=sample ;
  var x ;
run ;
```

Partial output from PROC UNIVARIATE

```
                      The UNIVARIATE Procedure
                           Variable:  x

                              Moments

N                            7    Sum Weights               7
Mean                2.64285714    Sum Observations       18.5
Std Deviation       1.30237878    Variance         1.69619048
Skewness            -0.4142638    Kurtosis         -1.9591546
Uncorrected SS           59.07    Corrected SS     10.1771429
Coeff Variation     49.2791969    Std Error Mean   0.49225291


                   Basic Statistical Measures

        Location                        Variability

   Mean      2.642857      Std Deviation          1.30238
   Median    3.100000      Variance               1.69619
   Mode      1.000000      Range                  3.00000
                           Interquartile Range    2.90000
```

(continued)

(continued)

```
                    Tests for Location: Mu0=0

        Test              -Statistic-      -----p Value------

        Student's t     t  5.368901      Pr >  |t|    0.0017
        Sign            M      3.5       Pr >= |M|    0.0156
        Signed Rank     S       14       Pr >= |S|    0.0156
```

PROC UNIVARIATE and PROC FASTCLUS: Calculating weighted medians

If the weights are integral, use a FREQ statement instead of a WEIGHT statement with PROC UNIVARIATE. If the weights are not integral, use PROC FASTCLUS MAXC=1 LEAST=1 to compute an approximate median as in the following example:

```
data w;
   input x w;
datalines;
1  0
3  1
4  2
4  3
7  5
99 10
;
run ;
proc univariate data=w;
  var x;
  freq w;
run;
proc fastclus data=w maxc=1 least=1;
  var x;
  weight w;
run;
```

The LEAST=1 option tells FASTCLUS to try to minimize the weighted sum of absolute deviations from the cluster centers. The algorithm is iterative and not exact.

Partial output from PROC UNIVARIATE and PROC FASTCLUS

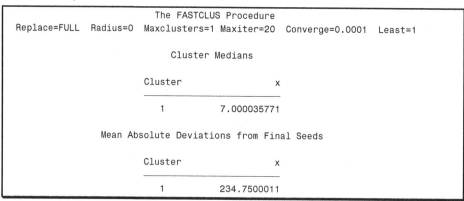

```
                       The FASTCLUS Procedure
Replace=FULL   Radius=0  Maxclusters=1 Maxiter=20  Converge=0.0001  Least=1

                        Cluster Medians

                  Cluster                x
                  _____
                     1          7.000035771

            Mean Absolute Deviations from Final Seeds

                  Cluster                x
                  _____
                     1          234.7500011
```

PROC REG: Determining whether to use intercepts

When performing a stepwise regression analysis and you are not sure whether you should consider an intercept or not, you can do the following. Create a new variable INTER containing the value 1 for each observation and include it in your MODEL statement. This is better than using the default INT option. The stepwise regression methods will show you whether INTER is a variable to take into account.

```
data DATASET;
   set DATASET;
   INTER=1;
run;
proc reg data=DATASET;
   model DEP = INDEP1 INDEP2 .. INTER
      / selection=rsquare ...;
run;
```

Chapter **10**

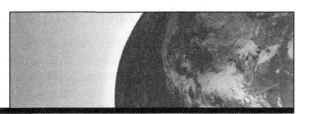

The PRINT Procedure

A better looking report with BY groups

Specifying the ID and BY statements in a PRINT procedure that has the same variable names (or lists of variable names) causes a special print layout. This will also work if the variables in the ID statement are the same as the first variables in the BY statement. The following examples show the standard layout and the special layout.

Standard code

```
proc sort data=sashelp.company ;
  by level1 level2 ;
run ;
proc print data=sashelp.company ;
  by level1 level2 ;
  var job1 n ;
run ;
```

Start of output

```
                               Subsidiary Reports

-------------------- LEVEL1=International Ai LEVEL2=LONDON --------------------

                                    Obs    JOB1                N

                                     1     MANAGER             1
                                     2     ASSISTANT           1
                                     3     MARKET. CONS.       1
                                     4     ASSISTANT           1
                                     5     SALES.-CONS.        1
                                     6     SALES CONS          1
                                     7     SALES CONS BERL     1
                                     8     MARKET. CONS.       1
                                     9     CONSULTANT S□D      1
                                    10     SALES.-CONS.        1
                                    11     SALES-TRAINEE       1
                                    12     CONSULTANT          1
                                    13     SALES-CONSMAINF     1
                                    14     ASSIST              1
                                    15     TRANSLATOR          1
```

(continued)

(continued)

```
--------------------LEVEL1=International Ai LEVEL2=NEW YORK --------------------

                                Obs     JOB1               N

                                 16     ASSISTANT          1
                                 17     ASSISTANT          1
                                 18     ASSISTANT          1
                                 19     RESPONS. FINANC    1
                                 20     MANAGER            1
                                 21     RECEPTIONIST       1
                                 22     RESPONSIBLE        1
                                 23     RECEPTION          1
                                 24     MANAGER            1
                                 25     ASSISTANT          1
                                 26     MANAGER            1
                                 27     PROD.MAN.MATERN    1
                                 28     ASSISTANT          1
                                 29     LYON RESP.         1
                                 30     INDUSTRY           1
                                 31     RESPONS. TERTIA    1
                                 32     PUBLIC             1
                                 33     AGENCE TERTIARE    1
                                 34     ASSISTANT          1
                                 35     MANAGER            1
                                 36     TECH.-CONS.        1
                                 37     TECH.-CONS         1
                                 38     ASSISTANT          1
                                 39     TRANSLATOR         1
                                 40     TECH. CONS.        1


-------------------- -- LEVEL1=International Ai LEVEL2=TOKYO --------------------

                                Obs     JOB1           N

                                 41     MANAGER        1
                                 42     ASSISTANT      1
                                 43     ACCOUNTANT     1
                                 44     ADMIN          1
                                 45     ASSIST.        1
                                 46     MARKETING      1
                                 47     MANAGER        1
                                 48     TRANSLATOR     1
```

Program using BY and ID statements

```
proc print data=sashelp.company ;
  by level1 level2 ;
  id level1 level2 ;
  var job1 n ;
run ;
```

Special output

```
                        Subsidiary Reports                        45

             LEVEL1          LEVEL2      JOB1            N

             International Ai   LONDON     MANAGER         1
                                          ASSISTANT       1
                                          MARKET. CONS.   1
                                          ASSISTANT       1
                                          SALES.-CONS.    1
                                          SALES CONS      1
                                          SALES CONS BERL 1
                                          MARKET. CONS.   1
                                          CONSULTANT SÜD  1
                                             SALES.-CONS.
                                          SALES-TRAINEE   1
                                          CONSULTANT      1
                                          SALES-CONSMAINF 1
                                          ASSIST          1
                                          TRANSLATOR      1

                              International Ai   NEW YORK   ASSISTANT       1
                                          ASSISTANT       1
                                          ASSISTANT       1
                                          RESPONS. FINANC 1
                                          MANAGER         1
                                          RECEPTIONIST    1
                                          RESPONSIBLE     1
                                          RECEPTION       1
                                          MANAGER         1
                                          ASSISTANT       1
                                          MANAGER         1
                                          PROD.MAN.MATERN 1
                                          ASSISTANT       1
                                          LYON RESP.      1
                                          INDUSTRY        1
                                          RESPONS. TERTIA 1
                                          PUBLIC          1
                                          AGENCE TERTIARE 1
                                          ASSISTANT       1
```

(continued)

(continued)

```
                                              MANAGER          1
                                              TECH.-CONS.      1
                                              TECH.-CONS       1
                                              ASSISTANT        1
                                              TRANSLATOR       1
                                              TECH. CONS.      1

                  International Ai    TOKYO   MANAGER          1
                                              ASSISTANT        1
                                              ACCOUNTANT       1
                                              ADMIN            1
                                              ASSIST.          1
                                              MARKETING        1
                                              MANAGER          1
                                              TRANSLATOR       1
```

Saving resources by specifying the WIDTH= option

You can save resources in your PROC PRINT by using WIDTH=FULL. Using the full width of the format for each column displayed means SAS doesn't have to calculate the optimum width for each column. Of course, you may generate more pages this way though.

The SAS Help and Documentation says that the WIDTH= option specifies what PROC PRINT uses as the column width when printing the data set. Column width must be one of the following:

FULL
prints the data set using the variable's formatted width as the column width.

MINIMUM|MIN
prints the data set using the minimum column width possible per page to print the data values.

UNIFORM|U
formats all pages uniformly using the variable's formatted width as the column width.

UNIFORMBY|UBY
formats all pages uniformly within a BY group using the variable's formatted width as the column width.

Labels are always displayed in BY groups

Here is a very simple thing to watch out for. Everyone knows that the LABEL
option in PROC PRINT determines whether variable labels are used for column
headings. However, variable labels are always used for BY groups (if they are
defined).

If the BY group variable has no label, or you specify a label var='', then the
variable name is used.

I know of one person who was quite confused because his BY group variable label
looked like a list of variable names.

The following example shows that the BY variable GROUP is displayed in the BY
line as its label EXPERIMENTAL GROUP.

```
proc sort data=sasuser.fitness ;
  by group ;
run;
proc print data=sasuser.fitness label ;
  by group ;
  var oxygen runpulse rstpulse ;
run ;
proc print data=sasuser.fitness ;
  by group ;
  var oxygen runpulse rstpulse ;
run ;
```

Output: with LABEL option

```
------------- Experimental group=0 --------------

                             Heart rate      Heart rate
                 Oxygen         while           while
     OBS      consumption      running         resting

      1          44.609          178             62
      2          45.313          185             62
      3          54.297          156             45
```

Output: without LABEL option

```
-------------- Experimental group=0 --------------

OBS     OXYGEN    RUNPULSE    RSTPULSE

  1     44.609      178          62
  2     45.313      185          62
  3     54.297      156          45
```

Chapter **11**

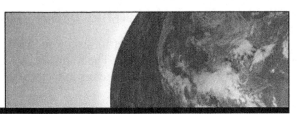

The FORMAT Procedure

Nesting formats within other formats

You can refer to other formats from within formats. You can also nest your formats up to five levels deep. The following code and log demonstrates how I created two formats, one of which refers to the other format as well as a standard SAS format.

```
proc format ;
  value loads
    5000-<6000 = 'Over 5,000'
    6000-<7000 = 'Over 6,000'
    7000-<8000 = 'Over 7,000'
    8000-<9000 = 'Over 8,000'
    other      = 'Mega!' ;
  value couple
    2 = 'Bingo!'
    5000-<10000 = [loads10.]
    other=[comma6.] ;
data _null_ ;
  input x ;
  put x couple. ;
  datalines ;
1
2
3
12
1234
5678
8888
9999
12345
;
run ;
```

```
4287   proc format ;
4288     value loads
4289       5000-<6000 = 'Over 5,000'
4290       6000-<7000 = 'Over 6,000'
4291       7000-<8000 = 'Over 7,000'
4292       8000-<9000 = 'Over 8,000'
4293       other      = 'Mega!' ;
NOTE: Format LOADS has been output.
4294     value couple
4295       2 = 'Bingo!'
4296       5000-<10000 = [loads10.]
4297       other=[comma6.] ;
NOTE: Format COUPLE has been output.

NOTE: PROCEDURE FORMAT used (Total process time):
      real time            0.10 seconds
      cpu time             0.01 seconds


4298   data _null_ ;
4299     input x ;
4300     put x couple. ;
4301     datalines ;

      1
Bingo!
      3
     12
 1,234
Over 5,000
Over 8,000
Mega!
12,345
NOTE: DATA statement used (Total process time):
      real time            0.04 seconds
      cpu time             0.00 seconds


4311   ;
4312   run ;
```

Modifying standard formats and informats

The use of existing formats and informats was covered in a previous tip, but here is a nice application of it.

If your format or informat doesn't do quite what you want, then create a new one based on the original. The new format or informat can handle those special cases that are not handled by the standard one.

The following example shows a DATA step that uses a standard numeric informat to input data, which causes errors due to the data having numerics, characters, blanks, and missing values. We then make a new informat that handles special values and reads numbers in using a standard numeric format.

```
data _null_ ;
  input number 8. ;
  put number= ;
datalines ;
10
Phil Mason
9.5
SUGI
;;
run ;
proc format ;
  invalue myfmt
    ' '     = 0
    .       = 0
    'A'-'Z' = 0
    'a'-'z' = 0
    other   = [8.] ;
data _null_ ;
  input number myfmt. ; * Use our modified informat ;
  put number= ;
datalines ;
10
Phil Mason
9.5
SUGI
;;
run ;
* Now we have no errors !;
* We could set values to a special missing value such as .A ;
*   which could then be selectively removed ;
```

```
1     data _null_ ;
2       input number 8. ;
3       put number= ;
4     datalines ;

number=10
NOTE: Invalid data for number in line 6 1-8.
number=.
RULE:        ----+----1----+----2----+----3----+----4----+----5----+----6-
   ---+----7----+----8----+----9----+----0
6          Phil Mason
number=.  _ERROR_=1 _N_=2
number=9.5
NOTE: Invalid data for number in line 8 1-8.
number=.
8          SUGI
number=.  _ERROR_=1 _N_=4
NOTE: DATA statement used (Total process time):
      real time            0.18 seconds
      cpu time             0.06 seconds


9     ;;
10    run ;
11    proc format ;
12      invalue myfmt
13        ' '      = 0
14        .        = 0
15        'A'-'Z' = 0
16        'a'-'z' = 0
17        other   = [8.] ;
NOTE: Informat MYFMT has been output.

NOTE: PROCEDURE FORMAT used (Total process time):
      real time            0.09 seconds
      cpu time             0.00 seconds


18    data _null_ ;
19      input number myfmt. ; * Use our modified informat ;
20      put number= ;
21    datalines ;

number=10
number=0
number=9.5
number=0
NOTE: DATA statement used (Total process time):
      real time            0.09 seconds
      cpu time             0.00 seconds
```

(continued)

(continued)

```
26    ;;
27    run ;
28    * Now we have no errors !;
29    * We could set values to a special missing value such as .A ;
30    *    which could then be selectively removed ;
```

Mixing character and numeric values in informats

Unquoted numerics in INVALUE statements of PROC FORMAT are treated as numbers, whereas they were previously treated as character values. This means that you can now handle character and numeric types with the one informat, as shown in this example.

```
Proc format ;
  invalue mixed
     1-10  = 1
     11-20 = 2
     'XYZ' = 9
     other=999 ;
run;
data in ;
  input info mixed. ;
  put "Input Data: " _infile_ / @13 info= ;
datalines ;
1
3.2
13
XYZ
A
;;
run ;
```

```
138   Proc format ;
139     invalue mixed
140        1-10  = 1
141        11-20 = 2
142        'XYZ' = 9
143        other=999 ;
NOTE: Informat MIXED is already on the library.
NOTE: Informat MIXED has been output.
144   run;

NOTE: PROCEDURE FORMAT used (Total process time):
      real time            0.00 seconds
      cpu time             0.00 seconds


145   data in ;
146     input info mixed. ;
147     put "Input Data: " _infile_ / @13 info= ;
148   datalines ;
```

(continued)

(continued)

```
Input Data: 1
           info=1
Input Data: 3.2
           info=1
Input Data: 13
           info=2
Input Data: XYZ
           info=9
Input Data: A
           info=999
NOTE: The data set WORK.IN has 5 observations and 1 variables.
NOTE: DATA statement used (Total process time):
      real time           0.01 seconds
      cpu time            0.01 seconds


154  ;;
155  run ;
```

Automatically rounding numbers

The ROUND option can be used with PROC FORMAT to display rounded numbers.

This option has several advantages:

- avoids doing rounding in a DATA step
- saves on DATA step coding
- retains the precision in the number
- can be used repeatedly in different programs

In the following example we use a format to display a number in thousands, rounded to the nearest thousand.

```
PROC FORMAT ;
  PICTURE THOU7C (MIN=7 MAX=7 ROUND)
                         .    = '    O'
     -999999500 <-  -99999500 = '999999' (PREFIX='-' MULT=.001)
     -99999500  <-< 0         = '00,009' (PREFIX='-' MULT=.001)
     0             -< 999999500 = '000,009' (MULT=.001)
     OTHER                    = '*******'  ;
NOTE: Format THOU7C has been output.
NOTE: The PROCEDURE FORMAT used 0.01 CPU seconds and 1476K.

data _null_ ;
  format a b c d thou7c. ;
  a=123499.99 ;
  b=123500 ;
  c=-123500 ;
  d=-123499.99 ;
  put _all_ ;
run ;

A=123 B=124 C=-124 D=-123 _ERROR_=0 _N_=1
NOTE: The DATA statement used 0.01 CPU seconds and 1476K.
```

Using formats in a table lookup

SAS programmers often make formats based on SAS data sets, which they then use to look up or translate data.

How to use a format for lookup

When you want to check whether a value is in a large set of values, there are many ways of doing so. Here are the three most obvious:

- Use OR operators, such as

```
IF name='fred' or name='john' or name='mike' ;
```

- Use the IN operator, such as

```
IF name in ('fred','john','mike') ;
```

- Use a PUT statement with a format, such as

```
IF put(name,$names.)='Y'
```

Format code

```
proc format ;
  value $names
    "phil" = "1"
    "chris"="2"
    "kristian"="3"
    "fiona"="4"
    "elaine"="5" ;
run ;
```

When you have many values to check against, the OR and IN statements may become difficult to code and inefficient to run, depending on the data. PROC FORMAT is quite efficient, because formats stay in memory and use binary searching to locate values. Creating the format can be time consuming though. To simplify the task, I created a macro that generates a format from a SAS data set.

Syntax: %MKFMT(LIBRARY.SERVS,$SERVS,servno,"Y",other="N",FMTLIB=1) ;

This creates a format from the SAS data set called LIBRARY.SERVS. The format is called $SERVS. Servno is used as the lookup value. If found then it returns "Y". Otherwise, it returns "N". I also specified FMTLIB=1 so that my format would be listed after being created. Note that you are required to put quotation marks around character values for the label and other parameters. This is so that you can alternatively enter numbers if you prefer. Here's an example of using formats in a table lookup.

```
%macro mkfmt(dset, fmtname, start, label, other=, library=library,
fmtlib=) ;
%* dset      sas dataset name ;
%* fmtname   name of format to create ;
%* start     variable to be used as START in format ;
%* label     variable to be user for LABEL in format ;
%* other     Optionally set all other values to this variable or
              literal;
%* library   Optionally override default format library to your own
              Library ;
%* fmtlib    Put any text here to list your format when created ;

data temptemp(keep=fmtname hlo &start label) ;
  retain fmtname "&fmtname"
  hlo ' ' ;
  set &dset
  end=eofeof ;
  label=&label ; * This could be a variable or a literal ;
  output ;

%if &other NE  %then
  %do ;
  if eofeof then
    do ;
      hlo='o' ;
      label=&other ;
      output ;
    end ;
%end ;

run ;

proc sort data=temptemp(rename=(&start=start)) nodupkey ;
  by start hlo ;
```

```
proc format library=&library
        %if "&fmtlib">"" %then
          fmtlib ;
          cntlin=temptemp ;
        %if "&fmtlib">"" %then
          select &fmtname ; ; * Make sure we only print 1 format
                                from lib ;

run ;

%mend mkfmt ;
```

Chapter **12**

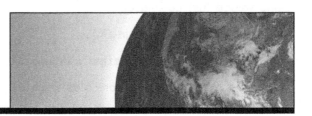

SQL

Automatic Data Dictionary information provided by SAS

A wealth of information exists in the SAS Help and Documentation. One such section relates to SASHELP views and SQL DICTIONARY tables. These are great sources of information about data sets, catalogs, libnames, etc.

PROC SQL DICTIONARY tables are a useful replacement for PROC CONTENTS, particularly when you want to get information about data sets into macros. Normally the dictionary tables can be accessed only under PROC SQL, but SAS provides a set of SQL views under the SASHELP libname, which allows access from normal DATA steps or procedures. (Enter DIR SASHELP on the command line, and you will see what's available.) DICTIONARY tables are excellent for finding out information such as the number of observations in a data set or whether a data set exists.

Try typing HELP SQL on the command line or in the SAS Help and Documentation for some good example code.

Here's an example (from SAS Help and Documentation) that shows all the variables in the SAS data set called SQL.EMPLOYE2:

```
proc sql;
create view vcol as
select * from dictionary.columns
where libname='SQL' and memname='EMPLOYE2';
NOTE: SQL view USER.VCOL has been defined.
proc print data=vcol label;
run;
```

OBS	LIBNAME	MEMNAME	MEMTYPE	NAME	TYPE	LENGTH	...
1	SQL	EMPLOYE2	DATA	NAME	char	20	

Here is what the SASHELP VIEWS selection gives you, followed by what the DICTIONARY TABLES selection shows:

PROC SQL: SASHELP views

Name of View	Code That SAS Used to Create View
Sashelp.vcatalg	select * from dictionary.catalogs;
Sashelp.vcolumn	select * from dictionary.columns;
Sashelp.vextfl	select * from dictionary.extfiles;
Sashelp.vindex	select * from dictionary.indexes;
Sashelp.vmacro	select * from dictionary.macros;
Sashelp.vmember	select * from dictionary.members;
Sashelp.voption	select * from dictionary.options;
Sashelp.vtable	select * from dictionary.tables;
Sashelp.vtitle	select * from dictionary.titles;
Sashelp.vview	select * from dictionary.views;

Sashelp.vsacces	select libname, memname from dictionary.members
	    where memtype = 'ACCESS'
	    order by libname, memname;

Sashelp.vscatlg	select libname, memname from dictionary.members
	    where memtype = 'CATALOG'
	    order by libname, memname;

Sashelp.vslib	select distinct(libname), path from dictionary.members order by libname;

Sashelp.vstable	select libname, memname from dictionary.members
	    where memtype = 'DATA'
	    order by libname, memname;

Sashelp.vstabvw	select libname, memname, memtype from dictionary.members
	    where memtype in ('VIEW', 'DATA')
	    order by libname, memname;

Sashelp.vsview	select libname, memname from dictionary.members where memtype = 'VIEW';

Dictionary.Catalogs

```
DICTIONARY.CATALOGS
   (
   libname  char(8)  label='Library Name',
   memname  char(8)  label='Member Name',
   memtype  char(8)  label='Member Type',
   objname  char(8)  label='Object Name',
   objtype  char(8)  label='Object Type',
   objdesc  char(40) label='Object Description',
   modified char(8)  label='Date Modified',
   alias    char(8)  label='Object Alias'
   );
```

Dictionary.Columns

```
DICTIONARY.COLUMNS
   (
   libname  char(8)  label='Library Name',
   memname  char(8)  label='Member Name',
   memtype  char(8)  label='Member Type',
   name     char(8)  label='Column Name',
   type     char(4)  label='Column Type',
   length   num      label='Column Length',
   npos     num      label='Column Position',
   varnum   num      label='Column Number in Table',
   label    char(40) label='Column Label',
   format   char(16) label='Column Format',
   informat char(16) label='Column Informat',
   idxusage char(9)  label='Column Index Type'
   );
```

Dictionary.Extfiles

```
DICTIONARY.EXTFILES
   (
   FILEREF  char(8)  label='FILEREF',
   xpath    char(80) label='Path Name',
   xengine  char(8)  label='Engine Name'
   );
```

Dictionary.Indexes

```
DICTIONARY.INDEXES
   (
   libname   char(8)  label='Library Name',
   memname   char(8)  label='Member Name',
   memtype   char(8)  label='Member Type',
   indxname  char(8)  label='Index Name',
   idxusage  char(9)  label='Column Index Type',
   name      char(8)  label='Column Name',
   indxpos   num      label='Position of Column in Concatenated Key',
   nomiss    char(3)  label='Nomiss Option',
   unique    char(3)  label='Unique Option'
   );
```

Dictionary.Macros

```
DICTIONARY.MACROS
   (
   SCOPE     char(9)    label='Macro Scope',
   NAME      char(8)    label='Macro Variable Name',
   OFFSET    num        label='Offset into Macro Variable',
   VALUE     char(200)  label='Macro Variable Value'
   );
```

Dictionary.Members

```
DICTIONARY.MEMBERS
   (
   libname   char(8)   label='Library Name',
   memname   char(8)   label='Member Name',
   memtype   char(8)   label='Member Type',
   engine    char(8)   label='Engine Name',
   index     char(8)   label='Indexes',
   path      char(80)  label='Path Name'
   );
```

Dictionary.Options

```
DICTIONARY.OPTIONS
   (
   optname   char(20)   label='Session Option Name',
   setting   char(200)  label='Session Option Setting',
   optdesc   char(80)   label='Option Description'
   );
```

Dictionary.Tables

```
DICTIONARY.TABLES
   (
   libname  char(8)  label='Library Name',
   memname  char(8)  label='Member Name',
   memtype  char(8)  label='Member Type',
   memlabel char(40) label='Dataset Label',
   typemem  char(8)  label='Dataset Type',
   crdate   num      format=datetime14. label='Date Created',
   modate   num      format=datetime14. label='Date Modified',
   nobs     num      label='Number of Observations',
   obslen   num      label='Observation Length',
   nvar     num      label='Number of Variables',
   protect  char(3)  label='Type of Password Protection',
   compress char(8)  label='Compression Routine',
   reuse    char(3)  label='Reuse Space',
   bufsize  num      label='Bufsize',
   delobs   num      label='Number of Deleted Observations',
   indxtype char(9)  label='Type of Indexes'
   );
```

Dictionary.Titles

```
DICTIONARY.TITLES
   (
   TYPE     char(1)   label='Title Location',
   NUMBER   num       label='Title Number',
   TEXT     char(200) label='Title Text'
   );
```

Dictionary.Views

```
DICTIONARY.VIEWS
   (
   libname char(8) label='Library Name',
   memname char(8) label='Member Name',
   memtype char(8) label='Member Type',
   engine  char(8) label='Engine Name'
   );
```

Using the _METHOD parameter in PROC SQL

The undocumented _METHOD parameter in PROC SQL provides a query plan
that describes what methods PROC SQL plans to use to execute the query.
Combining this with option MSGLEVEL=I is useful, because it specifies when
indexes are used for joins or provides information about processing in SQL.

```
30   proc sql _method ;
31   select retail.*
32     from sashelp.retail
33       left join
34         sashelp.prdsale
35       on retail.year=prdsale.year
36     order by retail.year ;

NOTE: SQL execution methods chosen are:

     sqxslct
         sqxjm
             sqxsort
                 sqxsrc( SASHELP.PRDSALE )
             sqxsort
                 sqxsrc( SASHELP.RETAIL )
```

SQL module codes used

The following list shows some of the SQL module codes that are used in listings
produced by using the _METHOD parameter.

```
sqxcrta    Create table as Select
sqxslct    Select
sqxjsl     Step Loop Join (Cartesian)
sqxjm      Merge Join
sqxjndx    Index Join
sqxjhsh    Hash Join
sqxsort    Sort
sqxsrc     Source Rows from table
sqxfil     Filter Rows
sqxsumg    Summary Statistics (with GROUP BY)
sqxsumn    Summary Statistics (not grouped)
sqxuniq    Distinct rows only
```

For more information, see the excellent SAS note by Paul Kent "TS-553: SQL
Joins—The Long and The Short of It" at http://support.sas.com/techsup/technote/
ts553.txt.

SQL views are now updatable (mostly)

You can update a data set referenced by an SQL view, providing the SQL view meets some criteria such as the following:

- Only one table is referenced.
- The table is not joined to another or linked through a set-operator.
- There are no subqueries.
- There is no ORDER BY.

You can update columns, as shown here, provided they are not derived columns.

```
proc sql ;
   create view test as select height/weight as ratio, * from
                                          sashelp.class ;
dm 'vt test' vt ;
```

After running this code, I can edit TEST using the Viewtable window, remembering to set it to Edit mode. Then any changes are reflected in SASHELP.CLASS, having been updated through the view.

To verify this, do the following to see what you have modified:

```
dm 'vt sashelp.class' vt;
```

Another way to update views is to use code such as that shown in the next example.

SQL to update a view

```
proc sql;
   update test
      set name='ABC';
dm 'vt test' vt ;
```

You can update a column in a view using the column's alias, but you cannot update a derived column (that is, a column produced by an expression).

Using the MONOTONIC function

One of the features of SQL is that there is no concept of an observation number in tables, as there is when using the DATA step with a SAS data set. In a data set, we can select data using an observation number and then use the data in reports. In SQL in SAS®9 and later, the MONOTONIC() function will return the equivalent of an observation number.

The following example uses the MONOTONIC() function to create a variable holding observation number and also selects data based on observation number. If you merely want a column number on each row, then you can use the NUMBER option in PROC SQL.

Code to select obs from 10 to 20, inclusive

```
proc sql;
  select monotonic() as rowno, *
  from sashelp.prdsale
  where 10 le monotonic() le 20 ;
quit;
```

Using =: in SQL

In many places in SAS software, you can use the colon modifier with various operators such as the equal sign so that you can test for character strings prefixed with the argument. For instance, to see if a name started with a "P" you could use:

```
If name=:'P' then flag=1 ;
```

However, in SQL you don't have the =:, >:, and <: operators. You can, however, use EQT, GTT, and LTT, which do the same thing.

```
proc sql;
   select *
   from sashelp.class
   where name eqt 'J' ;
quit;
```

Using conditional arithmetic

SUM is a standard SQL function; however, it has some extended uses when used in conjunction with other functions or expressions.

```
Select
   SUM (CASE FRED
           WHEN 'A' THEN AMOUNT
                    ELSE 0
       END) AS FREDAMT
   From data.set ;
```

This would cause the output variable FREDAMT to contain only the sum of the FRED 'A' records. SUM can also be used to sum across the columns in a row—i.e. SUM (A, B, C).

Providing values to use in place of missing values

In PROC SQL, the COALESCE function can be used to define a range of values for a variable, and the first non-missing value will be used. This is very useful if we want a value to be used if it is present, but if it is not we would like another value used. We can even provide a value to use as a default if all the variables specified are missing.

The following code will create a variable called c by using the value of a if it is non-missing. If a is missing, then it will use the value of b. However, if b is also missing, then it will use the special missing value .m.

```
data test ;
  input a b ;
  datalines ;
1 2
3 .
. 6
. .
;;
run ;
proc sql ;
  select coalesce(a,b,.m) as c
    from test ;
```

```
                                          c
                                     _____
                                          1
                                          3
                                          6
                                          M
```

Using values just calculated

You can use the CALCULATED keyword in SAS SQL to use values calculated in an SQL statement elsewhere in that statement. This avoids the need to recalculate the values, thereby saving resources. Use the CALCULATED keyword when you are using a variable in a WHERE clause that has been calculated in the current SQL statement. "And" can be used in the SELECT clause.

The following example avoids recalculating the value for use in the WHERE clause.

```
proc sql ;
  select style,
         bedrooms,
         price/sqfeet as value
  from sasuser.houses
  where calculated value > 55 ;
```

Examining resource usage in SQL

In SQL code that has more than one statement for each PROC SQL, the resource usage statistics for each statement are combined to give a total at the end of the procedure. This is the default action, because it takes SAS fewer resources to do this than to keep track of resource usage for each SQL statement.

If you are tuning your code and want to get the resource usage for each SQL statement, then you should specify the RESET STIMER statement. This will then give the resources for each individual SQL statement, which gives you more insight into the performance of your code.

The following example shows the PROC SQLs with identical SQL statements. The second has RESET STIMER specified.

```
2 proc sql ;
3 select * from sasuser.class where sex='F' ;
4 select * from sasuser.class where age>15 ;
NOTE: The PROCEDURE SQL used 0.03 CPU seconds and 1816K.
5 proc sql ;
6 reset stimer ;
NOTE: The SQL Statement used 0.00 CPU seconds and 1816K.
7 select * from sasuser.class where sex='F' ;
NOTE: The SQL Statement used 0.01 CPU seconds and 1816K.
8 select * from sasuser.class where age>15 ;
NOTE: The SQL Statement used 0.01 CPU seconds and 1816K.
```

Generating statements to define a data set or view structure

As an alternative to PROC CONTENTS or PROC DATASETS, you could use SQL to see the structure of a SAS data set or view. Use one of the following:

```
DESCRIBE VIEW view-name
```

or

```
DESCRIBE TABLE table-name
```

The output (which goes to the log) could then be copied in order to create a new data set or view.

```
   proc sql ;
      describe table sasuser.fitness ;

NOTE: SQL table SASUSER.FITNESS was created like:

create table SASUSER.FITNESS( label='Exercise/fitness study data set'
  bufsize=6144 )
  (
  AGE num label='Age in years',
  WEIGHT num label='Weight in kg',
  RUNTIME num label='Min. to run 1.5 miles',
  RSTPULSE num label='Heart rate while resting',
  RUNPULSE num label='Heart rate while running',
  MAXPULSE num label='Maximum heart rate',
  OXYGEN num label='Oxygen consumption',
  GROUP num label='Experimental group'
  );
```

Creating a range of macro variables from SQL with leading zeroes

In versions of SAS prior to SAS®9, you could create ranges of macro variables, but you could not use leading zeroes in the macro variable names. So in Release 8.2, you might end up with macro variables like var8, var9, var10. But in SAS®9, you could create variables like var08, var09, var10. This can make further use of those macro variables easier to code. See the following example.

```
proc sql noprint ;
   select name into :name01-:name19 from sashelp.class ;
```

Chapter **13**

Operating System (Mainly Windows)

Running SAS easily in batch under Windows

To those who use SAS under Windows, you will find many specific examples in this section to help you. For those who use SAS under UNIX, you should be able to apply most of the Windows techniques to your operating system, so this section should be useful to you. For other operating systems it will vary, but I would recommend looking through and seeing if you can apply these tips to your specific operating system.

Running SAS in batch is handy, because you can have a number of programs running in the background while you do other things on your PC. You can also schedule SAS programs to run when you are not at your PC, making use of the hours you are not at work for doing time-consuming runs.

When running SAS under Windows, you will have a range of actions associated with SAS programs in Windows Explorer by default. These can be selected by right-clicking on a SAS program in Windows Explorer. With SAS®9 the actions include:

- SASView (which opens the SAS System Viewer)
- open
- print
- print with SAS Viewer
- batch submit with SAS 9.1
- open with SAS Enterprise Guide 3.0
- open with SAS 9.1
- print with SAS
- submit with SAS 9.1

Note: To see some of these you need to have the SAS System Viewer and SAS Enterprise Guide software installed.

When you select one of these, a command is run passing the filename as a parameter to that command. To see these commands from Windows Explorer do the following:

1. Select **Tools** from the pull-down menu.

2. Select **Folder options**.

3. Select the **File Types** tab.

4. Scroll down the list to **SAS**.

5. Click the **Advanced** button. If you don't have it, then you need to click the **Restore** button to remove your customization.

6. Now you have a list of actions that appear when you right-click. You can choose a default action, add new actions, and edit existing actions.

7. Select **Batch Submit**, and click **Edit**.

8. You can now see the command used to invoke SAS in batch in the **Application used to perform action** field.

9. The part of the command that has "%1" is a substitute of the filename that you clicked before the command was run.

10. You can now change the command to use a customized one. The command that I use uses my configuration file so that I can use my autoexec to allocate libraries I need. On my system, the command is as follows:

```
C:\PROGRA~1\SASINS~1\SAS\V8\SAS.EXE "%1" -nologo -config
h:\mysasf~1\v8\batch.CFG -noaltlog
```

Note: When parts of a pathname are longer than eight characters, use the first six characters followed by a tilde (~) and a number (1 for first occurrence, 2 for second occurrence, etc.).

Copying data sets the fastest way

There are various ways to copy files or data sets. You will find that for large data sets, the time taken to copy them can vary a great deal depending on the method chosen. Some popular methods include the following:

DATA step

```
Data new.name ;
   Set old.name ;
Run ;
```

PROC COPY

```
Proc copy in=old out=new ;
   Select name ;
Run ;
```

Native operating system copy

Remember to copy indexes, audit files, etc. that may be associated with the data set being copied.

```
X 'copy c:\old\directory\name.sas7bdat c:\new\directory' ;
```

Copying via the operating system

I have found that the fastest way to make copies is usually the operating system COPY command. The following macro shows how to do this. The macro determines where your data sets reside from the librefs and issues the appropriate command.

```
%macro copyfile(from,to) ;
  %if %index(&from,.)>0 %then
    %do ;
      %let lib=%scan(&from,1,.) ;
      %let dset=%scan(&from,2,.) ;
    %end ;
  %else
    %do ;
      %let lib=work ;
      %let dset=&from ;
    %end ;
  %let fromfile=%sysfunc(pathname(&lib))\&dset..sas7bdat ;
  %if %index(&to,.)>0 %then
```

```
      %do ;
        %let lib=%scan(&to,1,.) ;
        %let dset=%scan(&to,2,.) ;
      %end ;
    %else
      %do ;
        %let lib=work ;
        %let dset=&to ;
      %end ;
    %let tofile=%sysfunc(pathname(&lib))\&dset..sas7bdat ;
    options noxwait xsync ;
    filename cmd1 pipe "erase &tofile" ;
    data _null_ ;
      infile cmd1 ;
      input ;
      put 'NOTE- COMMAND OUTPUT:' _infile_ ;
    run ;
    filename cmd2 pipe "copy ""&fromfile"" ""&tofile"" " ;
    data _null_ ;
      window msg irow=4 rows=9 columns=120
      #1 @6 'Copying file using the following command ...'
      #3 @1 "copy ""&fromfile"" ""&tofile"" " c=blue persist=yes ;
      display msg noinput ;
      infile cmd2 ;
      input ;
      put 'NOTE- COMMAND OUTPUT:' _infile_ ;
    run ;
%mend copyfile ;
/*%copyfile(x1,system.temp) ;*/
```

Running concurrent operating system commands

You can run more than one operating system command concurrently from SAS using the SYSTASK statement. The following code shows how I am running two commands in the sample SAS code. The first does a directory listing of all files and subdirectories on my C drive, putting the listing into a file. The second copies a file. Each one is given a task name and you tell SAS not to wait for the command to finish running before going on.

The WAITFOR statement then tells SAS to wait until all the named tasks have finished before going on.

For information about SYSTASK, see http://v9doc.sas.com/cgi-bin/sasdoc/cgihilt?file=/help/hostwin.hlp/win-stmt-systask.htm&query=systask#~1.

For information about WAITFOR, see http://v9doc.sas.com/cgi-bin/sasdoc/cgihilt?file=/help/hostwin.hlp/win-stmt-waitfor.htm&query=systask#~1.

```
systask command "dir c:\ /s >c:\results.txt" nowait taskname=dir ;
systask command "copy c:\test.txt d:" nowait taskname=copy ;
waitfor _all_ dir copy ;
%put Finished! ;
```

Using wildcards for file lists

In SAS 8 and later (depending on the operating system), you can use wildcards to describe external filenames defined through a fileref. This enables you to write more flexible code, which will match the files in existence as it runs. It also provides a shorthand way to describe a range of files.

The following example shows how I can read from all text files in a directory by using '*.txt' to match all files with a file type of txt.

```
filename c 'c:\*.txt' ;
data fred ;
  infile c filename=file ;
  input line $200. ;
 * write out the first 10 lines ;
  if _n_<10 then
    put file= line= ;
 run ;
```

```
312   filename c 'c:\*.txt' ;
313   data fred ;
314     infile c filename=file ;
315     input line $200. ;
316   * write out the first 10 lines ;
317    if _n_<10 then
318      put file= line= ;
319   run ;

NOTE: The infile C is:
      File Name=c:\CountCyclesWMVDecLog.txt,
      File List=c:\*.txt,RECFM=V,LRECL=256

file=c:\Count line=# dwFOURCC=32564d57, dFrameRate=30.000, 320x240,
  bInterlaceYUV411=0, bHostDeinterlace=1 Decoded on Mon Jan 09 09:02:58
  2006
NOTE: The infile C is:
      File Name=c:\hcwclear.txt,
      File List=c:\*.txt,RECFM=V,LRECL=256

NOTE: The infile C is:
      File Name=c:\slog.txt,
      File List=c:\*.txt,RECFM=V,LRECL=256

file=c:\slog. line=GET
  /serial_system/activate/activate.php?hwkey=1777315948&serial=9888776&s
  oftid=10&check=0 HTTP/1.0
```

(continued)

(continued)

```
file=c:\slog. line=Host: www.inertiasoftware.com
file=c:\slog. line=User-Agent: StarSyn 1.0

file=c:\slog. line=HTTP/1.0 200 OK

file=c:\slog. line=Date: Mon, 12 Dec 2005 17:30:34 GMT

file=c:\slog. line=Server: Apache/2.0.46 (Red Hat)

file=c:\slog. line=

file=c:\slog. line=
NOTE: The infile C is:
      File Name=c:\VIS.TXT,
      File List=c:\*.txt,RECFM=V,LRECL=256

NOTE: 2 records were read from the infile C.
      The minimum record length was 0.
      The maximum record length was 123.
NOTE: 1 record was read from the infile C.
      The minimum record length was 32.
      The maximum record length was 32.
NOTE: 30 records were read from the infile C.
      The minimum record length was 0.
      The maximum record length was 100.
NOTE: 42 records were read from the infile C.
      The minimum record length was 1.
      The maximum record length was 256.
      One or more lines were truncated.
NOTE: SAS went to a new line when INPUT statement reached past the end
      of a line.
NOTE: The data set WORK.FRED has 41 observations and 1 variables.
NOTE: DATA statement used (Total process time):
      real time              0.00 seconds
      cpu time               0.00 seconds
```

PC performance and the SAS System

The Technical Support Division at SAS Institute maintains a large collection of technical documents on the Web. The following methods are taken from one such document that discusses how to get the best performance from SAS. It also covers how to tune hardware and software, and can be found at:
http://ftp.sas.com/techsup/download/technote/ts684/ts684.html.

Here are some programming methods that will make your code as efficient as possible by reducing the input and output (I/O), keeping data in memory as much as possible, and reducing unnecessary data access.

- Create permanent SAS data sets instead of accessing flat files. Data sets are accessed more efficiently.

- Use the latest version of SAS data sets. There are usually performance improvements.

- Investigate SAS Scalable Performance Data Engine in SAS®9, which gives parallel data access developed for SAS SPD Server and is included with Base SAS for free.

- Choose a function for a task where it is appropriate. Earlier versions of SAS had far fewer functions and required coding for many more tasks.

- If loading data into Oracle, use bulk loading support (SAS®9).

- Eliminate unnecessary passes through the data. For example, eliminate multiple outputs per input.

- Read and write only the variables needed. Use DROP and KEEP.

- Subset your data using IF or WHERE statements.

- Use IF-THEN/ELSE structures instead of multiple IF-THEN structures.

- When using IF statements, type the IF statements with the most frequently occurring data values to the least frequently occurring data values to reduce execution time.

- Use indexes. Retrieving a subset of the data requires fewer I/O operations.

- Use temporary arrays, if possible. Retrieval times are shorter.

- Use the SASFILE statement, if appropriate. This keeps data sets in memory across step boundaries. SASFILE automatically sets enough buffers to load the entire data set if enough memory exists. Otherwise, the default BUFNO value is used.

- When you use indexes, the IDXNAME and IDXWHERE data set options allow a precise control of which indexes are used.

- Avoid using the TAGSORT option when running PROC SORT, if at all possible. PROC SORT requires approximately four times the data set size in free disk space for the sort utility files. TAGSORT reduces the amount of free disk space required, but the CPU time needed is greatly increased.

Importing and exporting between SAS and Microsoft Access

If you have SAS/ACCESS for PC File Formats software licensed, then it is now very easy to import and export data between SAS and Microsoft Access. You can reference Access tables directly with a LIBNAME statement. No engine is required. To read tables into SAS, use the libref in conjunction with the Microsoft Access table name to construct fully qualified SAS data set names (e.g. lib.table). To write a table to Access, use the libref and data set name, which becomes the table name. See the following log.

```
98    libname tabs 'x:\my documents\db1.mdb' ;
NOTE: Libref TABS was successfully assigned as follows:
      Engine:         ACCESS
      Physical Name: x:\my documents\db1.mdb
99    data x ;
100     set tabs.names ; * read table NAMES from database DB1 ;
101   run ;

NOTE: There were 3 observations read from the data set TABS.names.
NOTE: The data set WORK.X has 3 observations and 3 variables.
NOTE: DATA statement used (Total process time):
      real time           0.01 seconds
      cpu time            0.01 seconds


102   data tabs.new ; * Create a new table called NEW in database DB1 ;
103     set sashelp.class ;
104   run ;

NOTE: There were 19 observations read from the data set SASHELP.CLASS.
NOTE: The data set TABS.new has 19 observations and 5 variables.
NOTE: DATA statement used (Total process time):
      real time           0.01 seconds
      cpu time            0.02 seconds


105   libname tabs ;
NOTE: Libref TABS has been deassigned.
```

See http://v9doc.sas.com/cgi-bin/sasdoc/cgigdoc?file=../acpcref.hlp/ a002107496.htm for information about LIBNAME statement syntax, when used with PC Files.

Reading and writing SAS data sets within a ZIP file

Some people like to zip (compress) files to save space. Typically, when you then want to use the files, you first have to unzip (decompress) them. If you have a text file that has been zipped, then you can use pipes from SAS to read that file without first unzipping it. However, pipes can't be used to read SAS data sets from a zip file in this way. Pipes are used with FILENAME statements, and data sets must be read using LIBNAME statements.

There is a way to read and write SAS data sets that are stored in a zip file. This involves getting a product called ZIPMAGIC (for Windows platforms), which enables zip files to be treated like folders. You can then define your zip file with a LIBNAME statement and read or write data sets within the file. See the following log.

```
1     libname test 'C:\Sample SAS data.zip' ;
NOTE: Libref TEST was successfully assigned as follows:
      Engine:        V8
      Physical Name: C:\Sample SAS data.zip

2     proc print data=test.cars ;
3     run ;

NOTE: There were 116 observations read from the data set TEST.CARS.
NOTE: PROCEDURE PRINT used:
      real time           0.26 seconds
      cpu time            0.03 seconds


4     data test.new_thing ;
5       x=1 ;
6     run ;

NOTE: The data set TEST.NEW_THING has 1 observations and 1 variables.
NOTE: DATA statement used:
      real time           0.14 seconds
      cpu time            0.03 seconds
```

See http://www.aladdinsys.com/zipmagic/ for information and a free trial of ZIPMAGIC. This currently works only for Windows platforms.

Browsing external files

In SAS 8 and later, PROC FSLIST and the FSLIST command are part of Base SAS, which means you can use them even if you don't have SAS/FSP. They are useful if you want to browse the contents of text in a file from within SAS, because they open a window and display the file contents.

To browse a text file from the command line, you can enter the following command:

```
fslist 'c:\frame.html'
```

To open a selection window to enable you to choose a file to browse, you can enter the following on the command line:

```
fslist
```

Or you can run the procedure like this:

```
proc fslist file='c:\config.sas';
run ;
```

Sizing the screen space used by SAS

When you use SAS interactively, it is usually desirable to maximize the space available to your application. This tip will explain how to do so automatically.

The SAS Application Workspace window can be sized and its menu bar turned off when running an application in SAS under Windows. This is useful to ensure that maximum screen space is available for the application. Putting the following lines into your SAS configuration file (typically SASV9.CFG) or on the SAS command line will do the following:

- cause SAS to use 100% of the display area
- turn off the SAS Application Workspace menu bar

Part of CONFIG.SAS

```
-awsdef 0 0 100 100
-noawsmenu
```

Viewing tables with variable names, not labels

Many people use the VIEWTABLE command in SAS, which can be used in different ways, for example:

- from the command line `viewtable sashelp.class`
- abbreviated from the command line `vt sashelp.class`
- from the Explorer Window by double-clicking a data set or view
- from the Explorer Window by right-clicking a data set or view, and then selecting **Open**

By default when you view the table, you will see variable labels over each column. I know that some people would prefer to have variable names appear by default. So here is how to do it:

1. Click the Explorer Window to activate it, making the context-sensitive menus appropriate for it.

2. Select **Tools ▶ Options ▶ Explorer**.

3. Click the **Members** tab in SAS®9.

4. Double-click **Table** (or double-click **View**, depending on which you are changing).

5. Double-click **&Open**.

6. Now you can see the command that is issued when you double-click a table in the Explorer Window. It is probably `VIEWTABLE %8b.'%s'.DATA`.

7. Now add the following optional parameter to the end of command: `colheading=names`. This makes the command now `VIEWTABLE %8b.'%s'.DATA colheading=names`.

8. Exit the dialog boxes by clicking **OK**, and you are finished.

If you want to open the table in Form View rather than Table View, then you could also use the command `view=form`.

- `Colheading` can be either `names` or `labels`.

- `view` can be either `form` or `table`.

For more information, see http://support.sas.com/techsup/unotes/SN/005/005873.html.

Enhanced Editor tips

You can turn on line numbers by using either the NUMS command or by choosing **Tools ▶ Options ▶ Enhanced editor**.

Tools ▶ Options ▶ Enhanced editor can set different options for different file types (HTML, SAS, TXT, or SCL).

Using Find in Enhanced Editor

The Enhanced Editor was introduced in SAS 8 and has been improved in various ways in SAS®9. The old Program Editor is still available, so don't confuse the two. One improvement appears in the Find dialog box, which can be accessed by pressing CTRL+F or using the **Edit ▶ Find** menu.

You can use Find to look in all the text, the code, or the comments.

You can specify regular expression searches, which allow pattern matching. If you are unfamiliar with this, you can click the right-facing triangle next to the **Find text** box. This has descriptions of things that can be specified in an expression. By selecting one of these, the code will be entered in the **Find text** box, and can be customized.

This all works for **Replace** as well (CTRL+H or **Edit ▶ Replace**).

Some examples of regular expressions in a Find text box

Regular Expression	Explanation
[sme]date	matches "sdate," "mdate," or "edate"
^data	matches "data" when at the start of a line
var_[abc123]	matches "var_a," "var_b," "var_c," "var_1," "var_2," or "var_3"
_*name	matches 0 or more "*" characters, followed by "name," so it would match "_name," "name," "_____name," etc.
proc \w+	matches "proc " followed by one or more word characters so it would match "proc print," "proc datasets," etc. (in fact "proc *anything*")
data\b+\w+	matches "data" followed by one or more write space characters and then one or more word characters, so it would match "data *anything*"

More information on regular expressions can be found at http://support.sas.com/rnd/base/topics/datastep/perl_regexp/regexp.motivation.html though not all are supported by the Find dialog box.

Autosaving your SAS code

You can set SAS to automatically save your code regularly, which means if your system or SAS crashes you can retrieve the last saved version of your code. Autosave is set using **Tools ▶ Options ▶ Preferences ▶ Edit**. Set it to autosave every x minutes.

Autosaved code is saved to the users `temp` directory (see the TEMP environment variable)—for example, C:\Documents and Settings\masonp\Local Settings\Temp.

Programs from the Program Editor are autosaved into pgm.asv. From the Enhanced Editor, they are saved into Autosave of *filename*.$AS.

If a SAS program is loaded in, autosave does not save over it. I loaded a SAS program called gdevice2.sas into the Enhanced Editor. It was autosaved into my temp directory as Autosave of Gdevice2.$AS.

If you exit the SAS session and say you don't want to save the modified code, then the autosave is discarded. If SAS stops before you can do so, then the autosaved file is kept. It is not automatically loaded back into SAS when SAS is restarted, though. You could probably write a macro to do this if you want to.

Running Visual Basic macros in Microsoft Excel from SAS

Using Dynamic Data Exchange (DDE), you can send an Excel 4.0 DDE function call to execute a saved Excel Visual Basic macro. This works with all versions of Excel, including Excel 2000 and Excel XP.

File.xls is the name of the Excel file where the macro is stored and Macro2 is the name of the macro you want to run. **Note:** These names are case sensitive.

```
filename excdata dde 'Excel|System';
data _null_;
  file excdata;
  put ' RUN("File.xls!Macro2",FALSE)]';
run;
```

Creating a pivot table in Microsoft Excel directly from SAS

The following macro is quite innovative by using SAS to generate Visual Basic Script (VBS) code. The VBS code creates an Excel spreadsheet and then creates a pivot table within it, all based on parameters passed to a SAS macro. Remember, all SAS code in this book can be downloaded from the book's companion Web site.

```
/*****************************************************************************/
/* Title      : createpivottable.sas                                      */
/* Description: Exports a SAS Data Set to Excel and creates a Pivot Table  */
/* Parameters : inpfile - The name of the data set to be exported         */
/*              xlsheet - The name of the Excel file to create            */
/*              rcols   - The name of the SAS variables to be set as row   */
/*                        fields in the Pivot Table                        */
/*              hcols   - The name of the SAS variables to be set as column*/
/*                        fields in the Pivot Table                        */
/*              dfields - The name of the SAS variables to be set as data  */
/*                        fields in the Pivot Table                        */
/* Author     : Chris Brooks                                              */
/*              Office of National Statistics, UK                         */
/* Date       : June 2005                                                 */
/*                                                                        */
/* Change History:                                                        */
/*                                                                        */
/* Notes      : This has been tested using Windows XP Pro, SAS 9.1.3 and  */
/*              Excel2002 - there are no guarantees it will work with any  */
/*              other version of Excel as the Excel Object Model can      */
/*              (and does) change considerably between versions - you have */
/*              been warned!!!!                                           */
/*                                                                        */
/*              The parameters rcols, hcols and dfields are space separated*/
/*              "lists" of variables (see sample call)                    */
/*                                                                        */
/* Sample Call: %createpivottable(sashelp.class,'c:\sas\sample.xls',      */
/*              name age, sex,weight);                          */
/*                                                                        */
/*****************************************************************************/

%macro createpivottable(inpfile,xlsheet,rcols,hcols,dfields);

  /* First use Proc Export to create the Excel Workbook */

  proc export data=&inpfile outfile="&xlsheet" dbms=excel replace;
  run;

  data _null_;
```

(continued)

(continued)

```
     /* Open a text file which will be used to write VBA Commands to */

  %let filrf=pivvbs;
  %let rc=%sysfunc(filename(filrf,'c:\sas\pivot.vbs'));

    %if &rc ne 0 %then
        %put %sysfunc(sysmsg());

  /* Create an instance of the Excel Automation Server */

  %let fid=%sysfunc(fopen(&filrf,O));
  %if &rc ne 0 %then
        %put %sysfunc(sysmsg());
  %let rc=%sysfunc(fput(&fid,Set XL = CreateObject("Excel.Application")));

  /* Make Excel visible, otherwise there isn't a lot of point! */

    %let rc=%sysfunc(fwrite(&fid,-));
  %let rc=%sysfunc(fput(&fid,XL.Visible=True));

  /* Open the newly created workbook */

    %let rc=%sysfunc(fwrite(&fid,-));
  %let wstring=XL.Workbooks.Open "&xlsheet";

  /* Determine the last cell in the range */

  %let rc=%sysfunc(fput(&fid,&wstring));

    %let rc=%sysfunc(fwrite(&fid,-));
  %let rc=%sysfunc(fput(&fid,Xllastcell= xl.cells.specialcells(11).address));

    %let rc=%sysfunc(fwrite(&fid,-));

  /* Add a new worksheet to the workbook to hold the pivot table */

  %let rc=%sysfunc(fput(&fid,XL.Sheets.Add.name = "PivotTable"));

    %let rc=%sysfunc(fwrite(&fid,-));
  %let sname=%scan(&xlsheet,-2,\.);
  %let wstring=xldata="&sname";
  %let rc=%sysfunc(fput(&fid,&wstring));
  %let rc=%sysfunc(fwrite(&fid,-));
  %let rc=%sysfunc(fput(&fid,XL.Sheets(xldata).select));

  /* Start the pivot table wizard and set the range for the pivot table to the
data previously exported */
    %let rc=%sysfunc(fwrite(&fid,-));
  %let wstring=%nrstr(XL.ActiveSheet.PivotTableWizard
```

(continued)

(*continued*)

```
SourceType=xlDatabase,XL.Range("A1" & ":" &
  xllastcell),"Pivottable!R1C1",xldata));
    %let rc=%sysfunc(fput(&fid,&wstring);

      %let rc=%sysfunc(fwrite(&fid,-));



    /* Loop through the list of row fields and set them in the pivot table */

    %let i=0;
    %do %while(%scan(&rcols,&i+1,%str( )) ne %str( ));
      %let i = %eval(&i+1);
      %let var = %scan(&rcols,&i,%str( ));

      %let
rc=%sysfunc(fput(&fid,XL.ActiveSheet.PivotTables(xldata).PivotFields("&var").Ori
entation =1)) ;
      %let rc=%sysfunc(fwrite(&fid,-));
    %end;
    %let i=0;

    /* Loop through the list of column fields and set them in the pivot table */

    %do %while(%scan(&hcols,&i+1,%str( )) ne %str( ));
      %let i = %eval(&i+1);
      %let var = %scan(&hcols,&i,%str( ));

      %let
rc=%sysfunc(fput(&fid,XL.ActiveSheet.PivotTables(xldata).PivotFields("&var").Ori
entation =2)) ;
      %let rc=%sysfunc(fwrite(&fid,-));
    %end;

    /* Loop through the list of data fields and set them in the pivot table */

    %let i=0;
    %do %while(%scan(&dfields,&i+1,%str( )) ne %str( ));
      %let i = %eval(&i+1);
      %let var = %scan(&dfields,&i,%str( ));

      %let
rc=%sysfunc(fput(&fid,XL.ActiveSheet.PivotTables(xldata).PivotFields("&var").Ori
entation =4)) ;
      %let rc=%sysfunc(fwrite(&fid,-));

    %end;
```

(*continued*)

(continued)

```
   /* Hide the field list */

   %let rc=%sysfunc(fput(&fid,XL.Activeworkbook.ShowPivotTableFieldList =
 False));
   %let rc=%sysfunc(fwrite(&fid,-));

   /* Close the file */


   %let rc=%sysfunc(fclose(&fid));

   x "c:\sas\pivot.vbs";
 run;

%mend;

%createpivottable(sashelp.prdsale,c:\prdsale.xls,country region division,quarter
  year month,actual predict);
```

Exporting to Microsoft Excel

If you have SAS/ACCESS for PC File Formats software licensed, then it is now very easy to import and export data between SAS and Microsoft Excel. You can reference Excel spreadsheets directly with a LIBNAME statement. No engine is required. You can then refer to a spreadsheet using the libref and a worksheet by using a data set name. For instance in the following example, nice.test refers to the spreadsheet C:\nice.xls and within it the worksheet called test.

```
libname nice 'c:\nice.xls' ;
data nice.test ;
  set sashelp.class ;
run ;
libname nice ;
* Open the sheet ;
%sysexec "c:\nice.xls" ;
```

```
334  libname nice 'c:\nice.xls' ;
NOTE: Libref NICE was successfully assigned as follows:
      Engine:          EXCEL
      Physical Name: c:\nice.xls
335  data nice.test ;
336    set sashelp.class ;
337  run ;

NOTE: There were 19 observations read from the data set SASHELP.CLASS.
NOTE: The data set NICE.test has 19 observations and 5 variables.
NOTE: DATA statement used (Total process time):
      real time            0.09 seconds
      cpu time             0.01 seconds


338  libname nice ;
NOTE: Libref NICE has been deassigned.
339  * Open the sheet ;
340  %sysexec "c:\nice.xls" ;
```

This EXCEL engine greatly simplifies exporting data to Excel. The following log shows how I created an Excel file called test.xls, with a sheet called CLASS. The sheet lists variable names in the first row, followed by values on subsequent rows.

Note the error message demonstrating that there are some limitations with the EXCEL engine, preventing me from overwriting a sheet once I have created it. Following that, you can see that I can create more sheets within the file.

```
   libname out excel 'c:\test.xls' ;
   data out.class ; set sashelp.class ; run ;
   * try to replace data set ;
   data out.class ; set sashelp.class ; run ;
   * make a new data set ;
   data out.shoes ; set sashelp.shoes ; run ;
   * free it so we can read the spreadsheet from EXCEL ;
   libname out ;
```

```
341  libname out excel 'c:\test.xls' ;
NOTE: Libref OUT was successfully assigned as follows:
      Engine:         EXCEL
      Physical Name: c:\test.xls
342  data out.class ; set sashelp.class ; run ;

NOTE: There were 19 observations read from the data set SASHELP.CLASS.
NOTE: The data set OUT.class has 19 observations and 5 variables.
NOTE: DATA statement used (Total process time):
      real time           0.01 seconds
      cpu time            0.01 seconds


343  * try to replace data set ;
344  data out.class ; set sashelp.class ; run ;

ERROR: The MS Excel table class has been opened for OUTPUT. This table
       already exists, or there is a name conflict with an existing
       object. This table will not be replaced. This engine does not
       support the REPLACE option.
NOTE: The SAS System stopped processing this step because of errors.
NOTE: DATA statement used (Total process time):
      real time           0.01 seconds
      cpu time            0.01 seconds


345  * make a new data set ;
346  data out.shoes ; set sashelp.shoes ; run ;

NOTE: SAS variable labels, formats, and lengths are not written to DBMS
      tables.
NOTE: There were 395 observations read from the data set SASHELP.SHOES.
NOTE: The data set OUT.shoes has 395 observations and 7 variables.
NOTE: DATA statement used (Total process time):
      real time           0.26 seconds
      cpu time            0.03 seconds


347  * free it so we can read the spreadsheet from EXCEL ;
348  libname out ;
NOTE: Libref OUT has been deassigned.
```

Using DDE for customizing Microsoft Word output

The following program shows an example of how to use Dynamic Data Exchange (DDE) to send commands to Microsoft Word. This can be very useful when you can't quite get ODS to produce your ideal output.

The example uses commands to combine a graphic and a report, giving each a different page orientation and using Microsoft Word headers and footers.

The commands used with DDE for Microsoft Word are documented in the help file called wrdbasic.hlp, which can be found by searching the Internet. I found one reference to it at http://www.buoyantsolutions.net/PUBLIC/DOWNLOAD/wrdbasic.zip. Once you find this file, you will be able to do almost anything in Microsoft Word from a SAS program that you would otherwise need to do manually.

```
* make a sample report ;
ods rtf file='c:\sample.rtf' ;
proc print data=sashelp.class ; run ;
ods rtf close ;

* Make a sample graph ;
filename out 'c:\test.png' ;
goptions device=png gsfname=out ;
proc gchart data=sashelp.class ;
  hbar age ;
run ;
filename out ;

* Microsoft Word must already be running ;
filename word dde 'MSWORD|system' ;

* send DDE commands to MS WORD to combine files and create a new one ;
data _null_ ;
  file word ;
  put '[FileNew .Template = "normal.dot", .NewTemplate = 0]' ;
  put '[toggleportrait]' ;
  put '[ViewZoom .TwoPages]' ;
  put '[ViewFooter]' ;
  put '[FormatFont .Points=10, .Font="Arial", .Bold=1]' ;
  put '[FormatParagraph .Alignment=1]' ;
  put '[Insert "This is my footer"]' ;
  put '[ViewFooter]' ;
  put '[ViewHeader]' ;
```

```
      put '[Insert "This is my lovely header"]' ;
      put '[ViewHeader]' ;
      put '[InsertPicture .name="C:\test.png"]' ;
      put '[WordLeft]' ;
      put '[SelectCurWord]' ;
      put '[FormatPicture .scalex=150, .scaley=150]' ;
      put '[WordRight]' ;
      put '[insertpagebreak]' ;
      put '[InsertFile .name="C:\sample.rtf"]' ;
      put '[FileSaveAs .name="c:\test.doc"]' ;
      put '[FileClose]' ;
  run ;
```

Starting and minimizing programs from SAS

Sometimes you might like to start up a program from SAS, such as Microsoft Word, because you may want to carry out some DDE with that program. Under Windows you can use the START command to run a program, and by using the /MIN parameter you can also minimize that program once it begins running.

When you specify the program name to use, it seems that you can't specify the real path to the file you wish to run. Instead, you need to convert it to a DOS style path. This means that directory names cannot be longer than eight characters. This means that the first six characters are used, followed by a tilde (~), and then a number. The number refers to whether this directory is the first, second, third, etc. directory with the same first six characters. In the following example, I have three directories that start with Micros, and the one I want to use is the third one.

```
* don't wait for command to finish or synchronize with rest of SAS ;
options noxwait noxsync ;
* start MS Word and minimize it ;
/*x "start /min C:\Program Files\Microsoft
Office\Office10\winword.exe" ;*/
x "start /min C:\Progra~1\Micros~3\Office10\winword.exe" ;
```

You can specify the real path to the file, provided you enclose the long filenames in double quotation marks, and enclose the whole thing in single quotation marks. The code below works:

```
x '"C:\Program Files\Microsoft Office\Office10\winword.exe"' ;
```

START command syntax

Syntax: START ["title"] [/Dpath] [/I] [/MIN] [/MAX] [/SEPARATE | /SHARED]
[/LOW | /NORMAL | /HIGH | /REALTIME | /ABOVENORMAL |
/BELOWNORMAL] [/WAIT] [/B] [command/program]
[parameters]

In this syntax, the following definitions apply:

"title"   Title to display in window title bar.

path   Starting directory.

B   Start application without creating a new window. The application has ^C handling ignored. Unless the application enables ^C processing, ^Break is the only way to interrupt the application.

I	The new environment will be the original environment passed to the cmd.exe and not the current environment.
MIN	Start window minimized.
MAX	Start window maximized.
SEPARATE	Start 16-bit Windows program in separate memory space.
SHARED	Start 16-bit Windows program in shared memory space.
LOW	Start application in the IDLE priority class.
NORMAL	Start application in the NORMAL priority class.
HIGH	Start application in the HIGH priority class.
REALTIME	Start application in the REALTIME priority class.
ABOVENORMAL	Start application in the ABOVENORMAL priority class.
BELOWNORMAL	Start application in the BELOWNORMAL priority class.
WAIT	Start application and wait for it to terminate.
command/program	If it is an internal cmd command or a batch file, then the command processor is run with the /K switch to cmd.exe. This means that the window will remain after the command has been run.
	If it is not an internal cmd command or batch file, then it is a program and will run as either a windowed application or a console application.
parameters	These are the parameters passed to the command/program.

Getting the date, time, and size of a file other than a SAS file

Useful functions within SAS can tell you about SAS files (data sets, catalogs, etc.), but if you want information about other files, then you may need to use other techniques. Here is one that is handy under Windows and demonstrates some useful techniques:

1. Generate a directory listing and read it via a pipe.

2. Read the required information from that listing.

3. Write the information into macro variables, which are defined globally so they can be used throughout SAS.

4. Use field justification to ensure that our comma-formatted file size is left justified, rather than right justified.

The following macro code works on Windows XP, although you can easily alter it to work with UNIX or other operating systems. It takes a parameter, which is a command that produces a directory listing for a specific file. This listing is then analyzed to extract the date, time, and size from the directory listing, which is placed into global macro variables for use.

```
%macro getstats(dir_cmd) ;
  %global _date _time _size ;
  filename cmd pipe "&dir_cmd" ;
  data _null_ ;
    infile cmd truncover ;
    * This works on windows XP Professional, but on other version you
      might need to adjust the settings to
      read the information you want from different positions ;
    input #6  @1 date ddmmyy10.
              @13 time time5.
              @20 size comma17. ;
    * Now write the data to macro variables to be used ;
    call symput('_date',put(date,date9.)) ;
    call symput('_time',put(time,time5.)) ;
    * note we use left justification within formatted field , otherwise
      number is right justified within field ;
    call symput('_size',put(size,comma9. -1)) ;
  run ;
%mend getstats ;
%getstats(dir c:\windows\notepad.exe) ;
%put Date=&_date Time=&_time Size=&_size ;
```

```
387  %macro getstats(dir_cmd) ;
388    %global _date _time _size ;
389    filename cmd pipe "&dir_cmd" ;
390    data _null_ ;
391      infile cmd truncover ;
392     * This works on windows XP Professional, but on other version
            you might need to adjust the settings to
393        read the information you want from different positions ;
394      input #6  @1 date ddmmyy10.
395             @13 time time5.
396             @20 size comma17. ;
397     * Now write the data to macro variables to be used ;
398      call symput('_date',put(date,date9.)) ;
399      call symput('_time',put(time,time5.)) ;
400     * note we use left justification within formatted field ,
            otherwise number is right justified within field ;
401      call symput('_size',put(size,comma9. -1)) ;
402    run ;
403  %mend getstats ;
404  %getstats(dir c:\windows\notepad.exe) ;

NOTE: The infile CMD is:
      Unnamed Pipe Access Device,
      PROCESS=dir c:\windows\notepad.exe,RECFM=V,
      LRECL=256

NOTE: 8 records were read from the infile CMD.
      The minimum record length was 0.
      The maximum record length was 50.
NOTE: DATA statement used (Total process time):
      real time            0.04 seconds
      cpu time             0.01 seconds


405  %put Date=&_date Time=&_time Size=&_size ;
```

Chapter **14**

SAS/CONNECT

Connecting SAS sessions between mainframes

Something that SAS users sometimes misunderstand is that client/server doesn't always mean mainframe to PC, it can mean mainframe to mainframe or almost any platform to any other platform (PC to RS/6000, RS/6000 to HP, HP to z/OS, etc.). Where I work, we have SAS/CONNECT software available on most of our mainframe systems and on PC SAS. We run z/OS/ESA with a TCP network.

SAS/CONNECT allows you to use the three following types of client/server services. One SAS session becomes the client and another the server.

1. Compute Services use an RSUBMIT function to execute SAS code on the server.

2. Remote Library Services allow access to remote data libraries, moving data through the network as it is required. The LIBNAME statement would be specified as follows:

   ```
   LIBNAME libref <REMOTE> <'sas-data-library'> SERVER=rsessid
   <engine/host-options> ;
   ```

   The server is the Remote Session ID that you signed on with.

3. Data Transfer Services move a copy of data from one machine to another, for example, PROC UPLOAD, PROC DOWNLOAD.

The following example shows how to use SAS/CONNECT to connect two SAS sessions. After the connection is complete, the code can be sent from the originator to the one you connected to, which can run there. This is effectively a client/server relationship, though the machines can be any size. For example, you could connect from a mainframe (as a client) to a PC (as the server).

Example code to establish a link between two systems

```
* I have logged onto the mainframe and entered online SAS ;
* Now I tell SAS what protocol I will use to connect ;
* and what system to connect to (you can PING the system to see if its
  there) ;
options comamid=tcp
        remote=abc ;
* Now I tell SAS where my SAS/CONNECT logon script is ;
* The logon script tells SAS how to logon to the remote system ;
* filename rlink "ivmktg.xv02341.cntl(tcptso)" ;
* Now I tell SAS to go ahead and log on to the remote system ;
* make sure you are not already logged on to it ;
signon ;
* To cut off the link enter SIGNOFF on the command line.
```

Using SAS/CONNECT in batch mode

By default SAS/CONNECT scripts are set up to allow the user to interactively log on to remote systems. However, this can be automated so that the process can occur entirely in batch. This allows a SAS batch job to be connected from any mainframe system to any other(s) using SAS/CONNECT. This means that if a system is running out of resources, then you can run a program on another system, linking to the one where the data is (assuming your network can handle the data traffic).

Here is a PROC CONTENTS that I produced in batch, running on one machine and accessing data on another. This example was done from one z/OS mainframe SAS System to another over a TCP/IP network.

```
                        CONTENTS PROCEDURE
-----Directory-----
Libref:                                CHARM
Engine:                                SASE9
Physical Name:                         SYS1.PROD.D940715.SASLIB
Accessed through server:               SY2
Server's libref:                       SYS00016
Server's engine:                       V608
Views interpreted in server's execution: YES
Unit:                                  DISK
Volume:                                D00107
Disposition:                           OLD
Device:                                3380
Blocksize:                             23040
Blocks per Track:                      2
Total Library Blocks:                  330
Total Used Blocks:                     314
Total Free Blocks:                     16
Highest Used Block:                    314
Highest Formatted Block:               314
Members:                               1

               #   Name    Memtype  Indexes
               ---------------------------
               1   CHARM   DATA
```

To get this to work in batch you need to modify the SAS/CONNECT script, in this case SCRIPT (TCPTSO), which is set up to work in an online environment. You eliminate the script that is asking for input (INPUT statements) and add the data into the TYPE statements.

```
/*---------------------------Z/OS LOGON---------------------------*/
*  input 'Userid?';
   type 'user0001' LF;
   waitfor 'ENTER ACCOUNT', 30 seconds : nolog;
*   input 'Account?';
   type 'account code 2' LF;
   waitfor 'ENTER CURRENT PASSWORD', 60 seconds : nolog;
*   input nodisplay 'Password?';
   type 'secret1' LF;
```

This is my example JCL/SAS. Note the options where the system that you want to connect to is specified. FILENAME points to your script, which must be modified to include your user ID, account code, and password. Then LIBNAME specifies the system that you are connecting to in SERVER=.

You could link to several mainframes and access the data on each of them in the one program by specifying different SERVER= parms on various LIBNAME statements.

Screen shot

```
EDIT ---- USER0001.XVV1241.CNTL(CONNECT)  - 01.75 --------------
COLUMNS 001 072
COMMAND ===>                                            SCROLL
===> CSR
****** **************************** TOP OF
  DATA****************************
000001 //JOBSPM00 JOB 'ACCOUNT001','PM6342306',NOTIFY=&SYSUID,
000002 //         CLASS=U,MSGCLASS=X,MSGLEVEL=(1,1),REGION=2M
000003 //*
000004 //* CONNECT TO SY2
000005 //*
000006 //CONNECT  EXEC SAS
000007 //SYSIN    DD  *
000008 OPTIONS COMAMID=TCP REMOTE=SY2 ;
000009 FILENAME RLINK 'USER000.XVV1241.CNTL(TCPTSO)' ;
000010 SIGNON ;
000011
000012 LIBNAME CHARM SASE9 'SYS1.PROD.D940715.SASLIB'
000013         SERVER=SY2 DISP=SHR ;
000014
000015 PROC CONTENTS DATA=CHARM._ALL_ ;
000016 RUN ;
000017
000018 SIGNOFF ;
****** **************************** BOTTOM OF
  DATA****************************
```

Getting your IP address and connecting to your PC

Consider the case where you are developing some code at work that connects to another machine to run remotely, using SAS/CONNECT. You may want to work on this at home, but you are not able to connect to that machine. You could start another SAS session on your home PC, and use the same name as your remote machine at work to avoid changing your code.

The following example demonstrates two useful techniques. First is a way to automatically get the IP address of the machine you are running on. This works for Windows 2000, and may require some changes for other systems. Second is a way to log on to another session on your PC using a name of your choosing.

1. I use the IPCONFIG command through a pipe so I can read its output, which gives me my IP address. I use @'IP Address' to position the input pointer at the right place to read the IP address. I define all the characters I want to ignore as delimiters using DLM=. Finally, I put the parts of the IP address together and write them to a macro variable.

2. Now I make sure the SAS spawner program is running. This runs in the background and starts a new SAS session when I log on to the machine it is running on. As an example, the command I use to invoke the spawner is `C:\Program Files\SAS Institute\SAS\V8\spawner.exe -comamid tcp`. Now I assign either my IP address or PC name to a macro variable, which acts as the remote session ID. When I log on using the name of that macro variable, SAS will use the IP address (or PC name) to identify the system to connect to. The spawner then starts another SAS session, and I can RSUBMIT code to it.

See the SAS/CONNECT documentation for syntax about how to start the PC Spawner Program.

See the *SAS Companion for Microsoft Windows* for syntax about using unnamed pipes.

SAS program

```
*** Part 1 ***;
filename cmd pipe 'ipconfig' ;
data _null_ ;
  infile cmd dlm='.: ' ;
  input @'IP Address' n1 n2 n3 n4 3. ;
  IP_Address=compress(put(n1,3.)||'.' ||put(n2,3.)||'.'
                      ||put(n3,3.)||'.' ||put(n4,3.));
  call symput('ip',ip_address) ;
run ;
%put My IP address is &ip ;

*** Part 2 ***;
%let london=&ip;
/*%let london=homepc; * can alternatively use the PC name;*/
signon london ;
rsubmit london ;
  proc setinit ; run ;
endrsubmit ;
```

Chapter 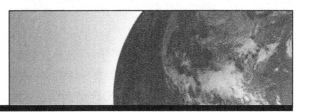 15

Output Delivery System

Using Java and ActiveX to generate static graphs

In SAS®9 there are two new graphics devices called ACTXIMG and JAVAIMG that can be used to create graphs. These produce very good-looking graphics but are not interactive graphics, such as ActiveX and Java. The files produced are actually in PNG format and by default will be 640x480 pixels (VGA). Try them out and see how easy it is to produce excellent looking output. The following graph is only 5.6 KB.

Sample code

```
goptions device=actximg ;
/*goptions device=javaimg ;*/
ods html body='c:\test.html'
        gpath='c:\'
        (url=none) ;
proc gchart data=sashelp.shoes ;
  vbar3d product / sumvar=sales ;
run ;
ods html close ;
```

Graph produced using ACTXIMG

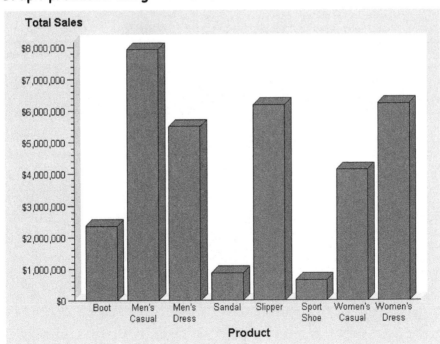

Using a Web browser to view HTML ODS output

By default SAS will use its internal browser to display HTML ODS output generated by SAS. You can change this to use either your system's default browser or a specific browser by using **Tools ▶ Options ▶ Preferences**, choosing the **Results** tab, and setting **View results using: to Preferred Web Browser**. This dialog box allows you to choose your default ODS style. Also, by clicking the **Web** tab, you can define what the preferred Web browser is.

Of course, the other way to view ODS output with a Web browser is to invoke one from within SAS using the WBROWSE command. The following code shows how this can be achieved. One advantage is that if you generate an HTML frame, you can then view the frame, rather than just the body.

```
ods html body='c:\body.html'
         contents='c:\contents.html'
         page='c:\page.html'
         frame='c:\frame.html' ;
proc sort data=sashelp.prdsale ;
  by country region ;
proc print data=sashelp.prdsale ;
  by country region ;
run ;
ods html close ;
dm "wbrowse 'c:\frame.html'" ;
```

Using multiple orientations in ODS

Sometimes you may want to produce a single document from ODS that has various pieces of output in various orientations, portrait and landscape. You can use the ORIENTATION= option to change the orientation for the next piece of ODS output generated. The following example shows how this can be done. Note that you need to tell ODS to look at the ORIENTATION= option again, hence the ODS RTF statement in the example. The following works only for some destinations, such as RTF and PDF. Support for more may be added.

```
Options orientation=landscape ;
Ods rtf file='c:\test.rtf' ;
Proc print data=sashelp.vmacro ;
Run ;
Options orientation=portrait ;
Ods rtf ; * notify rtf that orientation changed ;
Proc print data=sashelp.vmacro ;
Run ;
Ods rtf close ;
```

Generating graphs automatically for some procedures

A new feature available for some procedures in SAS®9 produces a graphic automatically for certain statistical procedures. One such procedure is PROC LIFETEST. To get the graph, enter ODS GRAPHICS ON, and then choose the graph required using the PLOTS= (variable) option in PROC LIFETEST.

Sample code

```
ods listing close ;
ods html file='lifetest.html' ;
ods graphics on;
proc lifetest data=sashelp.class;
   time age;
   survival confband=all plots=(hwb);
run;
ods graphics off;
ods html close;
```

Graph produced

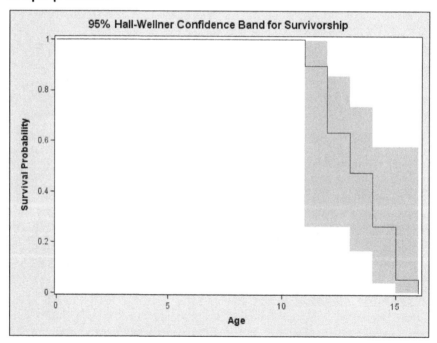

Adding page x of y in RTF and PDF

In SAS®9, if you want to add page numbers to your RTF output in the form of "page x of y," then you can use the inline formatting by specifying an escape character and {pageof}, which will generate RTF code to display *x of y* on each page.

Note: {pageof} works only for the RTF destination.

If you want to do this for the PDF or printer destination, you can use the in-line style directive {thispage}, which gives the current page number, and {lastpage}, which gives the last page number.

Sample code for RTF

```
ods escapechar = '\';
title 'This document will have page x of y '
     j=r 'Page \{pageof}' ;
ods rtf file='c:\test.rtf' ;
proc print data=sashelp.prdsale;
run;
ods rtf close;
```

Sample code for PDF

```
ods escapechar = '\';
title 'This document will have page x of y '
     j=r 'Page \{thispage} of \{lastpage}' ;
ods pdf file='c:\test.pdf' ;
proc print data=sashelp.prdsale;
run;
ods pdf close;
```

Adding page x of y in RTF in SAS 8

Using SAS 8.2, you can insert some raw RTF, which will be used by the word processor to display page x of y. This works nicely, although there is a much easier way to do it in SAS®9 (covered in the previous tip, "Adding page x of y in RTF and PDF"). This technique was discovered by Lauren Haworth, author of *Output Delivery System: The Basics*. She added page x of y using Microsoft Word, saved it as RTF, and then examined the RTF with Notepad to see what RTF code was used to implement page x of y. By inserting this as raw RTF, you can get the feature in SAS.

Using this technique, you can also discover other useful features of RTF and insert those into SAS ODS output.

Sample code for page x of y

```
ODS ESCAPECHAR="^";
footnote J=R "^R/RTF'{PAGE \field {\*\fldinst PAGE\*\MERGEFORMAT}}
{ OF  \field {\*\fldinst NUMPAGES \*\MERGEFORMAT} }'";
```

Sending data to Excel

The ODS destination PHTML (plain HTML) is great for exporting to Microsoft Excel. This was experimental in SAS 8.2 but fully supported in SAS®9. When I used the following code, I found that the HTML destination made a file of 16k, but PHTML made one of only 5k. On a bigger scale this would be a large saving in space and complexity.

```
ods html file='c:\html.xls' ;
ods phtml file='c:\phtml.xls' ;
ods htmlcss file='c:\htmlcss.xls' ;
proc print data=sashelp.class ;
run ;
ods _all_ close ;
ods listing;
```

Using native Excel formatting from ODS

It is possible to use native Excel formatting direct from ODS. This is done by producing HTML, which is imported by Excel. The HTML code contains embedded Microsoft Office XML commands, which set the formatting required. In the following example, a column of figures is displayed as fractions.

SAS program

```
ods html file='c:\both.xls' ;
data x ;
  do value=.1 to 1 by .1 ;
    fraction=value ;
    output ;
  end ;
run ;
proc print ;
  var value ;
  var fraction / style(data)={htmlstyle="mso-number-format:\#\/\#"};
run ;
ods html close ;
```

```
8     ods html file='c:\both.xls' ;
NOTE: Writing HTML Body file: c:\both.xls
9     data x ;
10      do value=.1 to 1 by .1 ;
11        fraction=value ;
12        output ;
13      end ;
14    run ;

NOTE: The data set WORK.X has 10 observations and 2 variables.
NOTE: DATA statement used (Total process time):
          real time         0.04 seconds
          cpu time          0.04 seconds


15    proc print ;
16      var value ;
17      var fraction / style(data)={htmlstyle="mso-number-
  format:\#\/\#"};
18    run ;

NOTE: There were 10 observations read from the data set WORK.X.
NOTE: PROCEDURE PRINT used (Total process time):
          real time         0.50 seconds
          cpu time          0.09 seconds

ods html close ;
```

Excel

 The SAS System

Obs	value	fraction
1	0.1	0/1
2	0.2	1/5
3	0.3	2/7
4	0.4	2/5
5	0.5	1/2
6	0.6	3/5
7	0.7	2/3
8	0.8	4/5
9	0.9	8/9
10	1	1/1

Adding page x of y in Excel reports

The wonders of ODS were revealed to me at PharmaSUG by Chevell Parker from SAS Institute. This tip is based on one of the many great examples in his paper "Generating Custom Excel Spreadsheets Using ODS."

Using the HTMLCSS destination, you can write an HTML file and CSS file. Because you name the spreadsheet using an XLS suffix, it will be opened by Excel. Excel will then import the HTML into a spreadsheet. The HEADTEXT= option in the ODS statement puts the text in quotation marks into our HTML code. That text uses special Microsoft Office XML commands to set a header and footer in the Excel file.

In the header use:

&P   current page number

&N   total number of pages

In the footer use:

&L   left justify text

&C   center text

&R   right justify text

&D   date

&T   time

Also, see the excellent paper by Chevell Parker at http://www2.sas.com/proceedings/sugi28/012-28.pdf.

SAS program

```
ods htmlcss file='c:\temp.xls'
            stylesheet="c:\temp.css"
            headtext='<style> @Page {mso-header-data:"Page &P of &N";
                                      mso-footer-data:"&Lleft text
                                      &Cpage &P&R&D&T"} ;
                      </style>' ;
proc print data=sashelp.prdsale ;
run ;
ods htmlcss close ;
```

Useful attributes with ODS in titles and footnotes

You can use attributes in titles and footnotes in SAS 8 and later. These work a bit like those that can be specified in SAS/GRAPH. These are not supported by all destinations but do work for RTF and PDF destinations, possibly more. You can specify things like:

- BOLD
- UNDERLINE
- ITALIC
- COLOR=foreground
- BCOLOR=background
- FONT=font
- HEIGHT=size
- JUSTIFY=just
- LINK=url

Sample SAS code

```
ods rtf file='c:\test.rtf' ;
Title1 justify=l bold 'Left'
       justify=c h=2 'Centre'
       f=arial j=right 'Right' ;
Title2 link='www.sas.com' 'SAS web site' ;
proc print data=sashelp.class ;
run ;
ods rtf close ;
```

Producing a spreadsheet for each BY group

The following program shows how to use ODS to produce a separate file for each BY group. This is done by using the NEWFILE=PAGE option. You use the HTML destination to produce files with an XLS suffix. This means that Excel will be used to open the file (on many systems, depending on preferences) when the files are opened; Excel then imports the HTML to display the data as a spreadsheet.

You also use the ODS HTML PATH statement to specify a base directory for all other ODS HTML files to use. This means that body files are written to c:\temp\html and will be called body.xls, body1.xls, body2.xls, etc.

You also use the HTML destination to create an HTML **contents** file. This produces some HTML with links to each of the spreadsheets, so you can conveniently see them all on one page and click on the one you want to display.

SAS program

```
ods listing close;
ods html path="c:\temp\"
        body="body.xls"
        contents="contents.html"
        newfile=page;
proc sort data=sashelp.prdsale ;
  by product ;
run ;
proc tabulate data=sashelp.prdsale ;
  by product ;
  class country region ;
  var actual predict ;
  table country all,
        region all,
          (actual predict)*sum ;
run ;
ods html close ;
dm "wbrowse 'c:\temp\contents.html'" wbrowse ;
```

Producing multi-column reports

In SAS®9 and later, there is a new ODS option for ODS printer and RTF called COLUMNS=, which allows you to choose the number of columns to produce in your output. The following example shows how this can be used to send output to various destinations and to select various numbers of columns by using macro variables.

SAS program

```
%let dest=rtf; * pdf, ps or rtf ;
%let cols=2 ;
ods &dest columns=&cols file="c:\test.&dest" ;
goptions rotate=landscape ;
proc print data=sashelp.shoes ;
  var region stores sales ;
run ;
ods &dest close ;
```

The following output shows a two-column format.

Obs	Region	Stores	Sales	Obs	Region	Stores	Sales
1	Africa	12	$29,761	29	Africa	24	$19,282
2	Africa	4	$67,242	30	Africa	1	$9,244
3	Africa	7	$76,793	31	Africa	3	$18,053
4	Africa	10	$62,819	32	Africa	18	$26,427
5	Africa	14	$68,641	33	Africa	11	$43,452
6	Africa	4	$1,690	34	Africa	7	$2,521
7	Africa	2	$51,541	35	Africa	1	$19,582
8	Africa	12	$108,942	36	Africa	6	$48,031
9	Africa	21	$21,297	37	Africa	16	$13,921
10	Africa	4	$63,206	38	Africa	5	$57,691
11	Africa	13	$123,743	39	Africa	10	$16,662
12	Africa	25	$29,198	40	Africa	11	$52,807
13	Africa	17	$64,891	41	Africa	10	$4,888
14	Africa	9	$2,617	42	Africa	1	$17,919
15	Africa	12	$90,648	43	Africa	3	$32,928
16	Africa	20	$4,846	44	Africa	8	$6,081
17	Africa	25	$360,209	45	Africa	3	$62,893
18	Africa	5	$4,051	46	Africa	2	$29,582
19	Africa	9	$10,532	47	Africa	9	$11,145
20	Africa	9	$13,732	48	Africa	5	$19,146
21	Africa	3	$2,259	49	Africa	2	$801
22	Africa	14	$328,474	50	Africa	1	$8,467
23	Africa	3	$14,095	51	Africa	25	$16,282
24	Africa	14	$8,365	52	Africa	1	$8,587
25	Africa	13	$17,337	53	Africa	19	$16,289
26	Africa	12	$39,452	54	Africa	12	$34,955
27	Africa	8	$5,172	55	Africa	10	$2,202
28	Africa	4	$42,682	56	Africa	3	$28,515

Obs	Region	Stores	Sales
57	Asia	1	$1,996
58	Asia	1	$3,033
59	Asia	1	$3,230
60	Asia	1	$3,019
61	Asia	1	$5,389
62	Asia	17	$60,712
63	Asia	1	$11,754
64	Asia	7	$116,333
65	Asia	3	$4,978
66	Asia	21	$149,013
67	Asia	1	$937
68	Asia	2	$20,448
69	Asia	7	$78,234
70	Asia	1	$1,155

Finding and using available ODS styles

To use a style in ODS, specify the STYLE= option in the ODS statement. STYLE= is valid in all markup destinations (i.e. not ODS OUTPUT and ODS LISTING). So the following would produce some HTML output that uses the DEFAULT style.

```
ods html file='test.html' style=default ;
Proc print data=sashelp.class ;
run ;
ods html close ;
```

There are a range of other styles available that can be used by specifying them under STYLE=. To get a list of those available, use the following program. Try out each of them to see what they look like.

Apart from using PROC TEMPLATE, you can see available styles by right-clicking **RESULTS** in the Results window, and selecting **TEMPLATES**. You can then navigate to **SASHELP.TMPLMST.STYLES** to see what's there. Also, if you double-click one of the styles, you will see the code used for that style.

You can also use the Display Manager command ODSTEMPLATES to open the Templates window.

For more styles, see the list for SAS 9.1.

Still want more? Well, you could buy the SAS Press publication *Instant ODS: Style Templates for the SAS Output Delivery System.* This CD is full of professionally designed styles. For details, see http://support.sas.com/publishing/bbu/companion_site/58824.html.

SAS program

```
proc template ;
  list styles ;
run ;
```

Output from SAS 8.2

```
              Listing of: SASUSER.TEMPLAT
              Path Filter is: Styles
              Sort by: PATH/ASCENDING

              Obs      Path                 Type


               1       Styles               Dir
               2       Styles.Newrtf        Style


        Listing of: SASHELP.TMPLMST
        Path Filter is: Styles
        Sort by: PATH/ASCENDING


        Obs     Path                      Type


         1      Styles                    Dir
         2      Styles.BarrettsBlue       Style
         3      Styles.Beige              Style
         4      Styles.Brick              Style
         5      Styles.Brown              Style
         6      Styles.D3d                Style
         7      Styles.Default            Style
         8      Styles.Minimal            Style
         9      Styles.NoFontDefault      Style
        10      Styles.Printer            Style
        11      Styles.Rtf                Style
        12      Styles.Sasweb             Style
        13      Styles.Statdoc            Style
        14      Styles.Theme              Style
        15      Styles.fancyPrinter       Style
        16      Styles.sansPrinter        Style
        17      Styles.sasdocPrinter      Style
        18      Styles.serifPrinter       Style
```

Output from SAS 9.1

```
Listing of: SASHELP.TMPLMST
Path Filter is: Styles
Sort by: PATH/ASCENDING

Obs    Path                    Type

 1     Styles                  Dir
 2     Styles.Analysis         Style
 3     Styles.Astronomy        Style
 4     Styles.Banker           Style
 5     Styles.BarrettsBlue     Style
 6     Styles.Beige            Style
 7     Styles.Brick            Style
 8     Styles.Brown            Style
 9     Styles.Curve            Style
10     Styles.D3d              Style
11     Styles.Default          Style
12     Styles.Education        Style
13     Styles.Electronics      Style
14     Styles.Festival         Style
15     Styles.Gears            Style
16     Styles.Journal          Style
17     Styles.Magnify          Style
18     Styles.Meadow           Style
19     Styles.Minimal          Style
20     Styles.Money            Style
21     Styles.NoFontDefault    Style
22     Styles.Normal           Style
23     Styles.Printer          Style
24     Styles.Rsvp             Style
25     Styles.Rtf              Style
26     Styles.Sasweb           Style
27     Styles.Science          Style
28     Styles.Seaside          Style
29     Styles.Sketch           Style
30     Styles.Statdoc          Style
31     Styles.Statistical      Style
32     Styles.Theme            Style
33     Styles.Torn             Style
34     Styles.Watercolor       Style
35     Styles.blockPrint       Style
36     Styles.fancyPrinter     Style
37     Styles.sansPrinter      Style
38     Styles.sasdocPrinter    Style
39     Styles.serifPrinter     Style
```

Changing attributes in PROC TABULATE

When using PROC TABULATE with ODS it is possible to change style attributes of various parts of your output. You can do this by using style overrides. Style overrides are specified as STYLE={defn}, where *defn* defines which style attributes you want to override. STYLE= can be abbreviated as s=.

Some (not all) useful style attributes appear in this table, followed by an example showing some places in PROC TABULATE in which style overrides can be specified.

Attribute	Use	Attribute	Use
Background	Background color	**URL**	Specify a link
Foreground	Foreground color	**Font_face**	Specify a font
Width	Cell width	**Font_size**	Size of font
Height	Cell height	**Just**	Justification

SAS code

```
data report ;
   input region $ citysize $ pop product $ saletype $
         quantity amount;
datalines ;
NC S  25000 A100 R 150  3750.00
NE S  37000 A100 R 200  5000.00
SO S  48000 A100 R 410 10250.00
WE S  32000 A100 R 180  4500.00
NC M 125000 A100 R 350  8750.00
NE M 237000 A100 R 600 15000.00
SO M 348000 A100 R 710 17750.00
WE M 432000 A100 R 780 19500.00
NE L 837000 A100 R 800 20000.00
SO L 748000 A100 R 760 19000.00
WE L 932000 A100 R 880 22000.00
NC S  25000 A100 W 150  3000.00
NE S  37000 A100 W 200  4000.00
WE S  32000 A100 W 180  3600.00
NC M 125000 A100 W 350  7000.00
NE M 237000 A100 W 600 12000.00
SO M 348000 A100 W 710 14200.00
WE M 432000 A100 W 780 15600.00
NC L 625000 A100 W 750 15000.00
NE L 837000 A100 W 800 16000.00
```

```
SO L 748000 A100 W 760 15200.00
WE L 932000 A100 W 880 17600.00
NC S  25000 A200 R 165  4125.00
NE S  37000 A200 R 215  5375.00
SO S  48000 A200 R 425 10425.00
WE S  32000 A200 R 195  4875.00
NC M 125000 A200 R 365  9125.00
NE M 237000 A200 R 615 15375.00
SO M 348000 A200 R 725 19125.00
WE M 432000 A200 R 795 19875.00
NE L 837000 A200 R 815 20375.00
SO L 748000 A200 R 775 19375.00
WE L 932000 A200 R 895 22375.00
NC S  25000 A200 W 165  3300.00
NE S  37000 A200 W 215  4300.00
WE S  32000 A200 W 195  3900.00
NC M 125000 A200 W 365  7300.00
NE M 237000 A200 W 615 12300.00
SO M 348000 A200 W 725 14500.00
WE M 432000 A200 W 795 15900.00
NC L 625000 A200 W 765 15300.00
NE L 837000 A200 W 815 16300.00
SO L 748000 A200 W 775 15500.00
WE L 932000 A200 W 895 17900.00
NC S  25000 A300 R 157  3925.00
NE S  37000 A300 R 208  5200.00
SO S  48000 A300 R 419 10475.00
WE S  32000 A300 R 186  4650.00
NC M 125000 A300 R 351  8725.00
NE M 237000 A300 R 610 15250.00
SO M 348000 A300 R 714 17850.00
WE M 432000 A300 R 785 19625.00
NE L 837000 A300 R 806 20150.00
SO L 748000 A300 R 768 19200.00
WE L 932000 A300 R 880 22000.00
NC S  25000 A300 W 157  3140.00
NE S  37000 A300 W 208  4160.00
WE S  32000 A300 W 186  3720.00
NC M 125000 A300 W 351  7020.00
NE M 237000 A300 W 610 12200.00
SO M 348000 A300 W 714 14280.00
WE M 432000 A300 W 785 15700.00
NC L 625000 A300 W 757 15140.00
NE L 837000 A300 W 806 16120.00
SO L 748000 A300 W 768 15360.00
WE L 932000 A300 W 880 17600.00
;
run;
```

```
proc format;
   value $salefmt 'R'='Retail'
      'W'='Wholesale';
   value $salecol 'R'='gray10'
      'W'='gray90';
   value $regcol  'NC'='gray20'
      'NE'='graya0'
      'SO'='CX00C400'
      'WE'='white';
   value cellcol  0-40000     = 'gray30'
  40001-90000 = 'gray50'
  other        = 'gray70';
run;
ods html ;
proc tabulate data=report s={foreground=grayb0};
   class region citysize saletype / s={foreground=graye0};
   classlev region citysize saletype / s={foreground=grayc0};
   var quantity amount / s={foreground=black};
   keyword all sum / s={foreground=white};
   format saletype $salefmt.;
   label region="Region" citysize="Citysize" saletype="Saletype";
   label quantity="Quantity" amount="Amount";
   keylabel all="Total";
   table all={label = "All Products" s={foreground=grayd0}},
   (region all)*(citysize all*{s={foreground=gray60}}),
   (saletype all)*(quantity*f=COMMA6. amount*f=dollar10.) /
s={background=gray80}
misstext={label="Missing" s={foreground=gray90}}
box={label="Region by Citysize by Saletype"
  s={foreground=gray40}};
run;
ods html close ;
```

Screenshot of output

All Products

Region by Citysize by Saletype		Saletype				Total	
		Quantity Sum	Amount Sum	Quantity Sum	Amount Sum	Quantity Sum	Amount Sum
Region	Citysize						
		Missing	Missing				
	Total	1,538	$38,400	3,810	$76,200	5,348	$114,600
	Citysize						
	Total	4,869	$121,725	4,869	$97,380	9,736	$219,105
	Citysize						
				Missing	Missing		
	Total	5,706	$143,450	4,452	$89,040	10,156	$232,490
	Citysize						
	Total	5,576	$139,400	5,576	$111,520	11,102	$250,920
Total	Citysize						
	Total	17,689	$442,975	18,707	$374,140	36,390	$817,115

Changing the look and feel of PROC REPORT output

When using PROC REPORT with ODS, it is possible to change style attributes of various parts of your output. You can do this by using style overrides. Style overrides are specified as STYLE={*defn*}, where *defn* defines which style attributes you want to override. STYLE= can be abbreviated as s=.

Here is an example showing some places in PROC REPORT in which style overrides can be specified.

SAS code

```
data report ;
input region $ citysize $ pop product $ saletype $
quantity amount;
datalines;
NC S 25000 A100 R 150 3750.00
NE S 37000 A100 R 200 5000.00
SO S 48000 A100 R 410 10250.00
WE S 32000 A100 R 180 4500.00
NC M 125000 A100 R 350 8750.00
NE M 237000 A100 R 600 15000.00
SO M 348000 A100 R 710 17750.00
WE M 432000 A100 R 780 19500.00
NE L 837000 A100 R 800 20000.00
SO L 748000 A100 R 760 19000.00
WE L 932000 A100 R 880 22000.00
NC S 25000 A100 W 150 3000.00
NE S 37000 A100 W 200 4000.00
WE S 32000 A100 W 180 3600.00
NC M 125000 A100 W 350 7000.00
NE M 237000 A100 W 600 12000.00
SO M 348000 A100 W 710 14200.00
WE M 432000 A100 W 780 15600.00
NC L 625000 A100 W 750 15000.00
NE L 837000 A100 W 800 16000.00
SO L 748000 A100 W 760 15200.00
WE L 932000 A100 W 880 17600.00
NC S 25000 A200 R 165 4125.00
NE S 37000 A200 R 215 5375.00
SO S 48000 A200 R 425 10425.00
WE S 32000 A200 R 195 4875.00
NC M 125000 A200 R 365 9125.00
NE M 237000 A200 R 615 15375.00
SO M 348000 A200 R 725 19125.00
WE M 432000 A200 R 795 19875.00
NE L 837000 A200 R 815 20375.00
SO L 748000 A200 R 775 19375.00
```

```
WE L 932000 A200 R 895 22375.00
NC S 25000 A200 W 165 3300.00
NE S 37000 A200 W 215 4300.00
WE S 32000 A200 W 195 3900.00
NC M 125000 A200 W 365 7300.00
NE M 237000 A200 W 615 12300.00
SO M 348000 A200 W 725 14500.00
WE M 432000 A200 W 795 15900.00
NC L 625000 A200 W 765 15300.00
NE L 837000 A200 W 815 16300.00
SO L 748000 A200 W 775 15500.00
WE L 932000 A200 W 895 17900.00
NC S 25000 A300 R 157 3925.00
NE S 37000 A300 R 208 5200.00
SO S 48000 A300 R 419 10475.00
WE S 32000 A300 R 186 4650.00
NC M 125000 A300 R 351 8725.00
NE M 237000 A300 R 610 15250.00
SO M 348000 A300 R 714 17850.00
WE M 432000 A300 R 785 19625.00
NE L 837000 A300 R 806 20150.00
SO L 748000 A300 R 768 19200.00
WE L 932000 A300 R 880 22000.00
NC S 25000 A300 W 157 3140.00
NE S 37000 A300 W 208 4160.00
WE S 32000 A300 W 186 3720.00
NC M 125000 A300 W 351 7020.00
NE M 237000 A300 W 610 12200.00
SO M 348000 A300 W 714 14280.00
WE M 432000 A300 W 785 15700.00
NC L 625000 A300 W 757 15140.00
NE L 837000 A300 W 806 16120.00
SO L 748000 A300 W 768 15360.00
WE L 932000 A300 W 880 17600.00
;
run;
```

```
proc format;
value $salefmt 'R'='Retail'
'W'='Wholesale';
value $salecol 'R'='gray10'
'W'='gray90';
value $regcol 'NC'='gray20'
'NE'='graya0'
'SO'='CX00C400'
'WE'='white';
value cellcol 0-40000 = 'gray30'
40001-90000 = 'gray50'
other = 'gray70';
run;
ods html ;
proc tabulate data=report s={foreground=grayb0};
class region citysize saletype / s={foreground=graye0};
classlev region citysize saletype / s={foreground=grayc0};
var quantity amount / s={foreground=black};
keyword all sum / s={foreground=white};
format saletype $salefmt.;
label region="Region" citysize="Citysize" saletype="Saletype";
label quantity="Quantity" amount="Amount";
keylabel all="Total";
table all={label = "All Products" s={foreground=grayd0}},
(region all)*(citysize all*{s={foreground=gray60}}),
(saletype all)*(quantity*f=COMMA6. amount*f=dollar10.) /
s={background=gray80}
misstext={label="Missing" s={foreground=gray90}}
box={label="Region by Citysize by Saletype"
s={foreground=gray40}};
run;
ods html close
```

All Products

Region by Citysize by Saletype		Saletype				Total	
		Quantity Sum	Amount Sum	Quantity Sum	Amount Sum	Quantity Sum	Amount Sum
Region	Citysize						
		Missing	*Missing*				
	Total	1,538	$38,400	3,810	$76,200	5,348	$114,800
	Citysize						
	Total	4,869	$121,725	4,869	$97,360	9,738	$219,105
	Citysize						
					Missing	*Missing*	
	Total	5,706	$143,450	4,452	$89,040	10,158	$232,490
	Citysize						
	Total	5,576	$139,400	5,576	$111,520	11,152	$250,920
Total	Citysize						
	Total	17,689	$442,975	18,707	$374,140	36,396	$817,115

Expanding your tagsets

The MARKUP destination in ODS is supported in SAS®9 and is experimental in SAS 8.2. You can, however, get advanced access to some of the new tagsets from SAS®9 by downloading the latest tagsets from http://support.sas.com/rnd/base/index-xml-resources.html. Simply go to this Web page, download the tagset definitions, which are in the form of a SAS program, and run them in SAS 8.2 or SAS®9. You will then have the latest tagsets available.

One tagset you get, which is not available in SAS 8.2, is HTML4. This is the default HTML tagset in SAS®9. This allows you to produce HTML Version 4 code, rather than Version 3.2, which the HTML destination produces (in SAS 8.2). The following log shows how to produce a file containing HTML Version 4 markup language.

```
5    ods markup tagset=html4 file='test.html' ;
WARNING: MARKUP is experimental in this release.
NOTE: Writing MARKUP file: test.html
6    proc means data=sashelp.class nway ;
7    run ;

NOTE: There were 19 observations read from the data set SASHELP.CLASS.
NOTE: PROCEDURE MEANS used:
        real time            0.05 seconds
        cpu time             0.01 seconds


ods markup close ;
```

Making a template to add a graphic

The following example shows how you can modify a template in ODS so that you can include a graphic at the start of any output you produce with that template. This can be useful if you want to include a logo or graph at the start of a report each time you generate a new report.

```
filename gsffile "test.jpg";
goptions gsfname=gsffile gsfmode=replace device=jpeg
        hsize=9cm vsize=6cm;
proc gplot data=sashelp.class;
 plot height*weight=sex;
run;

proc template;
  define style myRTF / store=work.templates;
    parent=styles.rtf;
    style table from table/
      preimage="test.jpg";
  end;
run;

ods path (prepend) work.templates;
ods rtf file="test.rtf" style=myRTF;
proc print data=sashelp.class;
run;
ods rtf close;
```

Writing to several ODS destinations at once

It's possible to write output generated from one piece of SAS code to multiple ODS destinations. They can either be different file names of the same file type, or different file types.

Code showing how to write to multiple destinations

```
ods html     file='c:\1.htm' ;
ods rtf      file='c:\2.rtf' ;
ods pdf      file='c:\3.pdf' ;
ods listing ;
proc print data=sashelp.class ;
run ;
ods _all_ close ;
```

Code showing how to write to multiple files of the same type

```
ods html(x)     file='c:\1.html' ;
ods html(1)     file='c:\2.html' ;
ods html(id=1)  file='c:\3.html' ;
ods html(sales) file='c:\4.html' ;
proc print data=sashelp.class ;
run ;
ods _all_ close ;
```

Note: If you close the _all_ destination, then this will close the LISTING destination as well. That means that if you produce any output, then it will not be sent anywhere, not even to the Output window. To reset the default, you should issue ODS LISTING.

Exporting to Excel using ODS

All of the following techniques will produce comma-delimited files, which can then be opened by Excel. The comma-separated value (CSV) destination produces a comma-separated file. The ODS CSVALL statement does as well, but also includes titles and footnotes and BY lines. HTML produces an HTML file, but the suffix XLS on the filename means that Excel opens the file, recognizes that it is ODS, and then imports the data along with formatting information.

```
Ods csv file='name.csv' ;
Ods csvall file='name2.csv' ;
Ods html file='name.xls' ;
Proc print data=sashelp.class ;
Run ;
Ods _all_ close ;
Ods listing;
```

Horizontal hi-lo chart

By default, SAS creates vertical hi-lo charts and unfortunately there is no way to create horizontal ones. What you can do is create a vertical chart, and then turn the axes values 90 degrees around on the bars, making the output appear as a horizontal chart.

SAS program

```
goptions reset=all ;
axis1 major=none minor=none label=none value=none;
axis2 value=(angle=90) label=none;
axis3 value=(angle=90);
symbol1 i=none;
symbol2 i=hilot;
proc gplot data=sasuser.houses;
   plot price*style=1 / vaxis=axis1 haxis=axis2;
   plot2 price*style=12 / vaxis=axis3;
run;
quit;
```

Note: This tip is taken from "Tips from the Techies Technical Support, SAS South Pacific" by Masrur Khan and Peter Mallik. You can find the full PowerPoint file at http://support.sas.com.

Getting the right special character in a graph

Many people who export graphics to Microsoft Word use the computer graphics metafile (CGM) device drivers. Drivers such as the CGM drivers have hardware fonts associated with them, which give high-quality results in output.

Each character of text that is displayed in a graph has an ASCII code associated with it. This ASCII code may have a different character assigned in different character sets or fonts. So if you type in one character and then produce a graph, you may get a different character displayed depending on which driver and font is being used.

In the following code, the ± (plus or minus) sign has been typed into the title statement, but comes out as a quotation mark when you produce the graph. This can be fixed by specifying a hardware font that has the correct symbol for that ASCII code.

See the following for more information on using hardware fonts: http://v9doc.sas.com/cgi-bin/sasdoc/cgigdoc?file=../graphref.hlp/ font-using-hardware-fonts.htm#font-alternative-hw-fonts.

SAS program

```
goptions reset=all;
GOPTIONS device=cgm gsfmode=replace gsfname=graph ;
filename graph "c:\test.cgm";


*--------------------------------------------;
*** This *does not* produce my plus/minus sign ***;
TITLE j=c "Intent-to-Treat, Survivial ± 1.5" ;
proc gchart data=sashelp.class ;
  vbar sex ;
run ;


*--------------------------------------------;
*** This *does* produce my plus/minus sign ***;
TITLE f=hwcgm005 j=c "Intent-to-Treat, Survivial ± 1.5" ;
proc gchart data=sashelp.class ;
  vbar sex ;
run ;
```

You can run PROC GDEVICE, select the driver, and use the CHARTYPE window to look at what hardware fonts are available for a device driver at http://v9doc.sas.com/cgi-bin/sasdoc/cgigdoc?file=../graphref.hlp/ gdevice-using.htm.

First graph without explicit hardware font

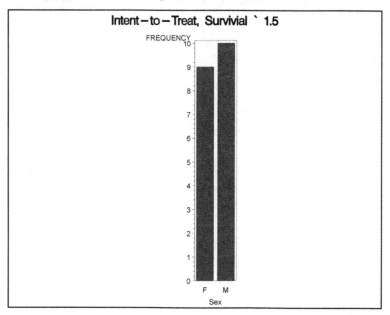

Second graph with explicit hardware font

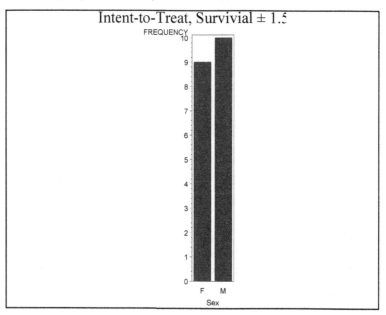

Hardware vs. software fonts in graphs

If you have ever been disappointed by the quality of text in graphs, then you may not have used hardware fonts. It's easy to use them, and if you're using Windows you can select true-type fonts easily. In the following example, I produce Portable Network Graphics (PNG) format graphs. (These have some advantages over some other formats, which I will cover another time.) Note that when using true-type fonts, you should put the font name in quotation marks. But, if you use software fonts, then you don't use the quotation marks (e.g. *goptions ftext=swiss ;*).

For information about the FTEXT goption, see http://v9doc.sas.com/cgi-bin/sasdoc/cgigdoc?file=../graphref.hlp/gopdict-ftext.htm.

SAS program

```
filename sw 'c:\software font.png' ; * file to save graph using
                                         software font ;
filename hw 'c:\hardware font.png' ; * file to save graph using
                                         hardware font ;
goptions reset=all gsfname=sw dev=png xmax=6 ymax=4;
proc gchart data=sashelp.class;
vbar sex / sumvar=height ;
run;
* produce second graph using the Arial Font with text height set to
  6% of total ;
goptions gsfname=hw ftext='Arial' htext=6pct ;
vbar sex / sumvar=height ;
run;
quit;
```

Software font

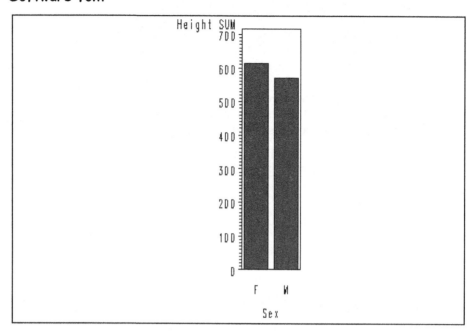

Hardware font

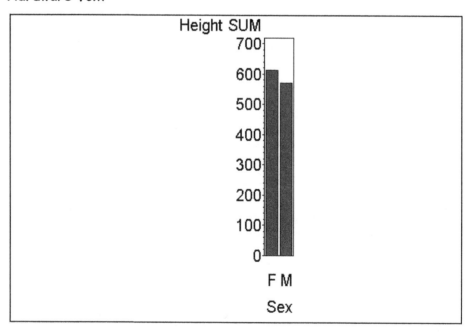

Inserting graphs and tables in a Word document

Here is some *simple* ODS code to show how easy it is to put a graph and table on a single page in a Microsoft Word document. Important features of the code are:

- `goption Reset=all` ensures all graphic options are reset to default before changing the ones you want to change

- `device=jpeg` specifies the device driver to use for producing a graph

- `ods rtf` specifies that you want to produce RTF output, which can be read by Microsoft Word

- `file='gt.rtf'` specifies the name of the RTF file you are making

- `startpage=no` tells ODS to not go to a new page after each procedure

SAS program

```
goptions reset=all device=jpeg ;
Ods rtf file='gt.rtf' startpage=no ;
proc gchart data=sashelp.class ;
  vbar3d age;
run;
proc print data=sashelp.class ;
run;
ods rtf close ;
```

Creating animated GIFs

SAS/GRAPH allows you to create animated GIF files. These files can contain a number of graphs in the one file. When these graphs are displayed through an application that supports them, you can see the graphs one by one. You can also define whether the sequence repeats and the time interval between each image.

For some nice examples of animated GIFs and the code to produce them, see http://support.sas.com/rnd/samples/graph/gifanimoverview.html.

SAS program

```
ods listing ;
filename anim 'c:\anim.gif' ;   /* file to create */
goptions device=gifanim         /* animated GIF driver */
         gsfname=anim           /* fileref to save file to */
         delay=100              /* 1/100s of a second between each
                                   image */
         gsfmode=replace        /* wipe over previous file */
         disposal=background ;  /* when graph is erased background
                                   color returns */
proc gchart data=sashelp.prdsale ;
  vbar3d prodtype ;
run ;

goptions gsfmode=append ;       /* append the next graph to existing
                                   image */
proc gplot data=sashelp.class ;
  plot height*weight ;
run ;

goptions gepilog='3b'x;         /* write end-of-file character after
                                   next graph */
proc gchart data=sashelp.prdsale ;
  hbar3d country ;
run;
```

Adding space at the beginning and end of cells in PROC REPORT output

Some simple things can be tricky to do in ODS. For instance, if you want space before and after values in each column, you can add spaces to each variable, making sure to convert numerics to character, but leading and trailing blanks are usually trimmed.

The following works with HTML 3, which is the default is SAS 8. In SAS®9, you would have to specify the destination HTML3.

Using `asis=yes` will stop the spaces being trimmed. You can then put spaces at the start and end of values using `pretext` and `posttext`. This avoids the need to change the values of variables to incorporate the spaces. *Cellpadding* can be used to define the white space on each of the four sides of text in a cell. In this case, we want none.

SAS program

```
ods html3 file='c:\test.html' ;
proc report data=sashelp.class nowd
            style={cellpadding=0}
            style(header)={cellpadding=0 pretext="   " posttext="   "
                          asis=yes}
            style(column)={cellpadding=0 pretext="   " posttext="   "
                          asis=yes} ;
  define sex / order ;
  define age / order ;
run ;
ods html3 close ;
```

Output

Name	Sex	Age	Height	Weight
Joyce	F	11	51.3	50.5
Jane		12	59.8	84.5
Louise			56.3	77
Alice		13	56.5	84
Barbara			65.3	98
Carol		14	62.8	102.5
Judy			64.3	90
Janet		15	62.5	112.5
Mary			66.5	112

Extract of HTML source

The following extract of HTML source code was obtained by selecting **View ▶ Source** from the browser when viewing the output. It shows the spaces before and after "Name" in the header row of the table. This demonstrates the effect of pretext and posttext.

```
<TD ALIGN=CENTER bgcolor="#B0B0B0"><PRE>
<font  face="Arial, Helvetica, sans-serif" size="4"
color="#0033AA"><b>   Name   </b></font></PRE>
</TD>
```

Comparing magnitudes of variables in categories in charts

The GAREABAR procedure in SAS/GRAPH lets you compare the magnitudes of two variables for each category of data using exact and relative magnitudes of values. It works only with ODS using the ActiveX or ACTIMGX driver, though.

The following example plots *sales* on the x-axis, relative percent of number of *salespersons* on the y-axis, with a bar for each *site*. Additionally each bar is sub-grouped by *quarter*.

SAS program

```
goptions reset=all device=activex ;

ods html file='c:\test.html' ;

data totals;
   input Site $ Quarter $ Sales Salespersons;
datalines;
Lima    1 4043.97    4
NY      1 4225.26   12
Rome    1 16543.97   6
Lima    2 3723.44    5
NY      2 4595.07   18
Rome    2 2558.29   10
Lima    3 4437.96    8
NY      3 5847.91   24
Rome    3 3789.85   14
Lima    4 6065.57   10
NY      4 23388.51  26
Rome    4 1509.08   16
;
proc gareabar data=totals;
   hbar site*salespersons /sumvar=sales
                           subgroup=quarter
                           rstat=SUM
                           wstat=PCT;
run ; quit ;

ods html close;
```

Output

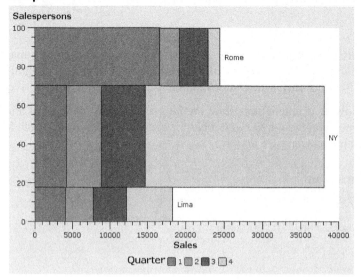

Making the correct size ActiveX for your resolution

The following program demonstrates two techniques.

First, you can change the size of an ActiveX control produced from SAS/GRAPH and ODS by using the goptions XPIXELS and YPIXELS.

And second, you can conveniently store settings for different screen sizes as macro parameters. You can then call up the desired group of parameters by simply setting another macro variable to the required value. In this example, you define two parameters for each of four different screen sizes, and call up the required one by simply using their names.

SAS program

```
* Define your preferred settings for various resolutions ;
%let qvga=xpixels=320  ypixels=240 ;
%let vga=xpixels=640   ypixels=480 ;
%let svga=xpixels=800  ypixels=600 ;
%let xga=xpixels=1024  ypixels=768 ;

* Select the resolution you want to use ;
%let resolution=vga;

ods html file='graph.htm' gpath='c:\' ;
* Choose the ACTIVEX driver with the appropriate resolution ;
goptions device=ActiveX &&&resolution ;
proc gchart data=sashelp.class ;
  vbar3d age / subgroup=sex ;
run ;
ods html close ;
```

Plotting details of slices in a pie graph

In SAS®9, there is a new parameter in PROC GCHART that can be used when making pie charts. It enables you to produce an inner pie overlay, showing major components that make up outer pie slices. This can be useful to get even more information into your chart.

```
ods HTML file='c:\test.html' gpath='c: \' ;
goptions reset=all device=png
         xmax=10 ymax=6            /* make PNG bigger */
         ftext='Arial' htext=4pct /* use some nice looking text */;

data countries;
  input country $ 1-14 region $16-26 Machinery;
  datalines;
Taiwan         Asia       6.1
Korea          Asia       4.6
Malaysia       Asia       4.4
Malaysia2      Asia       3.9
Malaysia4      Asia       3.9
Malaysia5      Asia       1.5
U.S.           U.S.       39.1
Belgium        Europe     2.6
Germany        Europe     7.8
United Kingdom Europe     3.9
France         Europe     3.9
Santa          Antarctica 1.1
Bob            Antarctica 1.0
Cydonia        Mars       1.1
Tims House     Mars       1.0
China          Asia       10.2
Malaysia3      Asia       3.9
;
run;
proc gchart;
  pie region / angle=320
               slice=outside
               percent=inside
               value=none
               sumvar=Machinery
               detail_percent=best
               detail=country
               descending ;
run; quit;
ods html close ;
; quit;
ods html close ;
```

Output

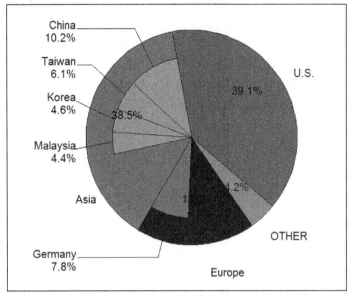

China 10.2%
Taiwan 6.1%
Korea 4.6%
Malaysia 4.4%
Asia
Germany 7.8%
Europe
38.5%
U.S. 39.1%
4.2%
OTHER

Changing resolution of graphs

You can use several settings in SAS/GRAPH to easily choose the resolution of graphs to produce. You may want to produce a low-resolution graph to use as a thumbnail, which when clicked takes you to a higher-resolution graph.

The following SAS macro demonstrates how you can choose a size and resolution for a graph by altering a few parameters:

- XMAX/YMAX—width and height of graphic area in inches, centimetres, or points

- XPIXELS/YPIXELS—width and height of graphic area in pixels

Horizontal dots per inch = number of dots / number of inches = xpixels / xmax

SAS program

```sas
%macro testres(x,y,dpi) ;
 * x   ... number of inches across graphic ;
 * y   ... number of inches across graphic ;
 * dpi ... resolution in dots per inch ;
  filename out "c:\test&dpi..png" ;
  goptions reset=all                      /* reset everything first */
           dev=png                        /* driver to use */
               xmax=&x in
           ymax=&y in
               xpixels=%sysevalf(&x*&dpi)
           ypixels=%sysevalf(&y*&dpi)
           ftext="SAS Monospace"      /* choose a nice font */
           htext=3 pct                /* make font a good size */
           gsfname=out                /* where to save graphic */ ;
  proc gchart data=sashelp.class ;
    hbar3d age / discrete ;
  run ; quit ;
%mend testres ;
%testres(6,4,600) ;
%testres(6,4,50) ;
```

6x4 inch, 600dpi, 8.6 mega-pixels, size=1kb

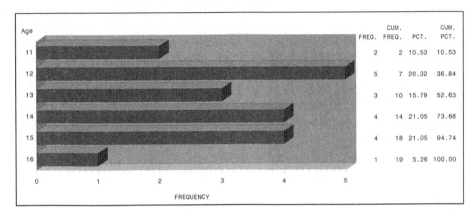

Age	FREQ.	CUM. FREQ.	PCT.	CUM. PCT.
11	2	2	10.53	10.53
12	5	7	26.32	36.84
13	3	10	15.79	52.63
14	4	14	21.05	73.68
15	4	18	21.05	94.74
16	1	19	5.26	100.00

6x4 inch, 50dpi, 0.06 mega-pixels, size=29kb

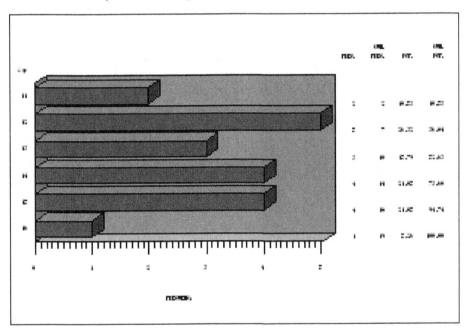

Putting interactive graphs on Web pages

ODS and some great graphic drivers make it easy to put interactive graphs onto Web pages. The following code demonstrates two methods. The first creates HTML code, which displays an interactive graph using an ActiveX control. This works great on Windows platforms. The second produces HTML code, which displays an interactive graph using a JAVA applet. This is great for Windows platforms and other platforms. Remember you need the appropriate control/applet installed, but you can add some HTML code to prompt the user to install it if needed.

SAS program

```
ods html file='c:\active.html' ;
goptions reset=all device=activex ;
proc gchart data=sashelp.prdsale ;
  vbar3d country / group=region subgroup=prodtype sumvar=actual ;
run ; quit ;
ods html close ;

ods html file='c:\java.html' ;
goptions reset=all device=java ;
proc gchart data=sashelp.prdsale ;
  vbar3d country / group=region subgroup=prodtype sumvar=actual ;
run ; quit ;
ods html close ;
```

Using flyover text in PROC REPORT

Flyover text appears (if defined) when you hover your mouse over something. ODS supports the creation of flyover text with PDF and HTML destinations. The following example shows how you can produce a report that shows first names, but when hovering the mouse over a name the whole name is displayed.

The following code works in HTML 3, which is the default HTML destination in SAS 8. In SAS®9, you must specify the destination HTML3.

SAS program

```
ods html3 file='c:\test.html' ;
data class ;
  retain fmtname '$full' ;
  length first last $ 20 sex $ 1 age 4 ;
  input first last sex age ;
  label=trim(first)||' '||last ;
datalines;
fred flintstone M 21
wilma flintstone F 19
ronald reagan M 99
barney rubble M 33
john thomas M 50
jenny thompson F 4
;
run ;
* Make a format to show full name when given first name ;
proc format cntlin=class(rename=(first=start)) ;
run ;
proc report data=class nowd ;
  columns first sex age ;
  define sex / order ;
  define age / order ;
  compute first ;
   * create flover text which will be full name, based on first name ;
    call define(_col_,
"style","style=[flyover="||quote(trim(put(first,$full.)))||"]");
  endcomp ;
run ;
ods html3 close ;
```

Output

first	sex	age
jenny	F	4
wilma		19
fred	M	21
barney		33
john		50
ronald	john thomas	99

Useful symbols in ODS

There are some useful symbols available throughout ODS, such as copyright and trademark symbols. These are easily accessed as the following code shows. You simply code a hexadecimal value for the one you want.

Copyright	'01'x
RegisteredTM	'02'x
Trademark	'04'x

These are described in a great paper at http://support.sas.com/rnd/base/topics/odsprinter/qual.pdf.

SAS program

```
ods html file='test.html' ;
data useful_symbols ;
Copyright='01'x ;
RegisteredTM='02'x;
Trademark='04'x;
run ;
proc print ;
run;
ods html close ;
```

Output

Obs	Copyright	RegisteredTM	Trademark
1	©	®	™

Making combined bar charts and plots the easy way

In SAS®9, there is a new SAS/GRAPH procedure that can make a combined vertical bar chart with a plot line on it. It is great for comparing two exact and relative magnitudes of values. It works only with ODS using the ActiveX or ACTIMGX driver, though.

SAS log

```
319  goptions reset=all device=activex ;
NOTE: Some of your options or statements may not be supported with the
   Activex or Java series of devices.  Graph defaults for these
      drivers may be different from other SAS/GRAPH device drivers.
   For further information, please contact Technical Support.
320
321  ods html file='c:\test.html' ;
NOTE: Writing HTML Body file: c:\test.html
322
323  proc gbarline data=sashelp.prdsale;
324    bar product / sumvar=actual ;
325    plot / sumvar=predict ;
326  run;

327  quit;

NOTE: There were 1440 observations read from the data set
   SASHELP.PRDSALE.
NOTE: PROCEDURE GBARLINE used (Total process time):
      real time            0.61 seconds
      cpu time             0.15 seconds


328
ods html close;
```

Screen shot

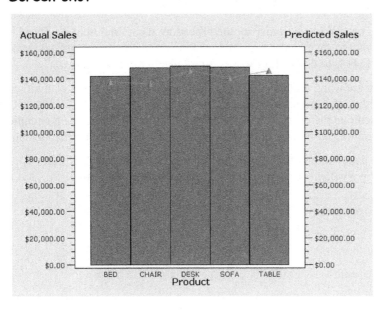

Changing procedure titles in ODS

Many procedures will display the procedure name in output produced by ODS. If you want to save some space and turn the procedure name off, you can use ODS NOPTITLE to do so. This works for all destinations.

If you are using a table of contents in HTML and PDF, then you will still get the procedure title there, but this can also be removed. Using ODS PROCLABEL ' ' will remove the procedure title, but it won't remove the space it occupies. If you want some text in its place, then you can specify that rather than a blank.

For a paper about ODS tips and techniques, see Lauren Haworth's Web site at http://www.laurenhaworth.com/pubs_current.htm#ODStips.

SAS program

```
ods html body='c:\test.html'
        contents='c:\contents.html'
        frame='c:\frame.html' ;
ods noptitle ; * turn off procedure title in body ;
ods proclabel ' ' ; * turn off procedure title in contents ;
title 'Sales frequencies' ;
proc freq data=sashelp.prdsale ;
  table country ;
run ;
ods html close ;
```

Using ODS markup to create DATA step code

ODS markup is an experimental ODS destination in SAS 8.2. It can display data by using one of many different markup languages. Additionally, it is very flexible by allowing the use of custom tagsets. These tagsets define how to lay out the data.

The following example demonstrates the flexibility of the markup destination by using a tagset that produces SAS DATA step code, which will reproduce the data selected.

For more information, see the paper "Reintroduction to ODS: The Philosophy of the Output Delivery System; or, How to Find Your Way Around All Those Features" at http://support.sas.com/rnd/base/topics/odsprinter/intro.pdf.

SAS code

```
proc template;
 define tagset Tagsets.datastep;
  notes "This is the Datastep definition";
  define event table;
   start:
    put "data;" NL;
   finish:
    put "run;" NL;
  end;
  define event row;
   finish:
    put NL;
  end;
  define event table_head;
   start:
    put "input ";
   finish:
    put ";";
  end;
  define event table_body;
   start:
    put "datalines;" NL;
  end;
  define event header;
   start:
    trigger data;
   finish:
    trigger data;
  end;
```

```
    define event data;
      start:
        put " " VALUE;
      end;
    end;
  run;

  ods markup type=datastep
             file="b_out.sas" ;
  proc print data=sashelp.class ;
  run ;
  ods markup close ;
```

Contents of b_out.sas

```
data;
input  Obs Name Sex Age Height Weight;
datalines;
 1 Alfred M 14 69.0 112.5
 2 Alice F 13 56.5  84.0
 3 Barbara F 13 65.3  98.0
 4 Carol F 14 62.8 102.5
 5 Henry M 14 63.5 102.5
 6 James M 12 57.3  83.0
 7 Jane F 12 59.8  84.5
 8 Janet F 15 62.5 112.5
 9 Jeffrey M 13 62.5  84.0
10 John M 12 59.0  99.5
11 Joyce F 11 51.3  50.5
12 Judy F 14 64.3  90.0
13 Louise F 12 56.3  77.0
14 Mary F 15 66.5 112.0
15 Philip M 16 72.0 150.0
16 Robert M 12 64.8 128.0
17 Ronald M 15 67.0 133.0
18 Thomas M 11 57.5  85.0
19 William M 15 66.5 112.0
run;
```

Note: In this case the DATA step won't work correctly because the code doesn't account for the fact that Name and Sex are character variables. However, the code can be manually fixed very easily.

Subscribing to *Your SAS Technology Report*

If you haven't subscribed to *Your SAS Technology Report*, I recommend you do so. Find instructions at http://www.sas.com/news/newsletter/index.html.

Index

A

ABOVENORMAL parameter, START
    command 288
Access (Microsoft) 268
ACF2 8
a-character-b method 108
ACTIMGX driver 341, 352
ActiveX controls
    combining bar charts/plots 352
    comparing magnitude of variables
        341–342
    correctly sizing 343
    generating static graphs 301
ACTXIMG graphics device 301
age, calculating 23
aliases for columns 247
all keyword 108, 129, 172
ALPHA= option, MEANS procedure 212
ampersand (&) 48
animated GIFs 338
a-numeric-b method 108
ANYDATE informat 101
APPEND procedure 187
application data security 8–9
Application Workspace window (SAS) 271
arguments
    DATA statement and 49
    forms for lists 26
arithmetic operators 31–32
ARM macros 10
arrays
    performance considerations 266
    sorting elements in 102–103
ASCII character set 190, 333
asterisk (*) 39, 79
ATTN command 126

B

B parameter, START command 287
Background attribute, TABULATE
        procedure 319
bar charts
    combining with plots 352–353
    pictures as patterns on 175–176
batch processing
    for SAS System 259–260
    SAS/CONNECT and 293–294
BCOLOR= option, ODS statement 311
BELOWNORMAL parameter, START
        command 288
BEST12. format 30
BEST12.2 format 21
bit flags in DATA steps 88
blanks
    See spaces/spacing
BOLD option, ODS statement 311
bookmarks 43
BREAK command
    DATA step debugger 57
    SYSERR automatic macro variable
        126
browsers 302
bulk loading 266
Business Intelligence Architecture 8

attributes
    changing 319–322
    in titles/footnotes 311
audit trails 4
AUTOEXEC.BAT file 69
automatic documentation 141–143
automatic keyword 129–130, 172
automatic macro variables 125–128
autosaving code 276
AUTOSCROLL setting 11–12

BXOR function
    bit flags 88
    data encryption 80–81
BY groups
    better looking reports with 220–223
    displaying labels 225–226
    page ejecting after 156
    producing spreadsheets for 312
    saving resources 224
    tuning SORT procedure 185
BY statement
    better looking reports 220–223
    displaying labels 225–226
    merge macros and 138
    minimizing I/O 7
    putting variables into titles 156–157
    tuning SORT procedure 13, 185
    WIDTH= option, PRINT procedure and 224
BYLINE option, OPTIONS procedure 156

C

CALCULATED keyword 252
calculations
    for age 23
    for factorials 23
    for pi 23
    for weighted medians 216–217
    in macros 133
    percentages relative to groups 204–205
    using values just calculated 252
CALENDAR procedure 82
CALL EXECUTE routine 40–42, 95
CALL LABEL routine 58
CALL RANUNI routine 24
CALL SYMPUT routine 49, 58
CANCEL option, RUN statement 61
case sensitivity
    COUNT function 18
    for variable names 90
    Visual Basic macro names 277

CATALOG procedure 172, 182
    STAT option 182
catalogs
    adding titles to graphs in 158
    DICTIONARY.CATALOGS table 243
    gaining space from members 182
    saving space in 6
CATX function 20
cell padding 339
CGM device drivers 333
character variables
    saving disk space 4
    SORTN routine 102
    specifying ranges 108
characters
    displaying for fonts 183–184
    in macro comments 134
    mixing with numeric values in informats 233–234
    pathname limitations 260
    sorting array elements 102
    special characters in graphs 333–334
CHART procedure 28
charts
    bar 175–176, 352–353
    comparing magnitude of variables in 341–342
    hi-lo 332
CHARTYPE window 333
CIMPORT procedure 187
CLASS statement 7
client/server environment 292
clipboard, accessing 104
CLIPLOG macro 112–113
CLM option, MEANS procedure 212
clock arithmetic 33
COALESCE function, SQL procedure 251
code generation, conditional 40–42
colon (:)
    as modifier 48, 249
    as wildcard 109
    in pattern matching 39

e-mail, sending 106–107
ENCRYPT data set option 8
encryption 8, 80–81
ENCRYPT=YES data set option 81
engines
 exporting to Excel 283
 nicknames for 166
 performance considerations 266
Enhanced Editor 274–275
ENTER command, DATA step debugger
 57
environment variables 69
EQT operator 249
ERROR: keyword 22
error messages
 checking for 76–77
 from variables in data sets 146
ERROR variable 110
%EVAL macro function 133
EXAMINE command, DATA step debugger
 57
Excel (Microsoft)
 adding page x of y to reports 310
 creating pivot tables 278–282
 exporting to 283–284, 331
 importing into 190
 native formatting in ODS 308–309
 running Visual Basic macros 277
 sending data to 307
exclusive OR operation 80–81
EXECUTE routine
 conditionally generating code 40–42
 running macro code from DATA steps
  95
 using compiled DATA steps 93–94
Explorer Window (SAS) 187, 272
exports
 between SAS and Microsoft Access
  268
 to Microsoft Excel 283–284, 331

external data/files
 browsing 270
 DICTIONARY.EXTFILES table 243
 editing in place 64
 saving graphs to 174
 tuning SORT procedure and 14
 wildcards for file lists 264–265
 wildcards for reading 79
 writing to 85

F

factorials, calculating 23
FASTCLUS procedure 216–217
 LEAST= option 216
 MAXC= option 216
field justification 289
FILE= option
 ODS statement 337
 PRINTTO procedure 190
file= option, FILE statement 98
FILE statement
 COLUMN= option 98
 DELIMITER= option 98
 DSD option 98
 FILENAME= option 98
 FILEVAR= option 98
 FLOWOVER option 98
 FOOTNOTES option 98
 HEADER= option 98
 in DATA steps 98
 LINE= option 98
 LINESIZE= option 98
 LINESLEFT= option 98
 MOD option 98
 NOFOOTNOTES option 98
 ODS= option 98
 OLD option 98
 PAGESIZE= option 98
 PUTLOG statement and 22
 sharing buffers 64
 STOPOVER option 98

HIPERSPACE engine option 185
horizontal hi-lo charts 332
HTML destination
    changing procedure titles 354
    flyover text in reports 349
    latest tagsets 328
    multiple graphs on 164–165
    native Excel formatting from ODS
        308–309
    spreadsheets for BY groups 312
    viewing with Web browsers 302
HTML3 destination 339–340, 349
HTMLCSS destination 310

I

I parameter, START command 288
IBUFNO= option, OPTIONS procedure
    114
ID statement 220–223
IDD (International Direct Dialing) prefix
    46
IDXNAME data set option 267
IDXWHERE data set option 267
IF statement
    performance considerations 266
    saving disk space 2
    WHERE statement and 72
IF-THEN/ELSE structures 266
imports
    between SAS and Microsoft Access
        268
    creating tab-separated output for
        190–191
    producing files for 137
IN operator 92, 236
%INCLUDE macro 40
INDENT option, TABULATE procedure
    198
indenting output 198
INDEX function 27

indexes
    DICTIONARY.INDEXES table 244
    performance considerations 266
    saving disk space 4
    views without 67–68
INFILE statement
    DLM= option 48, 295
    DSD option 48
    delimiters in 48, 295
    SHAREBUFFERS option 64
INFORMAT statement 38
informats
    date 101
    mixing character/numeric values
        233–234
    modifying 230–232
    reading unaligned data requiring 48
INPUT statement
    automatic macro variables 125
    reading unaligned data 48
    SAS/CONNECT scripts 293–294
    text value positioning 47
input/output
    minimizing 7
    performance considerations 266
    VIO 185
integers
    arithmetic calculations in macros 133
    IN operator and 92
integrity constraints 186–188
interactive graphs 348
intercepts 217
INTERNAL option, OPTIONS procedure
    114, 172–173
International Direct Dialing (IDD) prefix
    46
INTNX function 16–17
INVALUE statement, FORMAT procedure
    233
inverse trigonometry functions 23
IP addresses 295–296

MIN function 32
MIN parameter, START command 287–288
minimizing programs 287–288
minimum >< arithmetic operators 31–32
minus sign (-) 31, 82
missing values
    DATA steps and 82–84
    spaces and 29
    SQL procedure and 251
MMDDYYxw format 105
MOD function 33–34
MOD option, FILE statement 98
mode of continuous variables 214–215
MODEL statement, REG procedure 217
modulo arithmetic 33
MONOTONIC function, SQL procedure 248
MPRINT option, OPTIONS procedure 10
MSGLEVEL=I option, SQL procedure 246
MSYMTABMAX= option, OPTIONS procedure 136
multi-panel reports 197

N

N statistic 82
_N_ variable 110
NAMED option, REPORT procedure 199–200
naming statistics automatically 210–211
nesting formats 228–229
NEWFILE=PAGE option, ODS statement 312
NICKNAME procedure 166–168
nicknames 166–168
NMISS statistic 82
NOBS= option, SET statement 50–53
NOBS statistic 82
NOBYLINE option, OPTIONS procedure 156
NODATE option, TABULATE procedure 190

NOEQUALS option, SORT procedure 13, 185
NOFOOTNOTES option, FILE statement 98
NONUMBER option, TABULATE procedure 190
NOPTITLE option, ODS statement 354
NORMAL parameter, START command 288
normalization 3
NOROTATE option, GOPTIONS statement 155
NOSEPS option, TABULATE procedure 190, 201–202
-NOSLEEPWINDOW option 117
NOSTAX system option 9
NOTE: keyword 22
NOTSORTED option, SORT procedure 14, 185
NOUNBUFLOG option, OPTIONS procedure 114
NULL DATA step 7
NULL keyword 2, 49
null value
    integrity constraints and 186
    LENGTH function and 29–30
    treating blanks as 27
NUMBER option, SQL procedure 248
numbers
    arithmetic calculations in macros 133
    automatically rounding 235
    ensuring numeric value of 65
    in macro variables 21
    mixing with character values in informats 233–234
    random 24–25
    sorting array elements 102
numeric variables 4, 108
NUMS command 274
NWAY option, SUMMARY procedure 208–209

O

OBS= option, SET statement 51–52
observations
  determining number of 50–53
  reducing 13
  saving disk space 3
  tables and 248
ODS (Output Delivery System)
  adding page x of y to reports 305–306,
      310
  adding space in reports 339–340
  attributes in titles and footnotes 311
  changing attributes 319–322
  changing graph resolution 346–347
  changing procedure titles 354
  changing report output 323–327
  combining bar charts/plots 352–353
  comparing magnitude of variables
      341–342
  correctly sizing ActiveX 343
  creating animated GIFs 338
  creating DATA step code 355–356
  essential Web sites 178
  expanding tagsets 328
  exporting to Excel 331
  finding available styles 316–318
  flyover text in reports 349–350
  generating graphs automatically 304
  generating static graphs 301
  hardware vs. software fonts 335–336
  hi-lo charts 332
  inserting graphs/tables in Word
      documents 337
  interactive graphs on Web pages 348
  listing paper sizes 119
  multi-column reports 313–315
  native Excel formatting in 308–309
  plotting pie graph details 344–345
  sending data to Excel 307
  special characters in graphs 333–334
  styles available 172

  templates added to graphics 329
  useful symbols 351
  viewing HTML output 302
  viewing multiple orientations 303
ODS destination
  CSVALL statement 331
  FILE statement 98
  for information about 172
  FORMDLIM option 154
  HTML pages 164–165
  ODS markup 355–356
  PUT statement 96
  sending data to Excel 307
  TABULATE procedure and 192
  traffic lighting 195
  viewing HTML output 302
  writing to multiple 330
ODS markup 355–356
ODS= option, FILE statement 98
ODS statement
  attributes in titles/footnotes 311
  BCOLOR= option 311
  BOLD option 311
  changing attributes 319–322
  changing procedure titles 354
  changing report output 323–327
  COLOR= option 311
  COLUMNS= option 313–315
  exporting to Excel 331
  FILE= option 337
  finding available styles 316–318
  FONT= option 311
  generating graphics automatically 304
  HEADTEXT= option 310
  HEIGHT= option 311
  inserting graphs/tables in Word
      documents 337
  ITALIC option 311
  JUSTIFY= option 311
  LINK= option 311
  NEWFILE=PAGE option 312
  NOPTITLE option 354

security, application data 8–9
SELECT clause
    conditional processing and 62
    using values just calculated 252
Selection command 73
SEPARATE parameter, START command
      288
separator lines 201–202
SERVER= option, LIBNAME statement
      294
sessions, connecting 292
SET command, DATA step debugger 57
SET statement
    FIRSTOBS= option 51–52
    NOBS= option 50–53
    OBS= option 51–52
    reading variable values 99
    rearranging variables 38
SETINIT procedure 170, 172
SHAREBUFFERS option, INFILE
      statement 64
SHARED parameter, START command
      288
SLEEP function 117
software fonts 335–336
software tuning considerations 266
SORT procedure
    BY statement and 7
    integrity constraints and 187
    minimizing I/O 7
    NOEQUALS option 13, 185
    NOTSORTED option 14, 185
    performance considerations 267
    SORTDEV= option 185
    SORTPGM= option 13
    SORTSIZE= option 185
    TAGSORT option 13, 267
    tuning 13–14, 185
SORTC routine 102
SORTDEV= option, SORT procedure 185

SORTEDBY= data set option 185
sorting
    array elements 102–103
    indexes and 4
    tuning SORT procedure 13–14, 185
SORTN routine 102
SORTPGM= option, SORT procedure 13
SORTSIZE= option, SORT procedure 185
sounds-like operator 39
SOURCE option, OPTIONS procedure 10
SOURCE2 option, OPTIONS procedure
      10
source/program code
    automatic documentation 141–143
    autosaving 276
    commenting out 61
    data set passwords in 8
    saving disk space 4
spaces/spacing
    format modifiers and 48
    in reports 339–340
    in variable names 90
    missing values and 29
    treating as nulls 27
    trimming leading 21
    variables and 65
spawner programs 295
SPD Server (SAS) 266
special characters in graphs 333–334
SQL (Structured Query Language)
    conditional arithmetic and 250
    min/max confusion 32
    observations in data sets 50
    putting variable labels into titles 58
    saving disk space 2–3
SQL DICTIONARY tables 131, 241–245
SQL procedure
    COALESCE function 251
    colon modifiers in 249
    creating range of macro variables 255
    data dictionary information 131,
      241–245

ROW definition 203–204
RTS option 201
saving space with 201–202
TABLE variable 192
traffic lighting 195–196
TYPE variable 192
URL attribute 319
Width attribute 319
tagsets 328, 355
TAGSORT option, SORT procedure
 13, 267
tape data sets 52
TEMP environment variable 276
TEMPLATE procedure
 finding available styles 172, 316
 multiple graphs/tables on HTML pages
  164
templates, added to graphics 329
temporary data sets 2
testing, minimizing I/O while 7
text
 flyover 349–350
 searching 19
text value positioning 47
third-normal form 3
{thispage} style directive 305
tilde (~)
 as format modifier 48
 pathname and 260, 287
time intervals 16–17
TIME() function 93
TITLE statement 58
titles
 adding to graphs in catalogs 158
 attributes in 311
 changing procedure 354
 controlling size of 201
 DICTIONARY.TITLES table 245
 indenting 198
 putting BY variables into 156–157
 variable labels into 58–60
TKG= option, OPTIONS procedure 114

Topics command 73–74
Trademark symbol 351
traffic lighting 195–196
trailing blanks 21
traps, bugs and 72
TRIM function 29
truncation
 CATX function and 20
 format modifiers and 48
tuning considerations
 hardware/software 266
 options listed 10
 SORT procedure 13–14, 185
TYPE statement 293–294
TYPE variable, TABULATE procedure
 192

U

UCLM option, MEANS procedure 212
UNDERLINE option, ODS statement 311
underscore (_) 39
UNIVARIATE procedure
 calculating weighted medians 216–217
 FREQ statement 216
 mode of continuous variables 214–215
 WEIGHT statement 216
UNIX environment
 application data security 8
 reading external files in 79
 running SAS in batch 259
 SyncSort product 13
 SYSGET function 69
UPLOAD procedure 187, 292
URL attribute, TABULATE procedure 319
user keyword 129, 172
User library 120
utility procedures 181–188

V

variables
 See also macro variables
 adding with similar names 46

WIDTH=UBY option, PRINT procedure
224
wildcards
for file lists 264–265
for reading external files 79
in variables lists 109
Windows environment
accessing clipboard 104
application data security 8
encryption support 81
interactive graphs on Web pages 348
reading external files in 79
running SAS in batch 259–260
sizing screen space 271
START command 287–288
SYSGET function 69
ZIPMAGIC product 269
Windows Explorer 259–260
Word (Microsoft)
controlling from other programs 45
customizing output 285–286
inserting graphs/tables 337
starting 287
SYSITEMS system command 74
writing to 43
words, counting 18
Work library 120
WRAP option, REPORT procedure
199–200
wrapping lines 199–200
wrdbasic.hlp file 285

X

X statement 127
XMAX option, GOPTIONS statement 346
XML command (Microsoft Office) 308
XPIXELS option, GOPTIONS statement
343, 346

Y

YMAX option, GOPTIONS statement 346
Your SAS Technology Report 356
YPIXELS option, GOPTIONS statement
343, 346
YYMMDDxw format 105

Z

zeros, leading 255
ZIP files, data sets in 269
ZIPMAGIC product 269
z/OS
application data security 8–9
SyncSort product 13
tuning SORT procedure 185

Special Characters

: (colon)
as modifier 48, 249
as wildcard 109
in pattern matching 39
& (ampersand) 48
* (asterisk) 39, 79
- (minus sign) 31, 82
% (percent sign) 39
| (pipe) 2, 56
? (question mark) 79
" (quotation marks)
format modifiers and 48
in macro comments 134–135
pathnames and 287
_ (underscore) 39
+ (plus) operator 82
<> maximum operator 31–32
>< minimum operator 31–32
~ (tilde)
as format modifier 48
pathnames and 260, 287

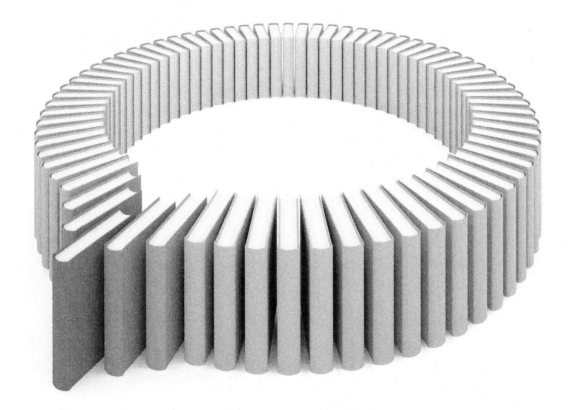

Gain Greater Insight into Your SAS® Software with SAS Books.

Discover all that you need on your journey to knowledge and empowerment.

support.sas.com/bookstore
for additional books and resources.

THE POWER TO KNOW®

CPSIA information can be obtained
at www.ICGtesting.com
Printed in the USA
BVOW10s0626280217
477310BV00003B/33/P